DESERT
FIRE

NIALL ARDEN
DESERT FIRE

THE **SAS** IN IRAQ – A SHOCKING TRUE STORY

HODDER &
STOUGHTON

First published in Great Britain in 2006 by Hodder & Stoughton
A division of Hodder Headline

A Hodder & Stoughton book

1

A CIP catalogue record for this title is available from the British Library

Hardback ISBN 0 340 89765 1
Trade paperback ISBN 0 340 89766 X
Typeset in Bembo by Hewer Text UK Ltd, Edinburgh

Printed and bound by
Mackays of Chatham Ltd, Chatham, Kent

Hodder Headline's policy is to use papers that are natural, renewable
and recyclable products and made from wood grown in sustainable
forests. The logging and manufacturing processes are expected to
conform to the environmental regulations of the country of origin.

Hodder & Stoughton Ltd
A division of Hodder Headline
338 Euston Road
London NW1 3BH

To my team. You were and are the best. You came with me to places no one should ever have to go and you stood with me all the way.

Contents

Part 3: Desert of No Return

ACHNOWLEDGEMENTS

Special thanks are due to the following without whom this book would not have been possible. Lieutenant Colonel Ian 'Tanky' Smith. Your last words to me with regard to this book were, 'Venture all, to dare all, to win all.' I promised I would and I have. Damien Lewis, for helping me shape the story, special thanks to you. Rupert Lancaster and staff at Hodder: a sincere and heartfelt thank you for having the courage and determination to publish *Desert Fire*. To Doug, for saving my backside I don't know how many times and for keeping my feet firmly on the ground. To Malcolm, Baby Steve, Pilot Steve, Guss, Athansa, Romero and the rest of the team, thank you for making my task a privilege and an honour and, of course, for allowing me to dish the dirt on all of you in this account. Shop Steve (you know who you are). To the makers of Land Rover, thank you for building a vehicle we were able to rely on – it worked every time when we needed it most. Andrew Lownie, my agent: this would not have been published but for your vision and foresight, determination and perseverance. Thank you. Last, but by no means least, to my lady Victoria: 'Shit happens', as you often reminded me; but for you my life would be a whole world of it. Thank you seems inadequate, and undervalues the depth and strength of my appreciation and love.

AUTHOR'S FOREWORD

I wrote this account to help me come to terms with the horrors that the men in my team and I endured in Iraq, where we had been saddled with a series of covert 'black' operations. Upon my return I felt alienated and dislocated from normal life; my friends, family and girlfriend all told me they felt estranged from me. I couldn't talk to anyone about what had happened there, the hellish experiences we had lived through. So I wrote down the story to communicate what I had survived, and what I couldn't tell them in person.

I felt compelled to write this story, despite the obvious risks involved. You will find in it plenty of horror, with religious, medieval, political and regional history − to make sense of the war, it's essential to have some grasp of its context and background. I have no axe to grind. I am not a cynical, embittered, disgruntled or angry ex-soldier desperate to be heard. I wrote the story as a way to deal with difficult feelings and emotions resulting from the war, which had changed me profoundly, as a man and as a soldier. I had no intention of anyone other than my family reading it, but they thought a wider audience would appreciate it, especially if it helped the bereaved to understand how and why their loved ones gave their lives.

I haven't changed the core facts as I wanted to keep as near to the truth as possible. But, as they say, 'Fact is often stranger than fiction.' Some of what you read may seem extraordinary, but the events described took place and are 100 per cent true.

Some events have been condensed or amalgamated into one place or scene, in an effort to keep the book to a manageable length. Most individuals' names and personalities have been changed for security reasons: some are still working in Special Forces or the Security Services. I have obfuscated some details of intelligence-gathering and operational procedures, and some items of equipment have been changed: I do not wish to endanger anyone's life.

Nothing within these pages constitutes a national threat, a breach of either protocol or security.

As Anthony Swofford wrote in his best-selling *Jarhead*, the true story of a US marine in the first Gulf War, 'All is not real but all is truth here.' I don't claim that my opinions are necessarily the right ones, but they are mine, and where they are not, I have said so. I have been as open and honest as I can be, especially when talking about my fears, weaknesses, motivation and hopes for the future.

In Iraq my team battled through episodes of combat no Special Forces soldier should have survived. We didn't fight with any belief in the war or in those who were manipulating the conflict from above: we did so only with a desperate will to live.

This story is packed with betrayal, dirty tricks and the loss of Allied lives – all in the service of the warped sense of political expediency that seems to have governed this war. When I discovered the true nature of our mission in Iraq, it shocked and sickened me – as it still does. No soldier should face the moral and ethical dilemmas with which we were confronted. When I returned to the UK I had to re-evaluate my life and my military career, which resulted in my decision to leave the armed services.

My story is likely to shock you. When you have finished reading it, I hope you'll understand why I felt it needed to be told.

PART ONE

DOGS OF WAR

1

PREPARE FOR WAR

It was in the autumn of 2002 that, out of the blue, Patrick, a former work colleague, contacted me and asked me to meet him in London. All he would tell me over the phone was that he had a 'job' to discuss with me. I had spent the last twenty years seesawing between various occupations in civilian life and Special Forces operations, which had taken me to Northern Ireland, the Balkans, Afghanistan and other more obscure corners of the world. I had also done several stints on counter-terrorism and surveillance work in the UK. Patrick was my 'controller' – he called me when the powers that be deemed my services were required.

I caught the London train in Ross-on-Wye, and as it trundled through the countryside I wondered what the operation might be. Momentum was building for war in Iraq, but the conflict still seemed less than certain and a long way off. In any case, in 1996 I had blotted my copybook in Bosnia: afterwards, during a severe dressing-down, I had been told I was not suited to Special Forces soldiering. Since then I had never been assigned to another overseas operation so I doubted that I'd be deployed to Iraq. Far more likely it would be a stint of surveillance work in the UK, keeping an eye on another bunch of undesirables.

As I gazed out of the window, I thought of that Bosnian operation. I had led a team of two SAS troopers and one CIA operator into the mountains on a covert, deniable operation. We had trekked in overland with all our weapons and survival kit, then spent weeks hiding in the forests, guiding in C130 Hercules aircraft that were dropping arms to Muslim enclaves under siege by the Serbs. Our orders had been crystal clear: we were only to engage the enemy if compromised – and even then, only if it was absolutely necessary. At all costs we were not to betray our positions or our mission – whatever we might see the Serbs doing to local civilians. The weapons we were helping to deliver would redress the balance of power between the Serb and Muslim forces to prevent further massacres and bring both sides to the negotiating table. Nothing was to get in the way of the 'bigger picture' objective of our mission.

Which was all very well until we had observed the Serbs 'necklacing' Muslim families in Maglaj village. From our concealed OP (observation post) high on the freezing hillside, we had watched as the picture-postcard snow scene had been turned into hell on earth. Serb thugs had taken an elderly couple, slung old tyres filled with petrol round their necks and set them alight, in front of their family – a younger couple with three daughters. We had heard that this barbaric practice took place in brutal wars in Africa, but this was Europe. As the grandparents' screams echoed across the valley and the family sobbed hysterically, we had held our fire. But it took a supreme effort of self-control, and I knew my men were itching to pull their triggers.

The following day, the Serb commander ordered his men to necklace the eldest daughter. I radioed for clearance to open fire, but it was denied repeatedly. My men begged me to give the order to engage the Serbs, and finally, as the Serb commander played a lighter flame across the girl's face, I decided to disobey my orders. I sent an urgent radio message to Headquarters: we had been spotted, I said, and would have to engage the enemy. Then we opened fire. We took out a dozen or more Serbs from our positions some six hundred metres above the village.

In the ensuing chaos, the family managed to escape. But by then the entire Serb Army in Maglaj was bearing down on us. We got out of Bosnia by the skin of our teeth. When I thought back on what I had done, I regretted none of it. I believed that I, and the men under my command, had done the right thing. Faced with similar circumstances in Iraq, or anywhere else, I believed I would do the same.

The train pulled into Paddington, and I made my way to Patrick's office, deep within the MoD complex at Whitehall. Patrick had cut his teeth working for E4, the surveillance wing of Special Branch, and had had a long career in counter-terrorism and covert operations as a former regular SAS officer. After the usual pleasantries he asked how I was getting on as a self-employed engineering designer. I guessed he knew that the business wasn't thriving. Over the years he had called me many times when a specific job or operation came up to which he felt my skills would be suited. Often he made clear that he had done a thorough check on my financial and domestic situation before he had got in touch. Invariably I would be down to my last penny and Patrick knew that it would be hard for me to turn down a juicy MoD contract.

This time he wondered if I was free to do some homeland-security surveillance for the Home Office – in other words, keep an eye on terrorist suspects in the UK. With al-Qaeda threats multiplying and too many suspected UK-based players, he needed operators and he needed them fast. The Home and Foreign Offices could call on former members of the Special Air Service (SAS) and Special Boat Service (SBS) for such work, or the Territorials. Operational again, we were known as

'Retreads' or 'Dunlops'. Being a former special forces officer still on the reserve list, I fell into that category.

Six months previously I had moved to Ross-on-Wye with Victoria, my new girlfriend. Since then, she had become our main breadwinner: with two ex-wives and four children, I was financially stretched. Also, I had recently promised myself – and, more importantly, my two youngest children – that I would not take on any jobs that might be dangerous or keep me away for long periods. Some nice, safe UK-based work, such as Patrick was offering, would suit me fine until one of my design projects paid off. For months I had been working on a replacement design for the SA80 assault rifle, the main British combat weapon. It was a perfect weapon on the range, but useless in dirty, dusty, sandy combat environments. However, my replacement was bogged down in MoD red tape. It had yet to win final approval – and earn anything. I accepted Patrick's offer and we went out to dinner. Over some good food and wine, the conversation turned to the probability of war in Iraq. We talked through various operational scenarios and the pros and cons of engaging the Iraqi military machine. Patrick confirmed that an Allied invasion was already a done deal – this, even though it was still many months away: 'Watch out for all the political bullshit over the next few months,' he said. 'It's all just a front – the invasion's a foregone conclusion. There'll be a lot of work to do out there.'

I caught the late train home and mulled over what had been discussed and what I'd just agreed to. I couldn't deny that I still got a buzz out of this type of work, and maybe that was partly why I'd accepted the job. But there had been a subtext to the conversation. Patrick had not told me about the certainty of war with Iraq for the fun of it. Despite the Bosnia debacle, he was dangling Iraq before me – knowing I'd be tempted by the prospect of an active operation overseas.

I spent an enjoyable weekend with Victoria and my two

youngest children. On Saturday we swam in the morning, went shopping in the afternoon and to the cinema that evening. On Sunday we went for a long walk in the hills, and I brought up the subject of Patrick's offer, especially making the point about Iraq. Victoria seemed distant but she told me I should do whatever made me happy and that she would be fine. 'Absolutely fine,' she repeated. I felt a pang of guilt as we walked along with the children skipping ahead of us. They were talking about our holiday in Spain the following spring, which we had just booked, blissfully unaware that I was about to be dragged back into the kind of military work I had promised them I'd given up for good.

On Sunday evening I went back to London for a follow-up talk with Patrick. We had arranged to meet at the Duke of York's Barracks, in Chelsea, a military base and headquarters for all UK Special Forces. No sooner had I arrived than I was introduced to Douglas, a former SSM (squadron sergeant major) from 22 SAS. Doug was a legendary figure within UK Special Forces circles – his reputation went before him and not everything said about him was particularly pleasant. This was the first time we had met face to face. At forty-seven he had been there, done it and printed the T-shirt, as far as Special Forces operations were concerned. Generally people were intimidated by his physical presence and icy-blue, killer stare. He was tall and rock-hard, with pure white hair swept back off his forehead, after the style of Count Dracula.

Doug was said to have an attitude problem with officers, but we seemed to hit it off. Patrick was a little surprised by how well Doug and I got on, even though I had been introduced to him as Major Arden, which marked me out as an officer and therefore a 'Rupert' – in Special Forces there was still an 'us' and 'them' barrier between the officers and men like Doug. By the end of the evening, though, it had been established that we would work together on the surveillance job. Over the coming weeks we would live in each other's pockets, so it was of crucial importance that we got on. Even the best of friends had ended up in fist-fights after many weeks on intensive operations.

For the next few weeks Doug and I spent a lot of time together – morning, noon and night – tracking several potentially dangerous individuals across the UK. Word soon got round in UK Special Forces Group Command – known as Head Shed – about Doug's and my operations. Our reports found their way into COBRA – the Cabinet Office Briefing Room, which is the nerve centre of all UK emergency and counter-terrorism operations. Then my report on Bosnia and the entire Yugoslav conflict – written after the Maglaj incident – was laid on the desks of several cabinet ministers. The Labour government wanted to know what had happened in the past when a hard-line dictator had been toppled from power. There were obvious parallels between the former Yugoslavia and Iraq, and deductions to be made on the most likely outcome if the UK and US ousted Saddam Hussein. At last, and ironically, my Balkans report was now being taken seriously by some in government.

After the Maglaj incident, I had been summoned to give an account of my actions and decisions. My explanation had gone down like the *Titanic*. The report on me concluded that I had shown total disregard for my own safety and that of my men, and had jeopardised the whole operation. I did not agree, so I had compiled a report on it, which went on to outline my thoughts on the ethics and management of the war. I had researched the history and background to the Balkans conflict, and pointed out that the disintegration of Yugoslavia, following the death of dictator Tito, had spawned it. With Saddam gone, Iraq might do likewise. I was informed that in writing the report I had 'overstepped the mark' and that I was dealing with issues 'well above my status'. I was deemed too much of a maverick and too idealistic to be considered for future operations. An idealist and a maverick? As far as I was concerned, those were just the qualities to be valued in a Special Forces soldier, the qualities that had made me want to join Special Forces in the first place, that had made me a fighter, a survivor, a pilgrim and a soldier. But, as far as the top brass were concerned, my orders had been crystal clear: *unless in danger of being compromised do not intervene.*

Around five weeks into our surveillance work I had an urgent call from Patrick. My Maglaj report had made waves and he'd had a request 'from the highest level' that I prepare an in-depth briefing and analysis of the potential consequences of removing Saddam Hussein from power. I left Doug to continue with what we were doing and set about it. I concluded that Iraq might disintegrate if Saddam were removed as the result of an Allied invasion, and that Allied forces stood in danger of being sucked into an interminable civil war. I submitted the briefing, expecting to hear little more about it, and rejoined Doug on the surveillance stake-out.

Just before Christmas Doug and I were told to report immediately to Head Shed. No sooner had we arrived than I was dragged through security and into a back room. I was met by Patrick and an officer from MI6 (the Secret Intelligence Service, or SIS). I helped myself to some coffee, and was surprised to see my personal file on the desk and the MI6 officer flicking through it. He ignored me as he selected sheets of paper with Post-it notes attached to them. My blood pressure rose. Suddenly he pulled out some ancient photographs of me from the 1980s, which I hadn't known existed. They showed me with some Iraqi and Iranian students I had befriended – and indicated that I had been under surveillance myself.

At the time I was in my early twenties, and a young gun in the SAS. One evening I had been walking home through Colchester, where I was living, when I was stopped by an Arabic-looking man. He was lost and asking for directions. His English was not good and others had ignored him. I had just started learning

Arabic as one of my specialist SAS skills, so I introduced myself and asked if he was all right. His face lit up: he had been walking around for most of the day, trying to find a particular address, and was now lost. I was heading the way he needed to go so I told him he could walk with me.

I soon noticed that he had a debilitating limp. The three-mile walk, which usually took me half an hour, lasted nearly an hour and a quarter. During that time I learnt that the man was an Iraqi, with an Iranian mother. He had been press-ganged into the Iraqi Army as Iraq was then at war with its neighbour, Iran, and had lost most of his right leg on his first day in action: he had been ordered to leave a trench and charge down an Iranian machine-gun emplacement. He had come to the UK to read philosophy and history at Essex University and this was his first week. When we arrived at his address he was so grateful that he insisted on taking me into his new home to meet his fellow students.

By chance I met him again several months later. By then he was teaching Arabic to supplement his income. I learnt a lot about the Iraqi peoples from him, especially their religious beliefs and culture, and also about the Iranians. Amazingly, his housemates were a mix of Iranians and Iraqis although the countries were still at war. None of them supported the conflict so they were now in exile, struggling to pay their way through university.

When my SAS masters found out about my friends I was told to distance myself from them on security grounds. When I asked why, I was told to abandon the friendships or leave the regiment. Eventually I agreed, although friendship and loyalty meant every-thing to me. Little did I know that I had been under surveillance. Now, after twenty years, those photographs had resurfaced.

As well as my personal file, I saw that the MI6 officer had a copy of my recent briefing on the Balkans and Iraq. In it I had argued that the best way to get rid of Saddam Hussein was to assassinate him. An Allied invasion of Iraq should be avoided. If

Saddam was removed, a replacement would be required immediately, and the majority of the Republican Guards units and the
Iraqi military infrastructure would have to remain in place, if a
repetition of the anarchy and bloodletting that had ravaged the
Balkans was not to be repeated. We could address human-rights
issues when the country was secure, and proper policing and legal
procedures had been implemented.

'You must be Major Niall Arden,' the MI6 officer announced,
when he glanced up from my file.

'Correct,' I replied.

'You had a good journey down here? No problem finding the
place?'

'Fine. It's not my first visit to the Duke of York's.'

'I see.' The MI6 officer returned to my file. 'I've been reading a
lot about you, Major.'

'I can see that.'

'And your . . . *interesting* views on Iraq vis-à-vis the Balkans
conflict.'

'You mean my report?'

'Yes. Not to beat about the bush, Major, your views on the
Iraq issue have upset quite a few people. Some ministers and
senior backbenchers.'

'I didn't write it to make people happy.'

'Indeed.' The MI6 officer glanced back at my file. 'One could
hardly say that your career to date has been distinguished by doing
that, could one, Major?'

'Sorry?'

'Making people happy – the top brass, politicians. Not really
your speciality, is it, Major?'

'I prefer to say what I think. A weakness in my line of business,
I know . . .'

'Look, Major, I'll cut to the chase. What qualifies you to write
such a report? You're not a diplomat. You're not a politician.

You're not a statistician or analyst. With all due respect, Major, you're a soldier and that does not qualify you to write such material with any authority.'

I glanced at Patrick, who was looking worried, drained my coffee and stood up to leave.

'Just where do you think you're going, Major?' the MI6 officer blurted out.

I stopped. 'I didn't come here to be lectured at or patronised by the likes of you. All right?'

With that, I winked at Patrick and left the room. I'd had dealings with MI6 before. Many officers did excellent work, but there were a few idiots – the pompous, arrogant pen-pushers who seemed to have something to prove. That guy fell into the latter category.

I'd gone no more than twenty metres down the corridor when I heard the door open behind me and Patrick hurried after me. He walked with me in silence for a while until we neared the entrance to the barracks, where I'd left Doug in a bar.

'Listen, Niall, the guy's a wanker, all right?' Patrick said, taking my arm to stop me. 'To be candid, we're all being leant on to come up with intelligence or analysis that validates the push for war. We're being made part of the process of legitimising it. The MI6 geek is no exception. He's under a lot of pressure – and your report goes against the grain.'

'All I did was point out a few simple facts,' I replied. 'Tito held Yugoslavia together for decades with an iron hand. When he died, anarchy, mayhem and genocide followed on an unprecedented scale. The Balkans went up in flames. It doesn't take a genius to see the parallels with Saddam's Iraq. The area's a tinderbox. If it goes up, the conflict could spread into Iran and even further afield. And if they do invade, they've got to keep the Iraqi Army and the police intact, like Allied forces did in Germany after 1945. That's all. Pretty damn straightforward, I'd have thought.'

'I know,' said Patrick, a little wearily. 'But figures in positions of power are arguing otherwise, saying that for the past fifty years all we've been doing is damping down the embers and perhaps it's time now to do what fire-fighters do and light the fuse in certain areas so it can burn itself out, but in a controlled way. Then we can set about rebuilding the region from scratch.'

'And you agree with that?'

'I didn't say that. I said we're being asked to come up with material to support that analysis. Look, I have to go. You won't be seeing that MI6 guy again – he was just here to break your balls. But there's a job I want to talk to you about, a big one. Stay on-side, Niall. It'll be well worth it. I'll call you.'

A few days later Patrick outlined the operation. In spite of the trouble my report had caused, Head Shed were aware of my experience in the region, as well as my knowledge of its religious and political set-up; my friendship with the Iraqi and Iranian students showed I could relate to people from that part of the world. Also, as several SAS courses had proven, I had a 'non-threatening' persona, which meant that I was a good listener and gained people's trust easily. Someone had decided that I was the ideal person to lead a very secret mission into northern Iraq several months ahead of the planned invasion. As Patrick was keen to point out, if I took it on, my mounting debts would be wiped out by the pay I'd receive.

He told me I would lead a team of SAS and SBS operators into northern Iraq to persuade the Kurdish Peshmerga guerrilla forces to join the Allies in the coming war, which was now a certainty. My team and I would fly to Turkey, where an FOB (forward operating base) was being set up for us at Konya USAF (United States Air Force) airbase. My role would be to liaise between the US Special Forces, CIA and MI6 agents and my own men, and lead the operation to bring the Peshmerga leaders on-side. The US and British governments wanted the Kurds to rise up against

Saddam in the north of the country at the same time as the Allied military machine invaded from the south.

I already knew a reasonable amount about the Kurds and their centuries-long struggle against various oppressors, Saddam being perhaps the worst of them all. They were fiercely independent, and natural enemies of Saddam's Ba'athist regime. Over the decades, Saddam had gassed them with chemical weapons at Halabja and bulldozed them into mass graves – thousands had been buried alive in the desert, including women and children. Kurdish mothers had hushed their children and hugged their babies as they were herded like cattle into huge ditches and the dirt simply bulldozed over them. But the mountains of northern Iraq had always offered them a refuge from which to wage guerrilla warfare. In recent years, Saddam's demoralised and under-equipped army had been little match for the spirited Kurdish Peshmerga fighters, and the hills of northern Iraq had become a no-go area for Iraq's armed forces.

It was clearly a vital task, and offered me the chance of real excitement and challenge. Although I was flattered to be asked, I was also acutely aware that I had been in similarly dangerous situations many times before, but now would be an especially bad time to get myself killed: I had a beautiful new woman in my life and we were planning a family. I'd promised her that I was going to settle down.

'All you need to do is go to Konya and discuss with the Peshmerga commanders their commitment to supporting our forces,' Patrick continued. 'Simple enough, isn't it?'

'And what if the Pesh don't fancy flying into Turkey for chats with me?'

'It's a fluid programme, Niall,' he replied. 'It's bound to evolve as you go along. That's what you're good at.'

'So it's SAS again, then?'

'Sorry?'

'SAS – suck it and see.'

I told Patrick I would only consider taking the operation if I could remain at our FOB in Turkey and oversee operations from there. I would send my units into the field if I had to, but I would not accompany them. I would remain in the rear with the gear, as they say. Then I might be able to justify the operation to Victoria and the children. Deep down, though, I knew I couldn't stick to that in the field. The pull of in-theatre operations would be irresistible. I guessed that Patrick knew me well enough to have grasped this – and that I had only said it to square my conscience.

He agreed to give me forty-eight hours to think it over. It was a tough decision. First, there was my family, of course, but I also had serious reservations about the war. If we wanted to get rid of Saddam, the intelligence I had read suggested that a targeted assassination was the best option. We'd take him out in one easy stroke, risk few of our own troops on the ground, and minimise Iraqi casualties. In the past we had had the opportunity to do it – the claims that he was too elusive and his security too tight for us to get at him were bullshit. Generally, we knew where he was at any given time and could have targeted him accordingly. But all I heard was war talk and briefings for an all-out invasion of Iraq. Senior government ministers and advisers were searching everywhere for the smallest piece of intelligence that would help to justify an invasion. The counter-argument that the war was all about snatching Iraq's oilfields didn't stand up either. If we wanted Saddam's oil we could have got it far easier and cheaper by simply negotiating to buy it from him direct. Circumventing the UN sanctions would have been simple, and Saddam had already suggested that we start buying his oil. But I still couldn't understand why.

I spent a day agonising over my decision, then called Patrick. I told him I would agree to the operation on two conditions: first, as I'd already said, that I remained in the rear with all the gear;

and, second, that I could select my team. Straight away, he agreed. As I hung up it crossed my mind that maybe he'd had trouble recruiting someone to lead the operation. And I had only accepted it because I needed the money.

I didn't have to ask Doug if he was up for it: he'd been alongside me throughout the negotiations, and took it as given that he would be in theatre as my right-hand man. So, I set about recruiting the others. First, I called Nick, an SAS veteran who'd been with me on the fateful Balkans operation. He was an ace operator with a sniper rifle, and had egged me on to open fire on the Serbs in Maglaj. He sounded pleased to hear from me, but I'd got barely half-way through outlining the Iraqi mission when he told me, in no uncertain terms, that he wasn't interested. 'Fuck off, mate,' he interrupted. 'You read the papers, or what? It's an immoral, illegal war. You do what you have to do but don't call me again, mate. I ain't interested.'

I knew that Nick had become a prison officer. He had a new wife and a son, and had supposedly turned his back on Special Forces operations. But that wasn't his main reason for refusing to join my team: 'It's totally morally indefensible, mate, this war,' he reiterated. 'Plus it's a cursed country, is Iraq, and you'd be wise to stay well away from it.'

I was deflated by his response – his position wasn't far removed from my own. But I'd agreed to the operation. Who the hell was I going to call next? I wondered. I decided to try Malcolm, an SBS operator I'd worked with in Afghanistan. He was known to the lads as 'The Snake', a reference to the legendary size of his manhood. Like Nick and the other men I planned to call, he had been flagged up by Head Shed as available for covert operations, but he was away in Norway on an Arctic-warfare leadership training course. I got a message through to him and he called me back.

'Yeah, mate,' he yelled. 'I'm your man. Whatever happens, count me in.'

His enthusiasm was cheering – just what I needed – and a relief after Nick's moralising. Next I called John, ex-22 SAS and another rock-solid operator. I'd known him since I joined 21 (v) SAS, and he'd also worked with me in Afghanistan. We'd been tasked with persuading the Mujahideen to sell us back some of the stinger anti-aircraft missiles that the Brits and the Americans had given them to shoot down Soviet Red Army choppers. He was short and stocky, known as 'Gori' – short for Gorilla – by his mates. Despite his wife's vociferous objections, which I could hear in the background, John agreed to join us.

Finally I spoke to Ian, another 22 SAS operator, whom I knew of old and who had been on the Bosnia operation. I wanted him, but as a reserve at this stage, because I was concerned about his fitness. 'My bags are packed, mate,' he said, 'and I'm as fit as a fucking seventeen-year-old. Ask my wife, mate. She'll tell you.' I told him he'd remain a reserve until he hit the gym, which I figured would inspire him to do just that.

I made one last round of calls and told all of the lads – Doug, John, Malcolm and Ian – that we'd meet a week later, on 15 December, at the Honourable Artillery Company barracks in London. We all knew it well as we'd done some FAC (forward air control) training there, and we needed to get fully kitted up.

On the arranged date we piled into Doug's Mitsubishi Shogun 4 × 4, and headed for Stirling Lines, the new SAS base at Creden Hill in Hereford. To Ian's disappointment, we left him in London, but the rest of us were buzzing. Small-team covert operations create a unique camaraderie between their members.

As we powered up the motorway, I was thinking about the operation. I knew it was going to be hard to convince the Kurds to join the Allied war effort against Saddam's forces. During Operation Desert Storm, the previous Gulf War, they had been called on by the Allies to rise up against Saddam and were abandoned to face his war machine alone. In the ensuing battles thousands of them were killed. While I knew that the Peshmerga had no problem fighting Saddam, whether they would trust us again and agree to work alongside us was another matter. It was going to be a challenge to convince their leaders that this time things would be different.

I was also wondering how I would explain to my children that I was going away again, even though I had promised I wouldn't. And how would Victoria react? When I'd tried to talk to her about it, she hadn't wanted to know where I was going. 'I know you'll always come back. I know you'll always be all right. I can feel it. Just go ahead and do what you have to do.' But I'd suspected she was trying to put a brave face on it, and that sooner or later I'd have to tell her when and where I was to be sent.

An hour or so into the journey, I started to brief the lads on who we would be teaming up with in theatre. Two seasoned Delta Force (the US nearest equivalent to the SAS) operators were waiting for us at Konya airbase, and two CIA operators had been supposed to join us, but one had shot himself in the foot and was out of action. Had he done it by accident or as a desperate measure to avoid the Iraq operation? I joked. It raised a laugh among the lads. We could also call on a unit from the SEALs (Sea Air Land – US Navy Special Forces), if we needed them. I admired the SEALs enormously, and believed they were almost on a par with the regular British SAS/SBS. Most of the UK Special Forces operators I knew had disparaged the Americans, but I had worked with US Special Forces on many previous occasions, and the SEALs had always accounted for themselves admirably.

As we approached Stirling Lines, on the outskirts of Hereford, our minds were on the task ahead of us: securing enough usable kit and weapons.

'Who's our contact here, then?' Malcolm asked.

'A lad named Steve,' I replied, 'a mate of Doug's.'

'Doug doesn't have any mates,' Malcolm interjected.

'Fuck off, Snakey,' said Doug.

'Well, Doug recommended him,' I continued, chuckling inwardly. The banter had started already. 'He injured himself on exercise and only just got back to duty. The rest of his troop are deployed in Saudi on a desert training op, and he's been left behind as a glorified blanket-stacker. According to Doug, he volunteered to help us get our shit together from Stores.'

'I always said Doug was a fucking homo,' John put in, 'and now he's got a nice boy at Stirling Lines. Either that or the sad old bastard just wants to feel younger by hanging around him.'

'You're just jealous, mate, 'cause an ape wouldn't shag you,' Doug shot back.

When we arrived we were met by the MoD police, who checked our details thoroughly as we were all new faces. Inside, none of us had a clue about the layout because the Regiment had only recently relocated there. It was early evening and already quite dark when we found the weapons store. No one seemed to be about, so for a while we stood around kicking our heels. Eventually Doug raised Steve on his mobile, and the young man soon appeared with a REME (Royal Electrical and Mechanical Engineers) armourer in tow. I was shocked by just how young he looked. Must be my age getting to me, I told myself. Oddly, you could have mistaken him for Doug's son: he had the same pale blue eyes and an almost identical haircut, the only difference being that his hair was dirty blond rather than white. He smiled and shook hands with each of us in turn.

The armourer didn't seem too pleased to see us. He didn't know any of us and we were not on Regimental strength at the camp – that is, we were not registered as part of 22 SAS. I wondered where Arthur, the old armourer, was with a touch of nostalgia. For years he'd been a permanent fixture at Stirling Lines, with a cigarette constantly hanging from his lip. If he'd still been there we'd have been met by a wall of cigarette smoke, a barrage of abuse, and he'd have gone on to sort out all the weapons we could have wished for with barely disguised enthusiasm.

We spent two days at the camp getting kitted up. Doug had the piss taken out of him by several of his former SAS troop: they told him they'd heard he was now a spook, working on covert operations. Before the Iranian embassy was stormed, on 5 May 1980, in Operation Nimrod, the SAS had routinely been used on deniable operations – 'black-flag jobs', as they are known. But afterwards world-wide media attention had meant that every man and his dog wanted to know all about the SAS, and the black-flag jobs started to fall to MI5 and MI6. It was soon realised, however, that a core of ex-SAS and ex-SBS, plus Special Forces Territorials, could be called upon for such operations, and would invariably do a far better job in the field. It was the genesis of operations such as ours.

Young Steve was eager to come with us, but I resisted bringing him on to the team, largely because of his youth and inexperience. But I soon saw that he could hold his own with the grizzled old thugs I had recruited. As ever, the banter centred on his and Doug's friendship – which did seem like some sort of surrogate father-son relationship. We all knew Doug's family history. He had been abandoned as a baby and left on the steps of a hospital, so never knew his real parents. He went on to be adopted by his foster parents after they had tried for years to have a baby of their own. But as soon as he was officially adopted, his foster mother fell pregnant. He joined the Army at age sixteen as a junior leader, moving on to the Parachute Regiment and eventually the SAS. Knowing his family background we all tried to convince Doug that Steve was his young brother from his real parents, as they looked so alike. At one point I inadvertently called him 'Baby Steve', and the name stuck. I was impressed with him and he seemed to fit in well. His personal report was excellent, and but for his recent accident he would already have been on the promotion ladder. Before we left I told him he could come on the operation if he could persuade his parent unit, 22 SAS, to release him.

We stashed our hoard of weapons and equipment in one of the storerooms at Stirling Lines. There was quite a pile: we'd taken all of the C7 Diemaco 5.56mm assault rifles in the store, 2 Hechler & Koch MP5-SKs, the shortened version of the classic Special Forces 9mm sub-machine-gun. Each of the Diemacos had a Hechler & Koch AG-36 40mm grenade-launcher slung beneath it, similar to an M203 40mm grenade-launcher but devastating and highly versatile. We nicked several 66mm LAWs (light anti-armour weapons), and several LAW 80s (94mm anti-armour weapons), shoulder-held disposable rocket-launchers. Each of us had a Sig Sauer P226 pistol as our personal handgun, and we managed to lift three Universal Service pistols as back-up. I got the only remaining Glock 17, and John signed out a Minimi 5.56mm light machine-gun SAW (squad assault weapon M249). Unfortunately, there had been no 7.62mm GPMG (general-purpose machine-gun), Doug's chosen weapon, but I was confident we could acquire some in theatre. We'd wanted some C8s but they'd gone too.

We bribed several people on the base to make sure our kit would still be there when we returned for it on 2 January, and Doug hinted at dire consequences if any of it went walkabout in the meantime. Then we set off for a weekend of socialising and team-bonding in London. We headed for the Victory Services Club, in Marble Arch, which caters for serving and retired military personnel. There, each took one of the cheap, spartan rooms – basically a bed and four walls – then hit town for a wild Saturday night. We had a curry on the King's Road, then went to Harry's Bar, on Sloane Square. We all drank far too much, which is about the best way I've ever found of discovering each person's idiosyncrasies before an operation.

Nursing a hangover on Sunday I watched, with incredulity, the TV news reports that showed politicians seeking a diplomatic resolution to the Iraq problem through the United Nations. We knew the truth, which was that the war would go ahead, no matter what. Once again, the British and American people were being treated like mushrooms – kept in the dark and fed on shit. And I could not shake off the feeling that I was involved in something that was morally indefensible.

Everything else I had done up to this point in my military career I could justify and live with. But the forthcoming Iraqi operation felt very wrong. I had accepted the job, and was probably beyond the point of no return, but that Sunday my instincts told me I should get up and leave while I still could. But as I looked at the lads, with the banter flying, I knew I couldn't. The die was cast.

2

INFIL IRAQ

I spent the Christmas break in Ross-on-Wye with Victoria and my two youngest children – it was my year to have them. The two eldest were spending Christmas with their mother. Victoria seemed to take it well. When I told her I was going on overseas operations again, Victoria said she had expected it. But as I watched my children open their presents on Christmas Day, sirens were screaming in my head. I knew they meant I shouldn't go to Iraq. I have to stay and see my children grow up, I kept telling myself. I have to be there for them. I've done my bit and some already.

When Victoria and I drove the children back to their mother, I found it hard to say goodbye to them. They knew I was going away again, but I had promised them it would be for a couple of months at most. But that didn't stop them crying. Eleven-year-old David clung to me and wouldn't let go.

I will see them again, I repeated to myself, as we drove home. But once more instinct was telling me not to go. I felt more than a little uneasy.

The following morning I kissed Victoria goodbye as she left for work. There were no lingering hugs or special words, just a simple kiss and then she was gone. Later, she told me she had driven round the corner and burst into floods of tears. I left lots of little notes for her to find around the house, then got into my car and headed off on the first leg of the journey to Iraq.

My drive to Hereford was tedious due to bad traffic, and when I arrived the others were already there, getting our kit sorted. I left the keys for my Vauxhall 4 × 4 with a sergeant I knew well, and told him he could use it while I was away. That turned out to have been a mistake: everyone used it on all manner of SAS excursions – as a squadron run-around and for off-roading across the nearby Black Mountains. I should have known better.

That night, we drove to RAF Lyneham to put John and Baby Steve – who had secured clearance to go from the Regiment – on board a C130 Hercules from No. 47 Squadron, RAF, with the kit and weapons. They were to take the slow route to Konya, via RAF Akrotiri in Cyprus. Doug, Malcolm and I would head to Gatwick and fly out in civilian gear with British Airways to Istanbul, then on to Konya in a private jet, courtesy of the CIA. Doug joked that if the operation was geared to getting me and my big mouth out of the picture, that was when the plane would nose-dive.

On the flight to Turkey, I took a look at the newspapers. Talk of war with Iraq was everywhere and Kofi Annan, the UN secretary general, was involved in last-ditch negotiations to avert conflict. I fell once again to pondering the operation ahead. Patrick had agreed that I would stay in Konya to meet and liaise with whichever Kurdish leaders the CIA and SEALs brought in to me. But I knew that wouldn't work. No way would the Kurds agree to hand over their weapons, board a US military helicopter and fly into Turkey to talk to me on my turf. The Turks wouldn't be too happy about it either: they had done almost everything they could to wipe out the Turkish Kurds. I would have to go in country and meet the Kurds on their own ground.

Half-way through the flight a young lad sitting next to Doug started mouthing off: he was against the war, he said, and would join the fight against the 'imperialist Americans and British'. When he stood up to use the toilets, Doug was up and after him. Malcolm followed, and I was more than a little relieved when he persuaded Doug to sit down again. At Istanbul we were whisked through Immigration and shown to the aircraft that would fly us on to Konya. As we climbed aboard the Learjet, an oversized loaf of a man was already hogging two seats. He was 'suited and booted', as we call it, in a three-piece suit with shoes so shiny you could see your face in them. He even had a briefcase handcuffed to his wrist. When Doug tried to squeeze past him he refused to budge from his two seats next to the door. 'If it's close to the door you want, mate, I'll pass you through it in a minute if you don't shift your fucking arse,' Doug announced, at full volume.

The man didn't reply.

'Fuck you, wanker,' Doug snapped, and sat down near the front of the aircraft.

A couple of men who were clearly US military boarded the Learjet and took up the remaining free seats, which left me to sit next to the loaf. During the flight, which took just under an hour, I tried to make conversation with him, but he would only give monosyllabic answers, and clutched the briefcase as though his life depended on it.

It was dark when we touched down to be greeted by a chill wind and snow-removal equipment clearing the parking area of the NATO E-3A Component AWAC's (Airborn Warning and Control) of the FMB (forward mounting base). When it comes to aircraft I'm a sad space cadet: if I hadn't made it into the SAS, I would have trained as a pilot. Konya, as a NATO FMB, was a hive of activity, with military aircraft constantly taking off and landing. As we stepped down from the Learjet I was impressed to see a giant SR71 aircraft taxiing across the airfield. The SR71 Blackbird is a US spy plane that flies on the edge of the earth's atmosphere; the crews have to wear spacesuits. I had assumed it only operated direct from the USA, but here it was, flying out of Konya. Its presence reinforced the seriousness of the coming conflict.

As we unloaded our kit, a US military Humvee jeep pulled up on the apron, and a US Army captain jumped out. He approached Doug and offered him a hand. Doug looked at it, then remembered his manners. 'Sorry, mate, bit jet-lagged,' he shouted above the aircraft noise.

'You Major Arden?' the US soldier shouted back.

'Fuck off, mate. Do I look like a ponce?'

'Sorry, bud. Thought you looked the most sensible and mature of you guys.'

They cracked up laughing, then Doug pointed at me. 'Ain't it obvious? He's the ponce, mate.'

The officer strode across to me. 'Major Arden? Captain Adrian Romero. I'm one of the Delta operators you'll be working with out here.'

He was about five foot eleven, tanned, almost Latino-looking, and exuded confidence. He was immediately likeable, with an easy, approachable manner. Behind us the besuited loaf was climbing down from the plane to be met by another US serviceman, who ushered him to a waiting vehicle. Hope that's the last we'll see of him, I thought, as we strode across to Romero's Humvee.

Within minutes Romero had taken us on a whirlwind tour of the base, ending up at a row of three Portakabins – our homes for the duration of the operation. Doug and I opted for the one that looked out on to the main runway so that I could watch aeroplanes. Malcolm took the one next to us for himself: he was convinced he'd be entertaining some of the females on the base, thereby doing his bit for Anglo-American relations. We reserved the third Portakabin for Baby Steve and John. Romero gave us an hour to settle in and unpack our kit. Then we'd get together for a heads-up (an informal meeting) in the base canteen.

We met up with Romero in a McDonald's trailer wagon, complete with double-arch logo. We ordered burgers, fries and coffee, then sat down for an informal meet and greet. First off, Romero introduced us to his fellow Delta Force operator, Athansa, whom we all acknowledged.

'OK, sir, what's the game plan?' Romero asked, getting down to business.

'It's Niall. We don't do "sir". And you tell me. Thought you'd have all the latest low-down.'

'You're kidding me, right?'

'Nope. I was told that once we were here you guys would have all the latest intel for us to start with.'

'Shit, no, we expected you to be bringing it with you,' Romero replied. 'We've been kicking our heels for two weeks with no idea what we're doing here.'

Doug, Malcolm and I grinned at each other.

'SNAFU, then,' Doug said.

'What?' Romero asked.

'SNAFU,' Doug repeated. 'Situation Normal – All Fucked Up.'

'Oh,' said Romero, and grinned. 'FUBAR is what we use.'

'Fucked Up Beyond All Recognition,' Athansa explained, in an exaggerated New Jersey accent. At first I thought it was put on, but soon discovered it was for real – and some Delta operators had a real problem working with him.

'Well, it looks like there's nothing else for it but to finish these –' I took a bite of my Big Mac – 'and get some sleep.'

That evening, after a stroll around the base, I went to bed. I tried out my mobile and I was pleased to discover that I could

send and receive text messages and even make calls to the UK. I
phoned Victoria, who was more than surprised to hear from me,
but our conversation was awkward – she and I had never been in
this position before. Victoria told me she was still going to have
my two youngest children at weekends, as we always did, to
maintain the routine. As we were saying goodbye a flight of F18
Hornet attack aircraft blasted down the runway, all but drowning
my voice, which upset her. Now she was in no doubt that I was in
a war zone and possibly in harm's way. I reminded her that I
would be safe in the rear with all the gear.

I hit my green maggot (army sleeping-bag) at 01.00 hours, but
Doug and Malcolm were still out on the prowl. I hoped Doug
was behaving himself – he had recently started dating Victoria's
friend and work colleague, Sara. As I lay there, trying to sleep, I
was a little concerned about the lack of intelligence and orders.
No one seemed to know to whom we reported or the scope of
our operation. But I had learnt a long time ago that sooner or later
all would become clear. The constant air traffic resulted in a
sleepless night, and by sun-up Doug still hadn't returned. I got out
of bed, shaved and got dressed in my uniform. I had a nice new
pair of desert boots, and decided to wear them. As a rule, you take
worn-in boots on operations, but this time I knew I had plenty of
time to wear them in, pounding around Konya airbase. I went to
look for my team and found Doug with Malcolm and Baby Steve,
somehow sharing two sleeping-bags between them.

'I don't want to know what you've been up to but I'll meet
you over at the McDonald's trailer for breakfast,' I told them.

The only reply I got was a series of grunts. John and Steve had
arrived in the early hours, met up with Doug and Malcolm and
decided to have a bottle of Bud, which naturally led to a few
more.

On my way to McDonald's, I spotted Romero and Athansa
doing their early-morning run round the base perimeter. I waved.

'Meet you in hangar six at eight-thirty,' Romero called as he ran past. 'Our CIA man has pitched up with all the details we need.'

John joined me for breakfast, but the others were still comatose. We spotted the loaf man from the Learjet heading towards hangar six, still with his briefcase attached to his wrist. I knew then that he was the CIA officer assigned to our team. And, after barely an hour together on a plane, he and Doug hated each other.

'Tell the lads to rest and I'll do the briefing alone,' I told John as I finished my coffee. At least that way I'd keep Doug and the CIA man apart for as long as possible. I wanted to suss the guy out properly: too many times in the past I had been forced to work with uptight, self-important individuals and I wasn't about to endure it again.

I entered hangar six warily and, to my surprise, the first person I saw was Tosh, an old SAS friend. He was dressed in civilian clothes but still looked every inch the classic SAS officer. He bounded over to me. 'Great to see you, Niall,' he said, as we shook hands. 'Didn't expect to see me, though, did you? Let me introduce you to our American colleague.'

As he ushered me towards the CIA man, Romero and Athansa appeared.

'Niall, meet Guss,' said Tosh, introducing me to the loaf. 'He's got all the relevant info and contacts and will be working closely with your team. Very closely indeed,' Tosh added, as I shook the man's hand.

From the way Tosh was scratching his head I knew that we were saddled with Guss, whether we liked it or not. I did my usual polite-greetings bit, and Guss launched into a hurried explanation as to why he had said nothing to me on the plane. He was on this great, all-encompassing mission with top-secret documents, he explained, and it was his first ever unsupervised operation. Anyone would be nervous and apprehensive in such a situation, he added. At least he knew how to take his job seriously.

We gathered round a collapsible table, grabbed some coffee and Guss flipped open his attaché case. Shortly, we were all engrossed in the paperwork. There were photos of some Kurdish leaders we were to try to contact, but only names and brief written descriptions of others. Gradually, Guss relaxed a little – he became positively perky when I told him to ditch the suit and get hold of some green gear to blend in with the rest of us. A little later, John joined us, introduced himself to Guss and Tosh, and started to study the documents.

Tosh and I had met at Hereford, then gone on to Camberley Officer Staff College together. I'd had no idea that he was coming on this operation, but it was great to have him there. It turned out that Patrick had asked him to join us: he'd wanted someone to act as the TCG (tasking and co-ordination group/tactical control group) officer to support me on the ground. Although he hadn't said so to me, Patrick hadn't believed I would stay in Turkey with the gear: he had known that I wouldn't be able to resist the challenge of the work. Instead Tosh would be our logistical back-up and comms (communications) man at base, while the rest of us were in the Kurdish areas of Iraq. He would also be our liaison link with Head Shed in the UK, and General Franks, the overall commander, in theatre.

We were now joined by another surprise member of the team, Dianne, a captain in the Royal Army Medical Corps, whom Patrick had recruited as our doctor, and to offer medical help to the Kurdish populations we would be dealing with. I thought we wouldn't need her – and seriously doubted that many Arab or Kurdish men would want a female doctor ministering to them. She was clearly nervous: this was her first covert operation, and she didn't know what would be expected of her.

I asked how she ended up on the operation. It turned out that she had only recently finished her training, and that the MoD had sponsored her through university on the understanding that she would put in six years' service with the armed forces. Ten male doctors had been approached to do the operation, but all had turned it down. Dianne had jumped at the chance. As she and I talked, I noticed that John was staring at the maps we had laid out on the table in front of us. I asked what was on his mind. 'Nothing, boss, honest,' he replied. But I sensed that something was eating him. I decided to tackle him later, when we were alone.

Doug, Malcolm and Steve finally surfaced just after eleven. I called an O (orders) group in one of our Portakabins, told them the good news about Guss, which went down like a lead balloon with Doug, then introduced them to Dianne.

'You male, female or a cross between the two?' Doug asked.

'Whatever you want me to be,' she replied. John and Malcolm roared with laughter.

The team spent the rest of the day poring over photographs and discussing which of the Kurdish leaders it seemed most likely that we could meet and bring on-side. One character in whom we were all immediately interested was Wajy Barzani, the head of the Kurds' own Special Forces. He was operating out of the north-western Iraqi mountains, which was where we wanted to start our operations. As he was fellow Special Forces, we thought we might be able to forge a natural bond with him. Also, MI6 and the CIA were already talking to him.

Later, I introduced the team to the Kurds' political and religious background. Doug groaned and disappeared with John to check our weapons, radios and other kit.

Over the weeks since I'd agreed to take on the operation I'd done some research. 'Peshmerga' means 'ready to die', and is the term used for all Kurdish fighters in northern Iraq. Most were loyal to either the Kurdistan Democratic Party (KDP) or the Patriotic Union of Kurdistan (PUK). The KDP was led by Massoud Barzani, Wajy's brother, and the PUK by Jalal Tala-bani, two of the main leaders we were seeking to recruit to the

Allied war effort. The KDP and PUK each had 25,000–30,000 men under arms, which was why we needed them on our side to fight against Saddam's forces in the north. Many were veterans, with years of combat experience gained from fighting either the Iraqis or, in some cases, each other. The fragile alliance that now existed between the two parties was only a recent development. Could they be organised and trusted to fight as a co-ordinated force?

I went on to talk about the makeup of the Kurdish guerrilla forces. The Peshmerga enjoyed near mythical status in Kurdish society. During numerous rebellions against successive regimes in Baghdad, they had been the Kurds' first and last line of defence, drawing on their hardiness and intimate knowledge of the Zagros mountains. For several years the CIA and MI6 had been working quietly in the region, and many of the Peshmerga had come down from the mountains to swap their baggy trousers and bandoliers for US-supplied fatigues and basic training in a more conventional military approach. I was eager to meet them.

Service in the Peshmerga force was voluntary, and while the majority were men, there was also a 500-strong women's battalion. It had been established in 1996, and was now commanded by twenty-seven-year-old Sirwa Ismael, and consisted of women whose husbands and loved ones had been killed by the Iraqi military. At a training camp outside the Kurdish city of Sulaymaniyah, young women were schooled in the arts of attack, ambush and sabotage, and the use of Soviet-era weapons.

Malcolm's ears had pricked up at the mention of women. He immediately volunteered to train and liaise with them. Both the KDP and PUK had set up military academies over the past decade, which taught maths, computer science and history as well as weapons' use, tactical awareness and strategy.

In terms of weaponry the Peshmerga had mainly small arms. Any artillery was old and salvaged from attacks on Iraqi positions.

AK47 assault rifles, some very old, were the standard weapon of a Peshmerga fighter, as well as RPGs (rocket-propelled grenades). AK47s could still be had for as little as twenty-five dollars in the arms bazaar at Arbil, the administrative heart of the Kurdish-run enclave in northern Iraq. They had no tanks or armoured vehicles, so Hi-lux Toyotas and pick-ups were the commonest forms of motor transport. Most Peshmerga travelled by donkey or on foot.

Having suffered horrendous losses in 1991, at the end of the first Gulf War – when the US had called on the Kurds to rise up against Saddam – the KDP and PUK had opened negotiations with the Iraqi government. In 1992, after an election of sorts, power in the Kurdish region was split almost fifty-fifty between the two parties. However, rivalry between them soon resulted in civil war, with the KDP mainly concentrated in the north and the PUK in the south. This continued until 1998, with both sides claiming jurisdiction over the whole of Iraqi Kurdistan. Then, leaders from both groups had signed a peace agreement brokered by the CIA and Washington.

Now it was our turn to liaise with the Kurdish groups and persuade them to organise co-ordinated opposition against Saddam's forces. To that end the CIA put together a joint-operations command centre (JOC) at their headquarters in Langley, Virginia. Much of the intel from there would reach us through Guss. Although my immediate mandate was a freewheeling one, we would be working under the nominal control of US Special Forces in northern Iraq. I had no problem with that because I enjoyed working with the US military. Now it was up to us to bring the Peshmerga into the fold.

After my lecture, we were given a couple of hair-raising flights in two UH60 Black Hawk helicopters, operated by the top-secret Helicopter Task Force 160, a black-operations aviation unit. Our British Special Forces choppers retain standard identification marks, indicating they are British military and RAF. All exterior signs are removed from covert-ops helicopters, so that operational deniability is assured if one is seen or shot down. However, the helicopters of Task Force 160 took secrecy to an altogether different level. The Black Hawks not only had all exterior markings removed, but each and every component and part number had been removed from inside them. If ever one went down behind enemy lines no one would be able to tell where it had come from. They had been put at our disposal for the Iraq mission. One of the pilots, another Steve, was on secondment from the RAF to Helicopter Task Force 160.

Later that evening I found Malcolm reading the intel reports on the female Peshmerga. He had become captivated by them. To him they were the twenty-first-century answer to the Amazons. I reminded myself to keep an eye on him in theatre. The Kurdish women's fight to prove their worth as soldiers had been tough, but they had built a reputation for bravery and skill in the battlefield. We all had to treat them with the greatest respect.

We spent the next couple of days preparing for the operation. Doug, Romero, John and Malcolm concentrated on the weapons and the gear, while Baby Steve, Tosh, Guss and I tried to formulate a working operational plan. The only person who seemed at a loss was Dianne, who must have checked and double-checked her medical and field-surgery kit a dozen or more times even after she was joined by a US Navy surgeon. Over dinner, Dianne exclaimed in frustration that she felt like a spare prick never knowing what to do with herself. Silence fell on our table, before Malcolm stood up and gleefully informed her he had more than enough spare prick ready and good to go, if she really did feel like one – which sent everyone at the table into fits of laughter.

Guss was receiving updated intelligence daily from the CIA and the NSA (National Security Agency), and as we studied it we got to know each other quite well. He had mellowed and opened up considerably since his arrival. Everyone kept telling him to go

with the flow, but I think he saw his first operation as a test he had
to pass in order to further his career with the CIA. Through
contacts in northern Iraq we had been able to open up dialogue
with three of the main Kurdish leaders. An Iraqi general had also
been in contact with Allied intelligence, claiming that he and his
soldiers were willing to defect. Although he withheld his identity
on security grounds, we agreed that we would try to meet up
with him in Kurdish Iraq in the near future. Naturally, our main
concern was whether he was genuine – or an Iraqi intelligence
trickster trying to ascertain Allied intentions for war.

After some deliberation we decided to enter northern Iraq via
the disputed Kurdish area nearest to the Turkish border. We
would work on the groups located there first, so that if it all went
pear-shaped we didn't have far to leg it for home. When we had
brought them on-side, we would move further in theatre. Our
SEAL team had arrived at Konya, and would be on constant
standby to rescue us if the need arose. Or, at least, that was the
plan. But the SEAL lads raised merry hell at being left on the
sidelines, as they saw it, so we agreed a compromise: a small
number of SEALs would join our team when we went in on the
initial operation. All being well, we would bring in the others as it
developed.

It took some serious arguing on my part to convince the SEALs
that I didn't need all of them in theatre at the start. Eventually I
pointed out that if I kept some in reserve, I could promise the
Kurdish leaders that more US Special Forces would become
available if they agreed to work with us. Finally they seemed to
accept this rather British logic. However, when they discovered
that I had completed the SEAL selection course some years earlier
at the US Navy Special Warfare Command Centre in Coronado,
they gave me their unqualified support. Sir Peter de la Billière,
then commander of the SAS, had instituted exchange tours
between ourselves and the US SEALs and Delta Force, then

decided we should prove how tough and versatile we were by undergoing the course. I was one of the first unfortunates to have this thrust upon me, but now I was glad I'd done it.

That evening Guss slapped in front of me a thick folder of the latest CIA intel on the Peshmerga. It was dated November. I asked how come this was the latest intel when it was already weeks old. Guss simply shrugged. It was what his agency was sending him, he said. It included a newspaper report filed by the *Guardian*'s Michael Howard, dated 26 November 2002. Top secret? I began to think that the CIA and MI6 had got cold feet about the war, and that intel was being cobbled together from whatever sources they could summon. As the start date for the war came closer, the intel grew thinner and thinner. No one wanted to commit themselves – and get the blame if everything went wrong.

Likewise the Peshmerga were circumspect about their support for any war. They didn't want to be left high and dry by Allied forces again to face an onslaught from Saddam's military. This time they wanted to meet us face to face on their turf and to have Allied Special Forces on the ground with them, among their fighters. Intel reports told me that their morale appeared high: despite their lack of heavy weaponry the Peshmerga were apparently 'ready and willing for action'. Both the PUK and the KDP maintained they could double their number of fighters, bringing in some forty thousand irregulars, which meant that each group would have around seventy thousand under their command.

The Kurds were the only armed opposition forces present on the ground in Iraq, and recognised that they were no match in a head-to-head with Saddam's tanks or helicopter gunships. Their constant request to us was for more weapons, plus anti-tank and anti-aircraft missiles. At the top of their shopping list, however, were chemical and biological warfare (CBW) suits and respirators.

We had arrived in Konya on 6 January and by the twelfth we were ready to go. I had decided that our earlier instincts had been right, and that our first meeting should be with Wajy Barzani, a seasoned, highly respected Peshmerga, head of their Special Forces, and younger brother of KDP head Massoud Barzani. By now I had all the intel on him that I needed so we set our departure time for the following evening at just after sundown. On the afternoon before we left I called Victoria, who was at work, and told her I had asked Tosh to email her any developments while I was in theatre. She said Sara was upset because Doug hadn't called her. 'He's out on the ranges so he can't,' I said. It wasn't true, of course, but I had to say something.

I'd just started strapping on my body armour when John came into my Portakabin and handed me a letter without a word. It was for his wife and children, and I knew he'd given it to me in case he didn't come out alive. I'd never seen him worried before, even when our backs had been against the wall in Afghanistan. It didn't bode well for the coming operation: all it takes is for one man in the team to lose confidence and the rest will follow. Everyone in the team had learnt to trust their gut instincts over the years, so if someone developed serious reservations about an operation, you listened: they were often uncannily accurate. I offered John the chance to stay behind with Tosh, but he said he'd be all right.

'Listen, John, I can't guarantee anything,' I told him, 'but we do have the best set-up going, as well as some serious back-up if we run into trouble. We're under the wing of the US military on this one – and they leave no one behind.'

After John had left, I ran through my copy of the US search-and-rescue manual. I hadn't forgotten the story of the ill-fated SAS Bravo Two Zero operation in the first Gulf War. They had been compromised on the ground only to discover that their radios and tacbes (tactical beacons, an emergency location and communications device) didn't work: they had been given the wrong frequencies.

At 16.00 hours we gathered in the hangar for the final pre-operation briefing. None of us recognised Guss in full desert combats, bristling with radio antennae and an M4 assault rifle, complete with an M203 40mm grenade-launcher. He had also shaved off his previously thick dark hair. When he saw that we were each wearing a dish–dash, an Arab robe, over our combats, and had shemaghs (headcloths) round our necks, he ran off to find some for himself.

When he got back, he asked why we had different assault rifles from him. Romero explained that they were the Canadian Diemaco C7s, the favoured weapon for UK and US Special Forces. Guss decided he wanted one too. Doug told him it would be useless to him as it wouldn't be zeroed in to suit his vision, but Guss went off anyway to find one, fuelling Doug's growing dislike of him. I could have told Guss to sit down and stop fucking around, but it was wiser to let him go: that way he would have no grievance against me or any excuse to sulk. I had learnt from past experience that it was little things like that which could cause the biggest problems in the field. Anyway, we were OK for time as the chopper wouldn't leave until 18.00 hours.

We double-checked the radio frequencies, batteries, weapons and our cover story, should we be caught – that we were mercenaries hired by the KDP – and then it was time for the off. I was glad we were finally getting on with it. Over the past few days we had received messages from the US and the UK that the operation was off, then delayed, then back on. If they sent another now I would ignore it and claim that we had been on our way to the chopper and had missed it. Just as we were about to leave, Admiral Gregory Johnson, US Navy commander, Allied forces southern Europe, appeared with an entourage of buttlickers, as Athansa referred to them. He was visiting and inspecting the AWACs. We vanished before he got near us.

Everyone, including Tosh, Dianne and the SEAL team lads, came out to see us off as we climbed aboard the awaiting Black Hawks. Tosh grabbed my hand, shook it, and yelled above the whine of the chopper's turbines that he'd keep Victoria updated daily. As soon as he'd said it, I had a powerful gut feeling that it wasn't a good idea, but I nodded, then climbed aboard. John, Doug, Malcolm, Baby Steve, Romero, Athansa, Guss and Ian, one of the SEAL team lads, were already inside. We looked a right bunch of bandits, in our dish-dashes and headcloths, bristling with weaponry. It crossed my mind that we were more likely to scare the Kurds off than befriend them. Then I heard Tosh yell through the open door of the chopper: 'Niall! If you don't make it back, mate, don't worry about Victoria. I'll look after her and keep her serviced for you.'

I smiled and gave him the thumbs-up. It was a clumsy attempt at boys' humour – and how could he know that I was already feeling unsettled about him and Victoria? The whine of the engines was ear-splitting now, and suddenly I remembered how much I hated helicopters. Ten crash landings over fourteen years was an unbeatable record as far as I was concerned. At least Steve, the RAF pilot, was at the Black Hawk's controls. Seconds later, we started to ascend. This was it. No going back now.

I put on a headset patched into the aircrew's intercom so I could talk to Pilot Steve. I had studied all I could about the Black Hawk helicopter and felt confident in its capabilities, but the Iraqis had a fully functioning air-defence system up and running, and there was always the chance that Allied aircraft might mistake us for an Iraqi chopper. To avoid any chance of friendly fire, Mark, Steve's co-pilot, was constantly talking to Allied aircraft in the region, identifying who we were: 'Red Fox Four, hello, AWACs, informing you of our bearing . . .'

Guss was looking anxious. Who wouldn't be on their first operation? I asked myself. I had assumed that he would be staying at Konya, but apparently the CIA wanted hands-on in theatre and Guss was their man. His confidence had taken a knock when his more experienced CIA partner had shot himself just before deployment. Like us, Guss suspected it might not have been an accident because shortly beforehand the man had told him he had a bad feeling about Iraq and wanted out.

It seemed an age before we banked hard right at the Tigris river and followed it south. Even at night we could see lush pastures and greenery, not desert as we had all imagined. As we approached the Iraqi border my heartbeat quickened. John looked across at me, and I mouthed, 'OK?' He grinned and gave me a thumbs-up. Doug was fast asleep. Malcolm was having trouble with his dish–dash and fidgeting with it. Baby Steve was watching the landscape that stretched away beneath us through the doorway. Romero and Athansa sat back to back, focused on their own thoughts. They had cut their teeth in Somalia in 1993, then in the Balkans and Afghanistan.

'Going dark, people,' said Steve, in my headset, then all illumination was switched off, including navigation and warning lights.

We dropped even lower, which jolted Doug awake. Pilot Steve was now operating on PNGs (passive night-vision goggles) and flying 'nape of the land', dangerously close to the ground. As we carved a path through the mountainous terrain the chopper was going all over the shop – up, down, left, right and up again. The aircrew were keeping radio chatter to a minimum now, in case Iraqi military were monitoring the airwaves. All I could hear was Mark warning Pilot Steve about what lay ahead, as he read the information off a computerised virtual-reality-type mock–up of the terrain. 'In fifty, turn five degrees left to avoid re-entrant peak . . .'

Soon Steve told us we were nearing our drop-off point: 'ETA LZ five, TOG [time on ground] less than one, please.'

I wiggled my index finger in a circular motion above my head – 'wind-up time' – indicating that we were nearly on target, be ready. When you'd been working as a team for a while, as we had, you developed a series of hand signals unique to yourselves, in addition to the basic fieldcraft hand signals taught to all soldiers. Before we knew it the Black Hawk had slowed to a hover, and Pilot Steve announced, 'Thank you all for flying with Black Hawk Mountain Tour Airways. We do hope you had an enjoyable flight and will be flying with us again soon.'

I was last off the chopper, and before the dust from its rotor wash had settled, the Black Hawk was out of sight. We lay in all-round defence and listened carefully for a few minutes. We were in a small gully and the ground was pretty flat all around us. Malcolm got on the radio and sent a short sitrep (situation report) to Tosh that we were down and to wait out. I checked the map and oriented it to the surrounding features. Sure enough, we looked to be bang on target. Ahead, there would be a disused church, our rendezvous point with Wajy Barzani in the morning, and other members of his following. The rest of us made for cover, while Romero and Athansa scouted forward to locate it and check it out. Within five minutes Romero made radio contact.

'Hello, India One Sunray, this is India Two. All clear, over.'

I pushed the throat mic up to my neck and whispered, 'India One Sunray, roger, out.'

We set off towards the church in the moonlight, down a shallow valley. On one side there was a dense grove of lemon and orange trees, and the forlorn old church. It had a square stone tower with a flat roof, and what would once have been an arched stained-glass window at one end. Unsurprisingly, there was no sign of life.

As Athansa and Romero skirted in a wider arc, checking the surrounding terrain, sweat trickled down my back although it was very cold. We were high in the mountains where the temperature dropped steeply at night, and the stars were all out, shining far more brightly than anyone who has never visited such a remote location could imagine. There was little or no light pollution.

Shortly after Romero and Athansa returned we heard packs of wild dogs moving about in the darkness. We had been warned about these dangerous animals and I did not want a hungry pack to pay us a visit now. We would have had to shoot off rounds, attracting every man and his donkey to the area. We could not light a fire to ward them off, either: at that height it would have been a beacon to Saddam – 'Come and get us!' As the night wore on Romero and Athansa set up booby-traps – claymores (directional charges that fire a hail of steel ball bearings), grenades and such like – in case of other unwanted visitors, but for manual detonation. We didn't want anything to set them off inadvertently.

We were in Kurdish-controlled territory and relatively safe from Saddam's forces, but I was too wired to sleep and ran through some common Arabic phrases, but I was pretty rusty. Malcolm offered me coffee from the Thermos he always kept by his side. We were not in covert-observation mode so the smell would not compromise our position. In any case, a bloody great helicopter had just landed a few hundred yards away and flown off again, and if that hadn't alerted anyone, coffee certainly wouldn't. As I took a sip, I caught a dark outline in the corner of my eye. As quickly as I turned, it was gone. I put the coffee down, Malcolm and I raised our weapons and looked towards a shadowy recess where the entrance to the old tower would once have been.

As we crept towards it, Malcolm pulled down his PNGs, muttering that he couldn't see anything. Suddenly a figure in what looked like a monk's habit loomed out of the darkness. I jumped, but my weapon was up and pointing at it. Slowly, the figure stepped forward and lowered his hood. Malcolm, clearly shocked, raised the PNGs – even with them, he hadn't seen the man. I kept my rifle on the man, who looked very old, while Malcolm did a quick body-search.

'I am no threat to you, my friends,' he said, in good, but accented English.

Malcolm finished frisking him and Romero came over, concerned that he and Athansa had missed the old man when they had searched the building.

Strangely, he didn't seem surprised by our arrival. I asked him who he was and what he was doing there. He said he was a Roman Catholic priest and had lived in a small underground crypt beneath the church, where he was safe from the wild dogs. He could not remember his exact age, but was in his late eighties, and had been there alone for nearly forty years. He had come here in the 1960s to check on the old church in this isolated valley, but the area was mainly Muslim and the Christians had long since left. On his first night there he had camped outside the ruined church. Even then there were wild dogs, so he had lit a big fire. While he was praying he had seen a ball of light descend from the sky. A figure had appeared and told him that one day, many years in the future, he would see another vision in the same spot, which would become a sacred place. The figure had vanished and the light had raced off across the sky.

'Fucking bizarre,' said Malcolm.

'So ET's been here, too,' Doug added. He'd heard the last part of the priest's tale.

For a while I sat with the old man, who looked at peace with himself and the world. He was very still and quiet, watching us. Now and then I caught him staring at me directly with a fixed smile. I wondered if he was a little mad. He didn't ask me anything about who we were or what we were doing there. As dawn broke and the first rays of sunlight streamed across the mountaintops, he grabbed my arm firmly. 'They will come and they will help you, but afterwards you must leave, please,' he said. 'There is only death waiting for you if you don't and there is much you have not completed with your life that you must.'

It occurred to me that he might have been put there by Wajy Barzani, as an early reception party to check us out, but as soon as the thought entered my mind I dismissed it. The man's age, his accent, his monk's robes – none of it fitted with him being a Kurdish plant. It was all very odd and surreal. For a start, how had he known we were there to meet anyone? No one had told him so. Yet he was predicting that the people we'd come to meet would give us the help we needed. And that 'only death' awaited us if we stayed too long.

John had been listening too. He looked troubled: after his earlier worries about the operation this was the last thing he needed. I like to keep an open mind but, right then, the old man's prophecy was unsettling. We had a quick chat, and I turned back to the priest. He was gone. After a few minutes' searching, there was still no sign of him. None of us could explain it.

'Fucking simple. He was a ghost,' said Doug. 'He just stepped into his parallel universe.'

'Probably was as the fucker – sorry, father, forgive me – didn't show up on my PNGs,' Malcolm whispered.

I could see that John was getting more and more agitated. To distract him, I told him to make the next radio call – we had set times to log in each day and if we missed one, Tosh would know that something was up. Malcolm and Romero went to check the underground crypt. After a few minutes Romero backoned me to join them. It was deserted.

'He was a fucking ghost, then,' Malcolm said, and thrust his torch under his chin to creepy effect.

Clearly no one had lived down there for decades.

However, we didn't have time to ponder the old man's disappearance as Wajy and his Kurdish fighters would be arriving shortly. Athansa got out his Tilley stove and rustled up breakfast for us from his MRE (meals, ready to eat) rations, while we kept alert for our visitors. They were due at 10.00 hours local time, but it was gone 14.00 before we spotted them coming up a winding track on donkeys. As they approached, Malcolm stood up to show himself and walked out to greet them, weapon shouldered as the rest of us covered him. It transpired that they were just the forward party. The rest had been delayed when the back axle had snapped on one of their vehicles.

As we made that first contact Guss was edgy and nervous, especially as he viewed the meeting as his responsibility – it was based on the intel he had provided – but within five minutes we were all acting like the best of friends and two young Peshmerga rushed away to inform Wajy Barzani that we were there. Half an hour later two Toyota Hi-lux vehicles packed with people came up the dirt track towards us. There never had been a broken rear axle; both jeeps were fine. They must have been playing it cautious, which was only right and proper and increased my respect for them.

As the Kurdish fighters got out of their vehicles and came towards us, I knew immediately which was Wajy Barzani. Even from a distance he was an impressive figure, and he looked about my age. He wore baggy black trousers, a white silk shirt, an embroidered goatskin waistcoat and a checked scarf, and had a shock of curly dark hair. Although I knew he was in traditional Kurdish dress, I couldn't help thinking it was a great 'Pirates of the Caribbean' look.

Fifteen minutes later we were sitting under a makeshift tent, erected by Barzani's men, and tucking into a hastily prepared meal of spicy goat's meat, unleavened bread, roasted vegetables and olives, a right royal picnic. Romero, Malcolm and Athansa took several Peshmerga and fanned them out across the area, giving them arcs of fire to cover for added security. But they wanted to work in pairs: the area was known to be haunted . . .

Wajy was friendly, and we got into a conversation about Mount Ararat. His English was quaint and peppered with out-of-date phrases. At 16,984 feet high Mount Ararat, a perfect pyramid shape, is called by the Kurds 'the Mountain of Fire'. It is the supposed resting place of Noah's Ark. Wajy asked me some questions about other biblical place names, and I realised he was testing me, trying to discover how much I knew about his region and its rich history.

'So, Sodom and Gomorrah, my friend, where is it found?'

'It's supposed to be at the bottom of the Dead Sea.'

'And Noah's Crossing?' Wajy lowered his sunglasses to reveal his calm yet determined gaze.

'A river near Kirkuk. Legend has it that that was where Noah made his crossing into these lands after the floods receded.'

'And Babylon?'

Eventually Wajy grinned and told me that he had never come across an 'outsider', as he referred to us, who knew as much as I did about their history, their beliefs and their sacred places. I told him that I had been sent to do this job because I loved the region and its native peoples, the Kurds. I hoped one day to live there myself. The last bit was political bullshit, but I wanted to connect with him on a human level.

As he warmed to us, Wajy introduced some of his female Peshmerga. I had told myself that they would be short, fat and clothed from head to toe in black, but I was staggered by their beauty. I had vowed to keep Malcolm on a tight leash but now even I was admiring them. Maybe it was the AK47s slung across their chests that did it for me. At one point Doug nudged me and told me to concentrate on my work, as I was smiling a little too often at a woman called Layla. Later we learnt that if you were a beautiful Kurdish woman, you were singled out for special attention from Saddam's henchmen. This was why so many had fled to the hills.

Wajy told me that some of his female Peshmerga had already seen front-line combat in action against Ansar al-Islam, an extremist Islamic group with suspected links to al-Qaeda, who occupied a string of villages on the border with Iran. 'Thankfully,' said Layla, 'we have not yet had any martyrs.' She smiled beautifully and had such elegance it was hard to imagine her in action on the front line.

After the meal as we sat drinking thick Kurdish coffee, Wajy complained that the US seemed reluctant to equip the Kurds with modern weaponry. When I asked him what he wanted, he glanced at his entourage as if to say, 'Now we're talking,' whipped out a roll of paper from under his goatskin waistcoat, rolled it out on the table and began to reel off a shopping list of arms and equipment – including gas masks and chemical-weapons suits.

As dusk approached the temperature dropped, and the Peshmerga were keen to leave the area. They had suggested the site as a meeting-point because of the belief that it was haunted so no one came there. Before they left, they asked us for MREs and radios – and, of course, for the gold sovereigns they were sure we all carried.

'I have read *Bravo Two Zero* many times,' said Wajy. 'I have read how you Special Forces types have those belts with gold coins stitched into your waistbands.'

I had to half undress to convince him that we were not carrying hidden hoards. I assured him that we could certainly organise some gold sovereigns for him, but explained that the MREs weren't a good idea. In the unlikely event that he and his men ran into an Iraqi army patrol, the discovery of US or British kit on them might alert the Iraqis to our presence.

Before he left, Wajy assured me repeatedly that he was willing to start offensive actions against Saddam Hussein at any time. In turn I emphasised that all attacks had to be carefully orchestrated and professionally executed if we were to succeed against Saddam's forces. I said that the Peshmerga were clearly able to operate with us like this. Wajy was pleased to hear that we viewed them as a professional and intelligent fighting force. We parted company, seemingly as friends, having agreed that my team and I would head down to Wajy's main base the next morning to continue our discussions.

As we prepared for our second night in the haunted valley, Guss came up to Doug and me. 'You know, sir – I mean, boss – I kinda reckon all that stuff about them being professional and intelligent . . . Gee, if that'd been me I'd have felt real patronised,' he murmured.

'That's 'cause you've got a big fucking chip on your shoulder, mate,' Doug retorted, before I had a chance to reply. Guss glared at him. They were shaping up to be trouble, no doubt about it.

John voiced his reservations about going to the Peshmerga base the next day. Indeed, it was a risk, but I'd agreed to show them that we trusted them. Some people there might not be sympathetic to Wajy, John pointed out, and, of course, there were Saddam's ubiquitous spies. He was right, of course, but we had no choice if we wanted to prove our worth to the Peshmerga. We decided to move higher up the valley to set up camp away from the church for the night – in case anyone had reported our presence and position to the enemy. Malcolm told us we were only doing it because we were afraid of the old priest coming back to spook us – but if it had got out that we were at the old church I didn't want to be caught sitting there.

As darkness descended we set up a well-defended position and settled in for the night. I sent a sitrep to Tosh, who responded that all was OK at his end. He added that he'd been chatting up Victoria via text messages. The radio network was secure, so there was no problem with him making jokes over the air, and I had a quiet laugh at the knowledge that the signal would have been monitored somewhere by Allied intelligence. But I still felt a twinge of unease about him and Victoria.

At around 21.00 hours Romero, Athansa, Doug and SEAL Ian went off on foot to do a CTR (close-target recce) of the village where Wajy had a temporary base. In the circumstances this was only a sensible precaution: 'Fail to prepare, prepare to fail,' as the saying goes. The village was around nine miles away from us, but they could get eyes on it from a vantage point some four miles short of it. They would use their night-vision equipment to observe, in case there was anything we should be aware of. They'd stay a couple of hours and be back by the early hours of the morning.

John and I settled down to keep watch as the remainder of the team grabbed some sleep. We were admiring the stars, lost in our own thoughts, when I noticed a pale blue light among the ruins of the old church. I nudged John and nodded in the direction of the eerie glow below us. We assumed it was an Iraqi hit team, using old-style NVGs (night-vision goggles), which give off a faint glow. As we prepared to wake the others I was considering whether fight or flight would be our best option when the light moved out of the front entrance, across what was left of the roof and straight up the church tower. Then the ball of light glided to the opposite side of the valley and disappeared over the forested ridge.

'What the fuck was that all about?' John whispered, breaking the eerie silence.

'No idea. ET? UFO? Flying orbs? God only knows.'

Such phenomena had always interested me, and for a moment I wished that I wasn't there as a soldier. This valley certainly had a 'presence' unlike anything else I'd experienced.

Around 05.00 hours Guss was anxious: our CTR patrol had

not returned. They had been due back at 04.45. We had agreed not to use our PRRs (personal-role radios, used for communications in theatre) unless we absolutely had to, in case the Iraqis were monitoring the airwaves. Also, we kept hearing packs of wild dogs roaming the valley floor. Shortly after the strange blue light had appeared, they had howled for several minutes, which spooked us.

My earpiece crackled three times with radio static: zzzt, zzzt, zzzt. This was the signal that they were coming in. When you're deployed on covert operations you can't shout, 'Halt, who goes there? Advance one and be recognised,' then demand passwords, for obvious reasons. All you do is depress your radio prestle switch to signal with radio static, which is inaudible to anyone else.

They came into camp, freezing cold after their night march, and Romero gave me the lowdown. The village seemed clean: there were no Iraqi military vehicles or personnel, as far as they could see. Doug and Malcolm joked that they were convinced they'd been followed on the long walk back. 'Fucking expected that dreadlocked fucker from *Predator* to fall out of one of the trees in front of me,' Doug concluded.

We were all sensible, no-nonsense soldiers but that valley was unnerving.

In the morning we gathered our kit together, made sure that we had left not a scrap of evidence of our presence, and headed for the village. With our dish-dashes on over our desert combats we didn't look out of place, but as we approached the village it seemed that every man, woman and child knew who we were and what we were doing there. As we traipsed past they stared at us as if we were aliens, and I wondered what they thought of us.

The main road was in a serious state of deterioration, and mud-faced houses with sheaths of tan-coloured sesame on the roofs fronted on to it. Turkeys scurried everywhere, while groups of men sat on stools, playing backgammon. Women passed us, dressed in black with veils across their faces, balancing baskets on their heads. It was as if we had stepped back hundreds of years. Only the service station and café told us that we were in the twenty-first century. A child shouted, 'Israelis! Israelis!' I knew that, over the years, Israeli Special Forces and intelligence people had been busy in the region, doing God only knew what.

Suddenly children were crowding around us, cheering and asking for sweets. To their delight, Romero and Athansa passed out handfuls of toffees. We stood around for ages, with no one too sure of what was going on, until Wajy appeared, with yet another beautiful Peshmerga woman on his arm.

'The day's looking up,' said Malcolm.

Wajy greeted me effusively and led me to his house, which was little different from any other in the village.

'I'll secure the area, boss. Can't be doing with another fucking history lesson,' Doug whispered, as we went in. He, John, Athansa and SEAL Ian went to take up positions around the village.

Meanwhile, Guss sent a sitrep that we were in location, and we settled down to what turned out to be a mammoth eating, drinking and talking session. I presumed the young woman was Wajy's wife, although he never said so. I was introduced to what I thought were his daughter and a young son, but again he was guarded. They might not have been his at all. Perhaps it was all a front. To begin with, the little girl was shy, but soon I was trying to eat with her sitting on my knee. She was showing me two little dolls, her only toys.

After we had eaten, Wajy got down to business, asking me if I had meant all that I'd said the previous day. He was openly unsure of me. On this type of op you never divulge any true personal details, and this generally works, so long as your story is tight and you don't trip yourself up. If you do, you immediately lose your target's trust and you might as well pack up and leave. Bearing in mind how much we needed Wajy and his Special Forces

Peshmerga on board, I decided to paint the canvas of my story as close to the truth as I dared: I knew that the Kurds would spot a lie or a bluff a mile off. So, when he asked me to tell him about my life and family, I knew how I had to respond. I glanced at Doug, who had rejoined us: his expression told me to go ahead, but to be discreet.

Suddenly Guss blundered in: 'We don't talk about that kind of stuff, sir.'

I could see that Doug was horrified.

'Normally, we don't,' I countered, as I bounced Wajy's little girl on my knee, 'but we do when we trust those we're dealing with.'

'Aha! So you trust me?' Wajy sat back and scrutinised me, arms folded.

'I'll be frank with you, Wajy,' I said, and met his eye. 'You've brought us into your home and let us meet your wife and lovely children.' I paused to let him correct me if he wanted to, but he didn't. 'Only a fool, or a man who does not care for his family, would risk a meeting such as this unless he trusted his guests. As you're no fool, and you clearly love your family, you must trust us.'

There was a long silence. Then Wajy broke into a huge smile. 'Ah, my friend, you are good, very good, and I am liking you more and more.' He ordered yet another round of coffee and I breathed a silent sigh of relief.

Wajy asked me to tell him my real name. When we had met the day before, I'd given him a false one, as had the rest of my team. It's standard operating procedure (SOP): if everything went wrong and the Peshmerga took us prisoner, Wajy couldn't call the press, give them our real names and play the hostage game. Both Doug and Guss looked anxious now, but I smiled at Wajy and told him I was called Simon, the name of a friend I'd grown up with.

'So, it is Simon,' Wajy confirmed. 'An easy name for us. Good . . . good.' He was leaning back, relaxing in his chair, now, the testing almost over.

It was mid-afternoon when I was taken to the centre of the village and shown a little river that snaked beneath an ancient bridge. Wajy claimed that this was where Noah had stopped on his journey through the Kurdish heartlands, as told in biblical traditions. I added a few details, which increased his faith in me. By the end of the day we had agreed to return within the week, by which time Wajy would have arranged for us to meet his brother, Massoud, the leader of the KDP, and other key Kurdish figures. We would rendezvous either in Wajy's village or at another secure location where I could present my plans for the Peshmerga to fight alongside coalition forces in the coming war.

As the cold of night fell over the hills we tabbed back to the haunted valley, with Doug setting a fast pace – Malcolm had been taking the piss out of his age, which spurred him on. We arrived at the LZ where Pilot Steve had dropped us off just as the Black Hawk landed. We climbed aboard and flew away from the valley fast and incredibly low, but not before I had taken a last look at the old church and remembered all the weird things that had happened there.

3

DEAR JOHN

We were all dozing in the rear of the chopper when an almighty bang thumped through the underbelly of the aircraft, jerking us awake. The co-pilot looked back at us, then burst into laughter. We had an American aircrew – I wondered where Steve had got to. Bang, The chopper had been hit again. This wasn't funny. I clambered across the open cargo area, put on the spare radio headset and demanded to know what was going on. The pilot told me there was nothing to worry about and that he'd fill me in once he'd put us down.

I sat down again and glanced at John, who was clearly stressing out. He looked like he'd be in tears at any moment. Nothing had seemed to scare him in the past and I'd never seen him like this before. When we put down at Konya airbase, I had to ease him out, as he was shaking so much. Tosh rushed across to greet us and check that John hadn't been hurt.

'I'm OK, guys, don't fuss,' John shouted, above the noise. 'Just a little airsick and feeling groggy. Dodgy food.' He pushed away my arm and walked off fast towards the Portakabins. I knew then that something was really getting to him.

Before I could head after him, Tosh grabbed me. We were

moving out of Konya, he told me, to a specially prepared FOB right on the Turkey–Iraq border, near Cizre. The new base had several advantages: it would allow us to come and go as we liked without attracting unwanted interest; it was shielded from prying eyes inside a gorge; and it was near the river Tigris, which made it easier for the pilots to navigate to and from base. I gave an in-depth debrief to Tosh, then he and Guss got on the comms to the UK and the US respectively, both keen to report the results of a largely successful operation.

I went to find John, but he wouldn't admit that anything was wrong. He said he must've picked up a bug, or maybe it was a dose of malaria coming back to haunt him. I decided I'd have to keep a close eye on him, then went and clobbered the pilot for the hair-raising flight. He explained we had been flying so low, at the helicopter's fastest speed, that every time it went over slightly raised ground the downwash bounced up and smashed into the aircraft's underbelly. Hence the loud bangs. He seemed to think it was all a great laugh. When Doug found out that the stunt had been about getting scrape marks from loose stones to impress the female mechanics, he was ready to bump the pilot across the tarmac.

When we had cleaned our weapons and stowed our kit I sloped off to call Victoria. We had a nice long chat and she told me to thank Tosh for his texts and emails – they'd been really funny. It sounded a bit odd, but I brushed it off and went on to ring my kids. I assured the two youngest I was OK, remaining in the rear with all the gear, just as I'd promised them. I felt bad lying to them, but it was better than worrying them with the truth. As I walked back to my Portakabin I thought again about John. I knew if I pushed it he might freak. Perhaps I should go ahead and let him – better it happened at the base than in the field. I decided to sleep on it and sound him out in the morning.

The following morning Tosh was organising our relocation to the Cizre FOB and getting nowhere fast. He was being too officious and demanding, so Romero took over with diplomacy and bribes, and we soon had what we needed. Guss, John, Doug and I decided to run through the latest CIA intel reports detailing Turkey's growing concern about the Peshmerga role in the coming war. The Turkish government feared they would rush headlong into Kirkuk, the Kurds' holiest city, and take immediate control of it. This Turkey viewed as unacceptable, probably because Kirkuk had the biggest oil reserves and refinery in Iraq. I recognised a name on one report: Dan Meany was one of the CIA operators on the ground with other Kurds. I knew him of old and asked Guss to arrange a meeting with him as soon as possible – I didn't want any overlap or, worse still, to risk a blue-on-blue (friendly fire) incident.

I was also concerned about the Turks' plans to send thousands of their own troops into Kurdish Iraq when the invasion started. They were arguing that they needed to sort out a specific Kurdish terrorist threat, and this was the ideal opportunity to do so. I knew that the Kurds would never agree to this. But if the Turks were not allowed to go ahead, they would refuse the US 4th Division permission to deploy into northern Iraq from their territory. Bloody marvellous, I thought. If the US 4th Division couldn't invade from Turkey, the US military couldn't offer the Kurds the heavy weapons and ground support they wanted. It was looking highly likely that the only support we'd be able to give was intel, air power and a handful of British and American Special Forces. I was relieved when the next intel I received confirmed that the US 173rd Airborne Division was stationed in Italy, being made ready to deploy into the northern sectors instead of the 4th.

As we considered the dilemma, John told me that the whole operation 'stank from tip to toe'. I sent him to the ranges to do some weapons firing with Athansa – hoped it would take his mind off things. But even Doug looked strained, which was unusual as he wasn't one for entertaining self-doubt. But at least I'd had prior warning of what might be about to happen. I couldn't promise massive US ground support in case Turkey pulled the plug so I had to come up with a convincing reason why Special Forces, coupled with air support, would be a more effective means of fighting in the area. We would be heavily reliant on the Peshmerga troops, but maybe that would play well with their egos. In any case, I didn't have another option.

Forty-eight hours later we touched down at our new base, and Tosh, who had flown in ahead of us, showed us round our tented home. The FOB consisted of a double helicopter landing area, a mobile workshop, an avgas (aviation fuel) holding area, a shower tent, food tent, weapons and ammo point, and several neat lines of four-man tents for us to crash in. Then there was the operations and planning tent, looking more like a marquee, with the medical tent and chemical deconta-mination unit beside it.

As we made ourselves at home Doug rushed off to be first on the laptops and email Sara. Tosh was looking pleased with his efforts when Athansa came over with several of the SEAL lads. They were somewhat perplexed. 'Hey, like, where's the range?' Athansa asked.

Tosh looked as if someone had just rammed a broom handle up his backside. 'Oh, shit.' Finally, he pointed at the helicopter landing area. 'Set one up there,' he said. Incredulity all round. 'You'll just have to put sentries out with flags,' he blurted out, 'so they can stop any firing when air traffic comes in.'

Athansa put his hand on Tosh's shoulder. 'Don't worry about it, bud,' he said, with a pitying smile. 'We'll go sort it out.'

At around 17.00 hours Guss ran out of the ops tent, Tosh following him. 'I've got you Dan Meany comin' over right now,' he announced proudly. 'He's on his way in one of our latest toys.'

Within minutes everyone was standing at the helipad, which had had a light sprinkling of water to keep the dust down. Suddenly, over the rim of the gorge, we saw an odd-looking aircraft. It was rather like a streamlined Apache attack helicopter, but stranger still, it was flying into the gorge fast – and sideways. We tried our hardest to look unimpressed as the pilot flew sideways across our landing zone, then hovered remarkably quietly and put down. Most ordinary helicopters can hover sideways but they can't fly sideways at nearly 70 m.p.h. as this one had, and I was impressed.

Dan Meany introduced himself to all like some conquering hero, jumping out of the chopper's hold sporting wrap-around Rayban sunglasses.

'Wanker,' Doug said aloud, before heading off to the food tent for more curry.

Dan Meany and I had first met in Afghanistan, many years before, and his vigorous handshake and over-the-top greeting drew questioning looks from the SEAL lads. Romero came over and shook his hand. He, too, had worked with Dan before, but they had not got on. I left the others to gawk at the chopper – which was an experimental RAH-66 Comanche – and headed off with Dan to the ops tent. Apart from being CIA, Dan was a mainstay player from Grey Fox, one of the most secretive military units in the US Armed Forces. Officially members of a unit named ISA (intelligence support activity), Grey Fox had been established by the Pentagon in 1981 to work as man-hunters, assassins and deep-penetration agents and was now a key part of the US military's 'black world' of undercover operations. Though heavily criticised by senior US officials for its 'lawlessness' and 'lack of control', post-9/11 it had been greatly expanded and its soldier-spies, part of Task Force 20, were now being tasked into Iraq.

Dan insisted that he would only talk to senior personnel. 'Need-to-know basis only,' he bellowed.

At that moment Doug came in with a mess tin of curry. Dan stared at him in a way that said, 'Why the hell are you here?' Without saying a word, Doug made it clear that he'd do as he chose.

As Dan, Tosh, Romero and I sat down, Doug started to pour himself some coffee.

'Mine's black, no sugar,' Dan said.

There was a moment's awkward silence. Doug stopped pouring, and looked at him. 'If there'd been a "please" I just might have,' he rasped, 'but as there wasn't, you can fucking pour your own.'

Dan was taken aback. 'Where's that good old British hospitality?' he asked, trying to make light of it. Doug sat down and stared at him.

In an instant Tosh had some coffee poured and in Dan's hand. But Doug, I knew, was a shrewd judge of character and suffered fools badly. Dan's dramatic arrival had not impressed him, and Romero's reservations had made things worse. I didn't need an atmosphere like this. I glanced at Doug and feigned a smile. He picked up the hint.

'I need some air, boss.' He got to his feet. 'Fill me in later.' As he passed me, he put his hand on my shoulder. 'Don't let that fucker drag us into anything truly silly,' he said, and left.

When I turned back to Dan his bravado and smile had vanished. 'OK – to business,' I said.

The intel Dan had brought was alarming, to say the least. We had promised the Kurds a supply of respirators, in case Saddam tried to use chemical weapons against them, but Dan laughed this off. According to him, the Americans had been working with Israeli teams for years in the region, and the Israelis knew just about all there was to know. There was no real threat from weapons of mass destruction (WMD) – it was political bullshit and media hype. Saddam had some chlorine gas, so they might supply the Kurds with some masks, but disposable ones only, which cost twenty-five cents apiece to manufacture.

'So, if there are no WMD, what on earth are we all doing here?' demanded Tosh.

'Hey, buddy, get real,' Dan replied. 'This is twenty-first-century warfare. Better get used to it.'

He was as full of self-importance and smugness as he had been in Afghanistan, and even Guss looked uncomfortable. I well remembered Dan's operations against the Soviets in Afghanistan. Then he had been liaising with the Afghan Mujahideen, and had suggested a policy to sow terror among the Soviet ranks: all Soviet prisoners would be strung up on poles, their stomachs cut open, intestines pulled out and slung over their heads. Men could live for hours, even days, like this, while insect and rodent life came to feast on them. The Russians reacted by bombing more and more villages, razing them to the ground. The Afghans retaliated and the situation spiralled out of control.

The Russians were forced to move men in ever-increasing numbers by helicopter to avoid losing them to the Mujahideen, as Dan and his fellow operators had predicted. As soon as they did this, US Stinger ground-to-air missile-launchers appeared. The Mujahideen had trouble operating them at first, so Dan and his mates demonstrated how to shoot down a helicopter filled with more than fifty Soviet soldiers, killing all on board in a ball of flame. At the time I could almost understand the reasoning behind this, and ultimately the strategy worked. Afghanistan became the Soviets' Vietnam and the venture nearly bankrupted the country.

We asked Dan to describe the gas masks he was offering. I'd imagined something like a surgical mask, made of paper with a rubber strap to hold it on, which would be of no use against many chemical agents and so they proved to be. He told us that we would deliver the first batches that became available to Wajy and his troops. Great, I thought. We would be in full NBC suits with expensive respirators as we handed them out. He went on to tell us that Turkey would certainly not allow the Kurds to take Kirkuk.

'Be interesting trying to stop them – Kirkuk means everything to them,' I said.

'Under no circumstances can they be allowed to take Kirkuk,' Dan repeated. 'Turkey and the US just won't allow it.'

'Guess that's got nothing to do with Kirkuk being the biggest oil-producing site in Iraq, then?' I countered.

'There's enough goddamn bleeding hearts and lefties going on about the war bein' all about oil without you guys joinin' in.' Dan leant across the table and lowered his voice. 'There are far bigger issues at stake here, boys, than you can possibly comprehend. So, can we just leave it at that? I'm here to help you guys.'

Patronising bastard, I thought.

Then he dropped an even bigger one on us. Washington had already agreed a deal with Ankara that would allow Turkish troops to occupy a large part of Kurdish territory during the war to oust Saddam. Romero was as alarmed as I: we knew what the consequences of that would be.

'The Peshmerga will never allow it,' I told Dan flatly. 'Do you want another internal war on your hands with the Kurds against Turkey? Because that's exactly what'll happen.'

'That's why you boys are going in and will be on their tails,' said Dan. 'If they overstep the mark and don't play by our rules, you'll have to remove the problem in whatever way you see fit. You'd better make sure that Wajy, Massoud and his lot are well educated on that point, or severe measures will be approved and actioned.'

For a minute I gazed at him in silence. 'Just how would you authorise and implement them?' I asked eventually.

Dan paused. 'You either deal with them suitably,' he said, 'or there may just be a friendly-fire incident. Who knows?'

At this point Romero got to his feet and shouldered his weapon. 'I saw enough of your shit before and I don't need to see any more now,' he spat. 'Friendly fire, eh, and us with them? So, does that mean us too?' Before Dan had a chance to reply, Romero stalked out.

'If you guys don't play the game, others will,' Dan went on, 'plus a solid bunch of SEAL guys out there will do just as they're ordered.'

'You're living in the past,' said Athansa, as he got up to leave. 'Things have changed and so have we. Better wise up fast or you'll need that fancy flying machine of yours to run as far as you can.' With that, he, too, walked out.

Guss, Tosh, Dan and I remained at the table. We sat there for some time in silence.

'Come on, guys, you know the score and the bigger picture here. This ain't no playground, and hard, nasty decisions have to be made. It's what we do,' Dan wheedled.

'It's what *you* do, maybe, but it's not our way,' I replied.

'Bullshit, man!' Dan exclaimed. 'You're educated and experienced. You know the game. *Make it happen.* Make those Kurdish friends of yours do as required. Do and promise whatever you have to, if you don't want it to turn nasty. We have people on the ground close to both Barzani brothers, and if we get intel back that they ain't playing the game our way extreme measures will be sanctioned. And if that happens, you'd better make sure you guys are well out of the way. Fuck! It was you who requested to meet me and wanted my help.'

'It wasn't your help we wanted, it was co-operation,' I shot back. 'You know the meaning of the word? I wanted us to meet so we could guarantee not to be working at cross-purposes with your people or overlap into each other's areas of responsibility.'

'You don't get it, do you?' Dan snapped. 'This is *all* my area of responsibility, and you are playing in my ballpark. So you're gonna have to play by my rules, whether you like it or not.'

Tosh looked at me uncertainly – probably thinking I was about to lash out. But I knew that if I did, we'd be the ones to suffer down the line. It doesn't pay to alienate people you may have to rely on later, no matter how unsavoury they may appear.

'OK, Dan, I'll keep this brief,' I said, trying to stay calm. 'You manage your team and I'll manage mine. On that basis I guarantee we'll keep the Kurds in the game, playing to our rules.'

'You can guarantee *that?*' he asked incredulously.

'Damn right I can – and I will,' I heard myself say.

And I knew that that was exactly what I had to do because so many lives were at risk. I would fly by the seat of my pants and react to the situation as it developed. I had to keep Dan on-side – with us, not against us. He might be ruthless, but he was also highly proficient and professional. He didn't endear himself to us, but he was not there to do so. The problem was, I didn't believe that the end always justified the means, and Dan did. Could it be right to cross the line of decency or ethical behaviour in defence of democratic principles? I didn't think so.

Dan 'reminded' us of how many 'so-called' Peshmerga were using the war as an excuse to feather their own nests. They were no more than gangsters wielding power in the Kurdish heartlands and gaining wealth from illegal dealings in stolen UN supplies.

He declined our offer of an evening meal, so we escorted him back to the Comanche helicopter. He climbed aboard and was whisked away. Things suddenly looked a lot darker.

That evening everyone grilled Guss. Had he known all along

about Dan's 'bigger-picture' scenario? They were both CIA, after all, and Guss had certainly seemed pretty sheepish during Dan's performance. Was that why his fellow CIA operator had so conveniently shot himself in the foot? He was at a loss – had no idea how to answer the accusations.

As far as I was concerned, shooting an enemy combatant was difficult enough, but slotting someone you had befriended was entirely unacceptable – and this was what Dan had said we must be prepared to do to the Kurds.

I broached the subject over dinner. Tosh said he would carry out whatever actions were required of him.

'I'd fucking do it, too,' Doug stated.

I knew that if Doug was ordered to do something, he would do it: he was that sort of soldier.

Half-way through the meal Guss rushed in with a signals sheet: it was intel on an Iraqi general who wanted to talk.

He was in command of a Special Republican Guards unit, perhaps even the élite Medina Guards based near Tikrit, Saddam Hussein's hometown. Allied commanders anticipated that some of the fiercest resistance from Iraqi forces would take place there, so the general's offer to negotiate and possibly defect was interesting. I began to talk about the town's history, hoping to take our minds off Dan's visit. I'd just got going when Doug said, 'Got to email Sara, boss. Don't mind if I leave you to it?' and escaped.

Tikrit had a long and well-known history in the Muslim world, I began. It was the birthplace of the great Sal ah-Din, or Saladin, as he was known in the West, who became one of the greatest Muslim commanders of all time, famed for his courage, compassion and chivalry. In 1187 his forces defeated the Crusader Knights at the battle of the Horns of Hattin, after which they lost control of Jerusalem. Saddam Hussein had attempted to present himself as a modern-day Saladin and would-be saviour of the Islamic world.

After the others had gone to bed, John and I sat up late, talking. Eventually I asked him what was eating him. He confided that he felt an overpowering sense of loss that he couldn't shake off. All he could think about was his wife and daughters: 'I should be at home with them, not out here. The whole world's going insane.' He'd had enough excitement and adventure and now just wanted to be with his family. 'I've lost my edge,' he said. 'I shouldn't have come.'

'I'll talk to Tosh in the morning and have you flown home.' Part of me wished I could go with him.

'My days of doing this are over,' John went on. 'I can't justify it any more, no matter how I dress it up. I just can't.'

I sat with him for an hour or so, then left him alone with his thoughts and went to bed.

The next morning I told Tosh I needed John flown out on the next available slot.

'Can I join the lads going in now, then?' he asked.

'No,' I said. I still needed him at the FOB as our main liaison with Northwood JOC (joint operations centre based in north-west London) and General Franks. I told him to send a signal back to Head Shed requesting Ian's immediate dispatch. He was on my reserve list and I knew he'd be out in a flash.

I was heading for the food tent to tell the rest of the team about John when Guss stopped me. 'Boss, we gotta be ready to leave first thing Thursday morning,' he said breathlessly. 'It's all been moved up a gear. I got a message from Wajy – he's eager to push things forward, and he's got us access to just about every player concerned.'

It was now Tuesday, which left us a full day to prepare for a major deployment in theatre. Instead of telling the team about John, I found myself calling an O group in the mess tent. I outlined the developments, then said I'd present a formal orders group the next day.

Tosh began to fret: 'You don't seem very busy – are you sure everything's covered?'

I checked that I had all the correct radio codes and frequencies, and glanced over the maps again. Several were dated from 1969, but that was all that had been available. We pulled in more maps from the Internet, blew them up to full size and sealed them in plastic. In fact, we had a mapping man, a US Air Force guy with a bank of computers linked to satellites at the FOB, so he could download the latest maps. Only trouble was, his hi-tech system wasn't working. When I told Tosh to calm down, he went off on one: we should abort, he said, until we had better maps.

Doug turned on him and let rip: 'That's why you'll always be a fucking REMF.' (Rear Echelon Mother Fucker).

There were times when I wished Doug would keep his mouth shut, and this was one of them. I placated Tosh by asking him to get in touch with Feltham, home of a major British Army mapping units and tell them we needed help. Then I ushered Doug off to sort out the SEAL lads. At last I was free to prepare a plan for the coming deployment.

On Thursday afternoon I called the team together for the final operation briefing. In normal circumstances I'd have had maps, codes and radio frequencies to give out, and the standard briefing information – ground, situation, mission, execution, service support, command and signals to run through, but the team already had the frequencies and details of our backup support, and knew the lie of the land. The only difference from our last trip into Iraq was that almost the whole complement of SEALs was coming with us. So, instead of the full briefing, I gave everyone what I hoped was a winning smile and told them three simple things: that our mission was to gain the Kurds' trust and get them on-side; that the situation was likely to change at a moment's notice; that we would be making it up as we went along.

I noticed that Guss was eyeing everyone, checking how they were dressed.

'Any problems, Guss?' I asked.

'Er, no, boss,' he replied sheepishly.

Guss had wanted to wait another twenty-four hours for maps and imaging courtesy of NPIC (National Photographic Inter-pretation Centre, Washington, DC), part of the CIA, but we'd agreed to meet Wajy and had to appear reliable so we were still leaving in accordance with the original time scale. Over the past few days we'd all noticed he was now eager to fit in, and copied what Romero and Athansa were doing. But just as he had his webbing set up as theirs was, Romero would change it. Sure enough, Guss would follow suit. Then the SEAL lads advised him on more ways to arrange his webbing, which confused him further.

As I'd finished the briefing I'd seen that Romero had placed a bright smiley-face sticker in the middle of his back. Suddenly, Athansa jumped up, said he'd forgotten his sticker and rushed out. That was too much for Guss and he had to ask. SEAL Ian told him that all Delta 'point-men' (patrol scouts) wear the sticker so that anyone behind would know they were friendly forces and not shoot them in the back. It had also been shown that a smiley-face sticker raised a smile, even with the enemy, which might just buy you vital seconds to get out of the line of enemy fire. Poor Guss rushed off to find himself a sticker and the rest of us collapsed into fits of laughter.

Just after he'd gone a fully geared-up figure came in, and the tent was suddenly filled with expletives. It was Ian, my reserve team member, ready to take over from John. He had comman-deered a US Humvee jeep and driven all the way from Konya to get to us on time.

At 18.00 hours we boarded the two Black Hawk helicopters, Pilot Steve beaming in the cockpit of one. Doug shuffled aboard next to me as Malcolm, our Ian and Guss all squeezed in among the kit, quickly followed by SEAL Ian and several SEAL team lads. One of them, Matt, looked like he'd been raised on manure and steroids, he was so big. He even dwarfed Guss, which was saying something. Romero and Athansa hopped aboard the second Black Hawk with the rest of the SEALs. Tosh and Dianne were standing nearby to see us off, Tosh still pissed off to be left behind.

As the Black Hawks powered up I suddenly spotted John. He ran across the helipad and hurled himself with his kit on to the lead chopper. 'You fuckers would be lost without me,' he yelled, and settled into the rear.

Malcolm and Doug looked pleased to see him. Our Ian glanced at me questioningly, as he was supposed to be John's replacement. Ian was an excellent operator, and I wasn't too happy that John had changed his mind at the last minute – but the chopper was airborne now so they'd both be coming in theatre with us.

As we pulled away from the FOB I knew it would be a while before I'd speak to Victoria and the children again. I didn't even have a picture of them as we were all 'person sterile'. We weren't wearing dog-tags or any other form of identification in case we were compromised and caught.

This was a real-time deniable operation. If captured we would resist interrogation for as long as possible, then let slip we were mercenaries working for the Kurds. We never took photographs of ourselves on these operations for obvious reasons, but I always had with me, safely tucked away in a waterproof bag on my webbing, a stuffed pink pig my daughter had given me. It had become my mascot, and I would put it in particular places – as if it was manning the gun in a CH53 for example – and photograph it. It's an exceptionally well-travelled pig!

In normal circumstances the US military has a policy of 'leave no man behind', which means that no soldier is abandoned on a battlefield. But with this mission all the US lads had been told that if the shit hit the fan no one would come for them, at least until the official start of hostilities. Their existence would be denied, and I knew the same rules went for us. They were all volunteers and part of CTJTF (Counter-terrorist Joint Task Force), made up from elements of what was SEAL Team 6, now DEVGRU (development group) under direct command of NAVSPEC-WARCOM (naval special warfare command), Delta Force and Helicopter Task Force 160, operating out of Fort Bragg. I'd told John earlier to remember that the Americans left no man behind, so now I hoped he wasn't harbouring any such illusion.

We'd been in the air barely fifty minutes when Pilot Steve told us we were almost there. We landed at a site three miles away from our previous landing zone at the disused church, in case the Iraqis had somehow been alerted to our presence. Within seconds we were all out and taking up positions of cover. Two minutes later, we were silent on the ground and the Black Hawks had gone. Then we were up and moving towards the village to link up with Wajy and his Peshmerga. John had asked to take point with Athansa, and I agreed. As we trudged down towards Wajy's village I grinned at the smiley-face stickers on everyone's back – Guss had fetched an entire sheet and insisted we all wore them. We'd told him that 'Smiley Faces' was code for Special Forces . . .

We stopped just short of the village, and I sent Romero and Malcolm in to meet up with Wajy. We waited half an hour, then Malcolm returned and said it was OK to enter. I designated an ERV (emergency rendezvous) point and left four of the SEALs, including big Matt, as a blocking and cut-off group a little up the valley in case we should need support and cover.

Wajy greeted me enthusiastically. His first question was about the gas masks and how many we had with us. He was relieved when I told him we had enough for the entire village and all his fighters. He told us that soon we would move deeper into the surrounding mountains, where we would find the Peshmerga leaders. First we would meet his brother, Massoud, the KDP leader, and if we got on with him, we would meet Jalal Talabani, the PUK leader. I wanted to see the PUK's special intelligence chief, too, Kosrat Rassul. Recently, he had been involved in serious run-ins with the CIA and MI6 officers who'd been trying to liaise with him. He was known to have a massive network of contacts and spies across Iraq, but all of that intel was being withheld from us because the CIA and MI6 boys had insulted him: they had questioned his integrity and certain claims he had made.

Bearing in mind Dan's comments and the intel on the Turkish view of the Kurds taking Kirkuk, I brought up the subject of the city. As soon as I mentioned its name, there were smiles all round. Wajy took out a note from his jacket and handed it to me. I tried to decipher the Arabic writing until Layla offered to read it aloud. She barely glanced at the words, which she knew by heart.

> Kurdistan without Kirkuk? NEVER! NEVER! NEVER!
> The fire in Kirkuk, the fire in Babagorgor,
> Is the fire in the heart of our Peshmerga,
> Is the fire that Mamosta Barzani carried,
> Is the fire in our flag,
> Is the fire in Newroz,
> NEVER WITHOUT KIRKUK!
> Kirkuk is, in fact and tradition, the heart of Kurdistan.

As soon as she had spoken those words I knew we were going to have a major problem over Kirkuk.

'At the moment, we're in the dark about US plans,' Wajy

remarked, 'but we can play an even more effective role than the Northern Alliance did in Afghanistan. We are much more organised than they were, and we have more experience. But we need resources.' He put the note back into his pocket. 'And if we men cannot do the job, or we fall, we have our sisters at our sides, and they are very, very scary.' He laughed. Layla and some of the other women laughed too, and the men nodded.

'It doesn't matter how long it takes, I will practise until I am the best shot in Iraq,' said Layla, raising a Soviet Dragunov sniper rifle. 'I know that we're still a male-dominated society, but women also make good Peshmerga. We are just as brave as the men.

'We should be active in building our future,' she went on, 'even if that means fighting alongside our men – there should be no discrimination.' Layla looked at me directly, and I could see the hurt in her dark eyes, the defiance and pride that coursed through her veins.

'And that is why we value your support,' I responded, trying to sound sincere, but feeling two-faced and deceitful.

We spent the next twenty-four hours in Wajy's house, waiting for the order to move out. Everything was primitive and so old you could almost smell its age, mixed with the scent of wooden floorboards, furniture and grass rope. An old framed photograph of Madame Mitterrand, the wife of the former French president, hung on the wall. I learnt that she had been a major supporter of the Kurds and was revered for it. I also spotted a smaller photograph of Jeffrey Archer. Apparently, he had raised funds for them in 2001. Talking with Layla I learnt that her family came from Kirkuk, once a predominantly Kurdish city situated in government-controlled territory. Six years ago her brother had been taken from their house by Iraqi Mukhabarat (secret police) and he had not been seen since.

As the hours passed and Wajy's confidence in us grew, I decided it was worth risking a little honesty and told him it was unlikely that US and British conventional ground forces would be deployed to the region. It was far more suited to guerrilla warfare, I explained, to the combination of Special Forces, air power and the Peshmerga. Wajy grasped what I was saying pretty quickly, but he was far from certain that other Kurdish leaders would agree. I assured him that we'd be with them all the way. There would be no repeat of 1991, when Allied forces had abandoned them to face Saddam alone. Wajy asked me to swear that we would be with them throughout the coming battle.

'I swear on my life and my children's life that it is so,' I announced solemnly. I knew that for the Kurds, a man's word was his bond, especially if he'd sworn on his family's lives. And I meant what I'd said. They were friendly, hospitable people, with an almost childlike innocence in how they viewed the world.

Eventually we were shown to a separate room to rest. Although I'd had little sleep over the last forty-eight hours, I dozed fitfully. Whenever I awoke, Doug was at the doorway, standing guard. Malcolm was trying to chat up Layla and her friends, and Guss was busy on the radio.

The air was cold when I got up. Malcolm handed me a mug of instant coffee from the British ration packs and Layla brought me an enormous breakfast of pitta bread, jam, fruit, olives and dried banana, which I ate politely, much to the amusement of Doug and Malcolm.

By 07.00 hours a convoy of Hi-lux Toyotas and assorted pick-ups assembled in the village. With little fanfare we set off up a winding dirt road that led into the mountains, Wajy in the lead vehicle. At each valley or gully a Peshmerga was waving, signalling that it was safe to continue. I checked our maps constantly, and Guss consulted his hand-held PLGR (precise lightweight GPS receiver). We had set up a trim pack in Romero's Toyota – a vehicle-mounted GPS system – to the delight of the Kurdish driver, who assumed it was now his to keep.

The journey was painfully slow, a long, bone-shaking ride with stops at all of the Kurdish checkpoints along the way. It was around 20.00 hours and dark when we reached our final destination. The Kurdish base was located precariously close to a series of Iraqi front-line observation positions on a nearby mountain range. But no one seemed concerned about this, and it was in an almost carnival-like atmosphere that we met Wajy's brother, Massoud Barzani.

'You fucking stay with me, boss, OK?' Doug ordered, placing a hand on my shoulder as we waited for Massoud and his heavily armed entourage to approach. 'Remember, you're the brains and I'm the brawn.'

Doug was standing on my immediate right, Romero to my left, while Guss, Malcolm and John were behind as Wajy introduced me to his brother. Massoud seemed a little intimidated by us, but I smiled and shook his hand. He only relaxed after Wajy had hugged me and declared that we had come to oust the evil regime of Saddam Hussein, and help them achieve their dreams of an independent Kurdistan. At this, a massive cheer went up from the crowd of Peshmerga. Instantly I felt guilty: that wasn't how those higher up in the chain of command saw it.

We were led into a cave and seemed to step back in time to a scene of medieval warfare. A labyrinth of passageways and galleries headed off in several different directions. We were allocated a branch and dumped our kit. Athansa and Guss went to set up a skywave radio net: they attached a thirty-metre length of signal cable to a standard radio set – our signal strength was reduced because we were deep underground.

Meanwhile I was introduced to the PUK representative, Khalid, who seemed pleased to meet us. Now that both leaders were with us, we had the Kurds pretty much sewn up. After some hours of discussion – the Kurds love to talk – I asked tentatively about Kosrat Rassul, the PUK's intelligence chief. Without a word, Khalid left the room. I wondered if I had pushed things too far.

'Fuck, you can waffle, boss,' Doug whispered. He'd been silent for hours. 'Glad I ain't your girlfriend.'

I stood up and stretched my legs. The coffee-pot was empty and I needed a caffeine fix. At that moment, Khalid returned with a serious, aggressive-looking man, whom he introduced as Kosrat Rassual, and set about making coffee. Immediately Kosrat began to talk. He asked the date set for the invasion of Iraq, and if we would stay with them throughout the conflict. How many men could we bring? And tanks? He wanted tanks. As he talked, I realised he was a very focused, no-nonsense individual.

My tone with him was different from the one I'd adopted with Wajy. Kosrat believed he was a man of destiny. He was convinced that the US would invade, no matter what world opinion or the UN said, and that the Kurds should be ready to seize the opportunity. He vowed that, with or without our help, they would take northern Iraq – and that he would capture Saddam Hussein personally. Doug laughed, and I could see that Kosrat was offended. I decided that the way to play him was to appear reverential, and use his enormous self-belief to our advantage.

'If you truly believe you can do these things, we'll do everything in our power to help you,' I told him.

'You would help us. Why?' Kosrat challenged me. 'Your MI6 people do not think we are capable of it, and openly mocked me for saying so.'

'Well, I believe you when you say you have many spies in Iraq, and close to Saddam,' I replied. 'The MI6 people were fools.'

'The American CIA men – the Grey Foxes – all they wanted was for me to hand over the names of my contacts so they could rush in, capture Saddam and take all the glory,' Kosrat continued resentfully.

After Dan's visit we had been more than aware of Grey Fox's presence in the area and knew that the CIA had leant on Kosrat and his people. Later that evening Guss sent a sitrep that we'd made positive progress with some major players in the PUK and KDP, but I knew that with Kosrat, there was still plenty of work to do.

That night, as I walked about the cave system checking on the lads, I felt as if I was in some ancient conflict of biblical times. Small campfires were lit, the smell of woodsmoke mixing with burning incense. Groups of men and women in Arab clothing were crouched round them, chatting and telling stories. It was only the modern weaponry that reminded me we were in the twenty-first century. I watched a woman strip and clean her AK47. Another was doing the same with an ancient US M60A3 machine-gun.

We spent the next four days befriending the KDP and PUK Kurds and briefing them on the forthcoming conflict. The SEAL lads had great fun trying to teach them fire mission procedures and how to co-ordinate airstrikes over the radio. There was no way that any of them would get to call one in, but it contributed towards building trust. John seemed perkier and was settling in well with the Peshmerga lads.

One of the caves had been set up as a TV room, and news came in that Turkey was rattled by the Kurds and threatening not to allow US troops through its borders into northern Iraq. Our Kurds became understandedly agitated.

I called a meeting and explained it was propaganda designed to mislead Saddam Hussein. General Franks was using a spy, codenamed April Fool, to furnish the Iraqis with intel, some of it genuine to boost credibility, that the Turkish hype was a bluff to lure Saddam's generals into keeping major forces in the north. False 'Top-secret' invasion plans, created by Cent Com (Central

Command), detailed the coalition decision (comprising US, UK, Australian, Kurdish and Polish) to build up only part of its forces in Kuwait while actually preparing major airborne assaults into northern Iraq above Tikrit. After that the US would fly in C17s with Bradley AFVs (armoured fighting vehicles) and tanks while helicopters flew in airborne troops. They would be reinforced by the 4th Infantry Division, which the Turkish government would allow, at the last minute, to enter Iraq and steamroll to Baghdad. I reminded the Peshmerga that they were the masters of guerrilla warfare, and better suited to fighting in that way, as conventional ground forces could throw up all manner of problems. I stressed that this was why we needed the Peshmerga to fight with us, and that this time we wouldn't abandon them.

On the morning of day four, Kosrat said he was leaving. I was still unsure that I'd won him over, and in our goodbye chat I gave him my word that we would be there to help him and his forces when the time came for war. He asked me about the sight on my weapon, and said he liked the look of it. It was a Bushnell HOLO sight, which uses advanced holographic technology to project an illuminated crosshair fifty metres in front of the weapon but with no forward light projection. I knew he wanted it, so I gave it to him. My team and I worked for a big firm that could afford to lose one. Kosrat thanked me effusively, then bade me an intense farewell. As his column of vehicles pulled away, I reckoned I'd done enough to bring him on-side.

After Guss had sent Tosh our regular sitrep, we received orders to pass on all of our intel about Kosrat Rassul, and where he was off to. Instinctively I knew this wasn't a good idea as I felt sure any intel would go straight to Dan Meany's lot in Grey Fox. Only God knew what they might do with it. I asked John, not Guss, to get on the radio and send limited information only – that he was still in our TAOR (tactical area of responsibility). I felt sure Grey

Fox wouldn't think twice about following and intercepting Kosrat to extract as much humint (human intelligence) from him as they could. If they did so – knowing Kosrat, as I did – it would be a complete disaster.

We stayed in the area for another two days, by which time Kosrat's group were well away. Since I had passed on my weapon sight to Kosrat, the rest of my team found their kit viewed by eager eyes. At one point an elderly Peshmerga got a little too possessive with Doug's AN/PVS 14 single-eye night-vision piece, an excellent, expensive item, but Doug was not going to part with it. Finally, John offered the old man a twin-eye AN/PVS 70 set. We were loath to use that type because if you got 'whited out', which happens when a sudden light, such as a flare or a phosphorous grenade, appears, both your eyes are affected: it takes fifteen minutes, sometimes longer, for them to readjust to the dark.

As the old Peshmerga showed off John's gift, there was an outburst of shouting in the valley below us, followed by shooting. Within a matter of minutes four terrified Iraqi soldiers were frogmarched into the camp. '*Jundi, jundi,*' one kept saying, the Arabic for 'private soldier'. It turned out that they had deserted their posts and been captured trying to head north to the Turkish border. One stood petrified, his mouth hanging open, unable to speak – this happens when someone is overcome by terror: the jaw drops and the muscles won't work to close it. The four Iraqis were only teenagers and I felt sorry for them, but Khalid assured me that if they were genuine deserters they would be well looked after.

As our operation was now largely complete, Guss called for some choppers to take us back to base. Tosh responded that they would pick us up at 01.00 hours that night, and gave the LZ location. Romero, Guss, Ian and big Matt, plus six other SEAL lads, agreed to stay with the Peshmerga to foster and reinforce our commitment to stick with them for the long haul, until we returned with a larger force. I'd asked Doug to stay as senior player, but received a frank negative response: 'Fuck off. I'd kill Guss within twenty-four hours, and you need me.' There was no arguing with that. Malcolm wanted to stay, but only because he was convinced he could get it on with Layla, so there was definitely no way he was staying. We offloaded most of our MREs and half our ammo for those staying behind, and at 23.00 hours we were ready to move. Two Peshmerga guides offered to show us the quickest, safest route to the LZ, missing many minefields, and Layla joined us, her Dragunov sniper rifle at the ready, which pleased Malcolm. 'Fucking knew she liked me,' he announced as we headed off down the mountainside in darkness.

It was 26 February, still the depths of the Kurdish winter, and bloody cold. But Doug opened up the pace and we were soon warm. Our Peshmerga guides kept up without any sign of tiredness, but I struggled. They kept stopping Doug to listen for enemy activity. Each time I checked our bearing and position on the map with my shiny new PLGR.

'These fuckers are like mountain goats,' John whispered during one of our halts.

The LZ turned out to be in the centre of a clearing about half the size of a football pitch and surrounded on all sides by steep rockfaces. There was no clear approach run and the only way in was to hover straight down between the steep sides. Pilot Steve would have fun pulling up here, I thought.

After the hike we were hot and breathless, but our Peshmerga guides hadn't even broken sweat. Eight miles may not sound much, but in the dark, in full combats, webbing, body armour, weapons and Arab dish-dashes, it had been quite an undertaking. Malcolm was moaning that he had friction burns between his legs. He wasn't the only one. I half undid my dish-dash to let the air get to me. We checked the immediate area for any present tenants, such as snakes, scorpions and the dreaded camel spiders the Peshmerga had warned us about, and settled down to wait in some cover.

As Doug spied out the wider area, using his PNGs, I noticed that John was looking anxious. After fifteen minutes we were confident that we were alone in the gorge, so I split the team into two groups ready to board the choppers when they arrived. The sky was sharply clear, the stars bright. In the silence, John became convinced that he could hear distant voices. At night sound travels further, especially in mountains, but I could hear nothing.

'Boss, I need to go take a look-see, just in case,' he whispered, and pointed in the direction from which he thought the voices were coming.

'OK, but don't go too far,' I whispered, reluctant to let him go. 'Take one of the SEAL lads with you and get on Athansa's chopper to save you crawling all the way back here.'

I indicated to Athansa that Maberley should go with John, and the two disappeared into the darkened landscape. Ten minutes passed. Then I heard the hiss of static on my radio.

'Hello, India One Sunray, this is India One Three, message. Over,' whispered John.

'India One Sunray, send. Over,' I replied.

'India One Three, there's definitely some Zulu hostiles active this way. Over.'

Jesus, I thought, what now? Almost on cue I heard the familiar thwoop-thwoop-thwoop as our helicopters closed in. If John had spotted the enemy it was too late to call off the choppers now.

'India One Sunray, maintain position and engage anything that comes your way. Over.'

'India One Three, roger. Out.' At least he had sounded calm, which was a relief.

No sooner had I put out a call to Athansa's group to watch for any enemy than the first Black Hawk broke the skyline behind me. Its downdraught blasted into us as it steadied and levelled out to make a fast landing. As it dropped into the gorge it moved forward, giving the second Black Hawk space to come in behind it.

'Hello, India One Sunray, this is Mike Foxtrot India One at your service,' came the unmistakable voice of Pilot Steve.

I stood up to usher the rest of my stick to the helicopter and glanced back at Layla, covering us, her weapon at the ready. She smiled. We were almost at the rear of the last Black Hawk, when the crack of AK47 fire opened up from the direction in which John and Maberley had disappeared. Green tracer rounds arched in our direction, dangerously close to the two Black Hawks.

'Hot LZ, you boys have one, repeat one, minute,' Pilot Steve shouted over the net.

For a split second I looked at Layla. I knew we couldn't abandon her and the two Peshmerga guides. Then I heard the awesome whir and burst of the Black Hawk's miniguns (also known as 'chain guns', a multi-barrelled 7.62mm machine-gun that puts down a wall of fire) as they opened up in the direction of the enemy. As red tracer streaked off, I know that John and Maberley were over there somewhere, engaging the enemy.

'*Cease your fire*,' I screamed over the net, jumping up and down and waving like a lunatic at the gunners, but they kept on firing – effectively: the incoming fire dropped to almost zero. But John and Maberley were somewhere out there, if they were still alive. '*Cease fire*,' I screamed again, and this time I heard Pilot Steve order them to stop.

'India One Three, come in.' I prayed John would reply.

Doug started to throw our kit and equipment on to the chopper as Baby Steve and Malcolm jumped aboard and scanned the area for John and Maberley. I kept radioing John's call sign.

Then Doug grabbed Layla and threw her into the chopper – she landed on top of Baby Steve

The snap of incoming tracer rounds started again, and several pinged loudly off the door spar between me and the mini-gunner, which prompted him to squeeze off another deadly salvo in their direction. Ahead, through swirling dust, I caught sight of Athansa bundling the two Peshmerga guides unceremoniously on to his Black Hawk, as more incoming rounds registered hits on their airframe. I had horrible visions of it going up in a ball of flame at any second.

Then came a squirt of static on my radio. My heart leapt as I heard John's breathless voice: 'India One Three, *contact*, in case you hadn't heard it,' he panted. 'I'm on way back in from your left flank, so blat away all you like.'

Everyone on the radio net must have heard because both pilots opened their throttles and the mini-gunners opened up in the direction of the enemy. As we crouched in the exposed open bay area of the chopper, I asked if we were all on board – I'd told John to get on to Athansa's chopper. Then Athansa radioed that he could see John and Maberley running towards him. I leant out just in time to see their silhouetted figures before they vanished in the haze of dust thrown up by Athansa's chopper.

'Good to go, boys,' Pilot Steve announced.

We lurched forward and were airborne as green tracer zipped past us, the odd round ricocheting off the airframe. A bullet smashed straight through the Perspex windscreen, but Pilot Steve didn't flinch and we carried on climbing. As both choppers clawed their way upwards, the door-gunners were firing in unison, down and forwards to where they could see muzzle flashes. Due to the forward momentum of the choppers we had no option but to fly straight over the enemy, and as we did so Doug was leaning out, firing his weapon from one side as Malcolm did the same on the other.

Suddenly the Black Hawk lunged violently – Steve had thrown it to one side as an RPG came up fast. It whooshed past far too close for comfort and I was flung across the loading bay. Doug grabbed me before I could fall out.

As I sat there, heart pounding, the enemy gunfire died away. I knew Doug and Malcolm were fine, and Layla was squashed between two SEALs, who had tried to shield her. But Baby Steve's hand was over his face. When he took it away I saw that his left eye was closed and covered with blood. But he gave me a thumbs-up: 'I'm OK – just a scratch.'

I grabbed the radio intercom: 'Steve, can you call the other bird and ask if John and Maberley are OK.' It had been a bloody close call.

'Boss, John isn't on it,' Steve replied. 'He threw Maberley on board as he'd been nicked in the thigh, and told Athansa he was jumping on with us.'

I turned immediately to check that I hadn't somehow missed John in the rear of our chopper. As my eyes darted from face to face, my stomach churned and I felt it cramp into a knot as I realised we'd left him behind. Grasping at straws, I asked Steve to reconfirm – John was famed for his practical jokes but if this was a joke I'd rip his head off when we got back to base.

'Negative, boss,' Steve replied. 'No duff. John's not on board.'

For a split second I was convinced I was about to throw up. Then: 'Put us all on the deck – now!' I yelled to Steve. I didn't know if we were in hostile territory but I couldn't leave John behind on the LZ.

We carried on for another two minutes until Steve found a suitably flat surface to put us down.

'Doug, take everyone else and put them on the first chopper,' I yelled at him. 'Get everyone back to the FOB. Organise a rescue team in case it's needed.'

'Fuck off, boss,' Doug yelled. 'I'm coming with you,

whatever you're doing. We've got enough old hands here to mount our own fucking search-and-rescue. That's what we're trained for.'

'Doug, I'm not fucking about on this one,' I yelled back. 'You get on that chopper, sort Steve's eye out, get them all back to base. I only need the crew, the loadies and Ian for this one.' I glanced over at Ian, who gave me a nervous thumbs-up. 'That way, if we go down it's only us. And I need you to make bloody sure we get a CSAR (combat search and rescue) chopper in the air and over to our ERV. You got it?'

I grabbed my map, studied it fast for a suitable ERV point, still trying to convince myself we wouldn't need it, then pulled out a Chinagraph pen and scrawled the co-ordinates on Doug's hand. 'Just in case,' I shouted.

'Ain't leaving you, boss,' Doug yelled back.

'Mate, you have to and I haven't time to argue. They won't expect us to come straight back in and maybe they haven't even noticed John yet. And I need you as back-up to keep our word with the Pesh in case it all goes pear-shaped.'

I shoved Doug in the direction of the other Black Hawk. He gave me one of his famous cold stares, still questioning the logic of my plan, then decided to go along with it.

'If we go down and you hear nothing,' I yelled at him, as I climbed back aboard our Black Hawk, 'make sure that fucking CSAR bird is at the ERV location by 04.00 regardless. And make bloody sure we have F16s or F18s up and ready, should we need them.'

Doug signed acknowledgement and started for the other chopper.

'OK, Steve, fast and low and put us back on to the LZ,' I told him.

Pilot Steve turned and stared at me, as if he hadn't heard properly. 'That's right, mate, put us back on the LZ,' I repeated.

Steve shrugged, gave me a thumbs-up and turned back to his controls. As we lifted off again, the two mini-gunners racked up their weapons, ready for more action. We climbed and banked hard as the other Black Hawk disappeared, and then we were heading back towards the hot LZ. I tried calling John on his PRR, but all I got back was silence and static.

4

BLACK HAWK DOWN

Before I'd had time to consider things, I felt the Black Hawk lurch upwards, as Steve pulled the aircraft to an almost abrupt stop. Then we were on the ground. The Iraqis opened up immediately, tracer zipping all over the place. The mini-gunners answered in kind, pumping thousands of rounds towards the enemy positions. One AK bullet hit the collecting bag under the port-side mini-gun, and hundreds of spent cartridges went rolling across the chopper. I leant slightly out of the port-side doorway, searching for John among the chaos of the LZ.

Steve raised the Black Hawk off the ground and into a stable hover, then eased the nose to the right so that both miniguns could be brought to bear on the enemy. The airframe shuddered as something big whacked into us. The helicopter lurched to port and Steve fought to control it. The noise was deafening as the miniguns fired and the engines whined. As we levelled out, I moved back into the cargo area. All of a sudden I saw John's head bob up beside the doorway. But as he went to throw on his weapon and grab hold, we lurched upwards and he disappeared. But Steve had spotted him, and dumped the Black Hawk back on to the ground.

John grabbed hold of the doorframe and I lunged forward, holding on to the grab rail, my C7 slung across my chest, and reached down with my right hand to John. Just as I had him, another almighty thump reverberated through the airframe, knocking us all backwards. John's eyes widened as I started to lose my grip on him, the engines groaning as Steve fought to control the violently jolting Black Hawk. I lunged forward again to John – the chopper had begun climbing rapidly now. As I did so I could see .50-cal tracer rounds arcing towards us. I was staring into John's eyes, about to haul him in with Ian's help, when, *bang!*, followed by an instant hissing and fizzing noise and a bright glow as a .50-cal tracer flung me across the cargo area.

I felt the biggest thump of my life. A bullet had smashed into my upper chest area. I landed hard against the opposite door jamb, as another .50-cal bullet smashed into the port side of the airframe, pushing the entire chopper upwards and almost over. The mini-gunner grabbed me just in time to stop me falling out the other side.

The adrenaline was pumping so hard that I couldn't even feel where I'd been hit, but I knew I was probably seriously hurt as our body armour was not designed to stop .50-cal. Any second now the pain would strike, I thought. Just then, I saw John's fingers on the edge of the doorway footstep, still holding on. He was totally exposed as he hung out of the chopper, the .50-cal pounding away at us. I scrambled back, leant out and grabbed his arm. Ian took the other, but it was difficult to haul him in as the helicopter was lurching violently from side to side. I knew that if I stood or knelt to get better leverage I would probably be hit again – the amount of fire directed at us was incredible. John stared up at me, helpless. Ian and I glanced at each other, and then we were on our knees and pulling for all we were worth.

I let out a yell as we hauled John over the side rail and into the cargo area. There was a sickening thump at the rear and the helicopter spun. Red warning lights flashed and alarms sounded. Steve swore, opened the throttle, raised the collective and tried to force the aircraft upwards. For two or three seconds we climbed and then we seemed to freeze in mid-air before the stricken aircraft began a backwards downslide to our starboard side. Steve was struggling with the controls as we plunged and reeled towards the ground. When co-pilot Mark unplugged his headset and seat harness, followed closely by the starboard mini-gunner, I knew we were going down.

The sensation as we lost power and fell towards the earth, with small-arms fire still rattling along the airframe, was hideous. Amazingly, the port-side mini-gunner kept firing as the chopper lurched further on to its side. I looked to my left, which was now straight down as the ground rushed up to greet us. Thwack! Thwack! Thwack! Shards of rotor blade flew off in all directions. The chopper's rear crashed into undergrowth and the main body smacked on to the ground. With a sickening crump the chopper finally came to rest, a broken mess lying on its starboard side.

Black Hawks had been specially designed for what are termed hard landings and ours certainly qualified. The port-side mini-gunner on the upper side of the chopper was still firing away, and incoming rounds thumped into the aircraft's exposed underbelly. It was reinforced and armour-plated, but there was every chance that it would burst into flames at any moment. As we gathered ourselves in the rear and prepared to fight our way out, John sat with his head cradled in his hands. At least he was alive and with us, I told myself, as I went to cock my C7. It was jammed. I checked it and realised the .50-cal bullet that had hit me had gone clean through the main working parts of my weapon, wrecking it. I was lucky it had – it must have slowed the bullet before it ploughed through my chest webbing, emergency escape and evasion kit, the solid ceramic trauma plate and almost all the way through my body armour. If it hadn't, I'd have been dead.

The minigun stopped firing when it ran out of ammo but co-pilot Mark had to drag the gunner off it – he was still squeezing the trigger causing the electrics to turn the barrels. Pilot Steve cocked his Beretta M9 pistol and I looked up at our only exit: through the open port doorway, which happened to have a bright tracer show dancing across it. Then we heard a massive bang on the underside of the chopper, followed by the familiar thump-thump-thump of the .50-cal firing. There was a series of similarly massive bangs as the rounds smashed into the chopper's under-belly, which clearly couldn't shield us for long.

'It ain't gonna hold,' Steve yelled.

'Do we surrender?' shouted Mark, and everyone looked at me.

As far as I was concerned it was a dumb question. 'Surrender?' I yelled, then took out my Glock 17 and cocked it. 'We ain't here, remember.'

'Oh, so this is just a bad dream, then?' Ian grinned. 'Well, that's OK. I was starting to get worried for a moment.' He glanced up at the tracer whizzing overhead, then forward to the cockpit, which was now just a shower of sparks and filled with swirling smoke.

I kicked John's foot. He looked up at me with a bewildered expression. He was dazed and in a state of trauma. 'Get ready to move, mate,' I shouted. His eyes were wide with shock. 'It's OK, mate, this isn't your doing,' I yelled in his ear. 'Now, come on, let's make it count.'

He nodded, and I thrust his Minimi back into his hands. I was about to stand up when Ian opened up with his C7 Diemaco right next to my right ear, firing literally between Steve and me into the cockpit area where two figures had appeared outside with AK47s. It was definitely time to go. One RPG or grenade hurled inside and we were all dead. There was no way out of the chopper but the upper side door. Suicidal though this seemed at first, there was a foot and a half's clear space that couldn't be reached by the enemy fire, as it was shielded by the floor door-runner. Somehow, we had to shimmy out on to the upper side of the helicopter and roll off out of the way of any fire.

Ian volunteered to go first and, without a moment's hesitation, he jumped up and gripped the upper doorframe. With us shoving at his legs he threw himself out and slid from view. John went next, yelling, 'Don't push me up so fucking high,' as we rammed him through the door. Incoming rounds were still slapping on the chopper's underbelly, with the odd massive whack from an impacting .50-cal. Pilot Steve tried to usher me out next, but I lifted him out with the help of the mini-gunner. Mark went next, and a bullet caught his buttocks. He was followed by the two mini-gunners, who paused on the upper side of the chopper to reach down and help me out. Without them I'd have been well and truly trapped.

As I rolled out my ears were ringing from the loud crack of bullets snapping past me. I hit the ground hard, rolling over and forwards, and somehow came up in a crouch with my Glock in my hands. Ian had already started to skirt forwards, keeping the helicopter between him and those firing at us, and we all followed him, quickly getting into some cover. We had presumed that those firing at us were Iraqis, until Mark came up with the unlikely suggestion they might be Peshmerga, mistaking us for an Iraqi chopper.

'English, you bastards – *English!*' John yelled, and suddenly we were laughing.

There was plenty of fire coming in our direction, though most was still concentrated on the chopper. Mark was fumbling in a satchel he was carrying. Then he twisted a fuse timer and lobbed it back inside the helicopter. 'OK,' he announced, with a grin. 'We all gotta leave – like now.'

We didn't need telling twice and set off after Ian, weapons at the aim as we disappeared into the underbrush. After two minutes we stopped and checked that we were all together. The Iraqis were still firing at the stricken Black Hawk, obviously not realising we'd left it, when suddenly it exploded in a huge ball of flame, the shockwaves rolling out across the gorge and the surrounding hills. Mark's satchel charge hadn't been powerful enough to destroy the aircraft totally but it had rendered it useless to the enemy.

We got up and hurried along until we found some rocky cover at the base of a steep climb where we paused to take stock. The two mini-gunners were now carrying just their M4 assault rifles, and both were still wearing their aviation helmets. Pilot Steve inspected Mark's wound – a shallow bullet burn. In the distance we could still hear shouting and the odd shot. It would not take the Iraqis long to figure out the direction we had taken, as there were only two routes out of the gorge: south into the valley below us, or north towards the higher mountains. It would be pretty obvious that we weren't going to head south: that was where they had been firing from.

As we considered our options, John repeated: 'I'm sorry, boss. I'm so sorry, boss. I'm sorry, boss . . .'

I grabbed his shoulder with my left hand and brought my face close to his. 'Mate, listen, shit happens, OK? We're fine. Not your fault, OK? So, let's deal with the biz here and now, and you can buy us a drink later.'

'Yeah, and make mine a fucking treble,' Ian added.

I checked my map. I was glad I'd made Doug go ahead with the other Black Hawk as I knew he'd kick up merry hell when they got to base. A CSAR chopper would be in the air by now. As I raised my left arm to put away my map, an intense wave of pain flooded through me, stopping my breath. I choked up some blood. Fuck, I thought. Maybe I was more hurt than I'd thought. Although my weapon and body armour had stopped the .50-cal round, the energy from it had obviously thumped me hard, the hydrostatic shock ripping through my organs. The human body is mainly water, and the ripple of shockwaves from a bullet impact radiates through the body. It can kill, if it disrupts the heart rhythms or badly damages the liver or kidneys.

I could taste more blood in my mouth now, and my left lung was burning. Also my torso was swelling, making my body armour and chest webbing feel like a straitjacket. I took out some Ibuprofen painkillers and crunched three, without any water.

'You OK, boss?' John asked. He had noticed I was injured, which seemed to jolt him out of his trauma.

I nodded, but I was in a lot of pain. Mark took out his emergency tacbe as a message came through on it from a nearby F16 pilot. It was a valuable bit of kit: it could be used in bleeper mode to pinpoint a missing patrol to Allied aircraft, or for voice communications with any friendly forces in a twelve-kilometre radius. Mark had had the presence of mind to activate his as soon as it had become obvious we were tail-ending down in the Black Hawk. Luckily, the F16 aircraft was already in the area, policing the Kurdish no-fly zone set up after the first Gulf War. Mark gave our position to the pilot, and asked him to pass on the information that we were heading for the ERV. I told Ian to request the F16 pilot to waste the crash site.

'Hello, Foxtrot Four One One, fire mission. Over,' Ian said, speaking into Mark's tacbe.

'Foxtrot Four One One here, fire mission co-ordinates?' came back the calm voice of the F16 pilot.

Ian confirmed them, so that the F16 didn't target our co-ordinates in error, but the pilot seemed to have lost us as we received no confirmatory response. We repeated the call several times, then decided to put out a call to any air cover in the region. At the start of the operation we'd been given predesignated call signs, which would indicate to any Allied pilot that we were Special Forces and in trouble.

'Fire mission out to all support,' Ian kept repeating, but there was no response.

Just as we were losing hope, the original F16 pilot made contact again, and confirmed he would deploy ordnance on target as requested. I loved the way US pilots referred to bombs as 'ordnance'. We decided to use the cover of the airstrike to put as much distance as possible between us and the enemy. We would head directly for the ERV, and try to make it out of there fast. We had the two tacbes that Mark and Steve were carrying; other than that we had our personal radios for inter-team communications. And we were pretty lightly armed, having left most of our ammo with Guss, Romero and the others up in the hills.

We listened intently for the noise of the F16's jet engines, which kept coming and going as it made its approach run through the winding valleys and hills. Suddenly, an explosion erupted near to the downed Black Hawk, but a little short of the mark. This was the pilot dropping a marker bomb so we could help him correct his aim.

'Up two and fire for effect,' Ian told the pilot via the tacbe, meaning he should drop everything he had on the target.

'Roger, fire for effect,' came the response.

'Fire in the hole, people,' Ian announced, and handed the tacbe back to Mark.

We saw a brilliant flash, followed by three more in quick succession, then heard the rumbling staccato of explosions. Overhead there was the scream of jet engines throttling up to pull away fast, after-burners streaking a trail of brilliant orange red across the sky. This was quickly followed by another set of four explosions, as the second F16 dumped its munitions on target.

As the percussion of the bombs reached us, we got to our feet and headed north-west at a fast jog, Mark cursing his wound. I'd rather have had a burn across my arse than the searing pain that racked my entire upper body, I thought. As we hurried towards the ERV, gunfire started up behind us again. I glanced over my shoulder and saw vehicle headlights probing the darkness, bouncing up and down as the bastards gave chase. This wasn't good news. There was no way we could outrun vehicles, even in this terrain, and if we climbed to higher ground we would not make the ERV in time.

After fifteen minutes' jogging, we reached a section of dirt track that ran through a narrow, rocky defile. Fresh vehicle tracks were in evidence, so it was a reasonable guess that our pursuers would come this way. I called a halt to set an ambush there. Part of me was worried: it was such an obvious ambush point that the Iraqis might dismount to scout round it, but I didn't have time to entertain such fears. Indecision or hesitation might prove fatal. We had two claymore mines, one Minimi light machine-gun, three assault rifles and three pistols between us. I did the fastest sighting of an ambush I've ever achieved, as Ian set the claymores. Then I lay down next to John, who was again on the edge of losing it, and tried to reassure him that all would be OK. I told the aircrew not to open fire until I had detonated the Claymores and then only in controlled bursts. I made Mark and Steve silence their tacbes.

We lay still for fifteen long minutes. John breathed in short sharp gasps, trying desperately to hold himself together. I considered taking the Minimi off him as it was our only serious firepower. But I decided against it: it would push him over the edge and then we'd really be in trouble. Four sets of lights were bouncing towards us in the dark.

'My girls, my girls, I must see my girls again,' John moaned as the lights drew nearer to the ambush point. He kept repeating it, and eventually I had to nudge him hard. For years he had been a diamond soldier, always focused and calm under fire, but now something had snapped. It happens, even with long-term experienced operators.

As the first vehicle came into view, its headlights blinding, I waited until it was practically upon us, then squeezed the hand-held trigger device three times, click, click, click. There was a massive explosion, followed by John laying down a murderous barrage with the Minimi. He might have cracked up, but he could still use a weapon when he needed to, almost as if he were acting on autopilot. Click, click, click, again, and the second claymore detonated. The front vehicle stopped dead in its tracks, with one headlight still working and white smoke billowing from its bonnet. The Iraqi soldiers started bailing out but they were mown down and lay screaming on the ground, silhouetted in the stark light of the vehicles behind them.

The three other vehicles behind stopped and Iraqi soldiers debussed amazingly fast, ran off into the brush and dived for cover. I didn't fire my pistol – a waste of ammo at that range. The Iraqis were firing in all directions, as orders were bellowed into the darkness. John pumped away with short bursts as our two mini-gunners fired their M4 assault rifles. Ian took single aimed shots in rapid succession. The front vehicle was alight now, first with just a few flames licking out of the sides of the bonnet, then exploding as the fuel tank ignited.

That was our cue to vacate the area and I jumped up, closely followed by John and the rest of the team. As I straightened to run, I coughed up more blood and had to spit it out.

After half an hour or so of fast tabbing, we stopped and took cover to assess our situation. I checked the map and the PLGR GPS, as Steve and Mark got on their tacbes. Behind us we could see slow-moving vehicle lights. They were still tracking us. The odd shot rang out, probably from some nervous point-man made to walk out front. We all carried small sarbes (surface to air rescue beacons, like a mini version of the tacbe) in our webbing belts, and I thought now was the best time to activate them in case we got separated. If the CSAR chopper failed to show, or we failed to make it to the ERV, we'd have to tab it out to safer ground. We were about to switch on the sarbes when John had a quiet word in my ear: 'Listen, boss, leave me here and I'll delay the fuckers for you,' he whispered, too calmly for my liking. 'Come on, admit it – it's my fault we're in this mess.'

'Fuck that,' I replied. 'Leave you, mate, and it'll have been a waste of a perfectly good helicopter. Wasn't your fault. If anyone's, it was mine.'

Before he could reply, we noticed movement on the hillside above us and to our left. More Iraqi soldiers were coming down on foot from positions up on the ridge. For a second, I reconsidered whether John and I should stay to create a diversion, so that the rest could get away. But as I looked around the area, it was clear that we all stood out in the bright, moonlit night. Thoughts of my children entered my mind, but I pushed them aside. We'd really be in the shit if we were captured now. Our cover about being mercenaries was fine, but how would we explain two helicopter pilots and their gunners?

'Get on the net and see if those bomb jockeys have anything else they can drop for us,' I whispered to Mark.

As quietly as he could, with just a slight crackle of static, Mark sent out a call to any air support. The response came back immediately, like a loudspeaker in the still of the night.

'Negative but can confirm CSAR en route,' the pilot announced. 'Will hold position and buzz them until our relief arrives.'

It was a joy to hear that the chopper was on its way, but I wondered how far off the F16s relief aircraft were. Time was not on our side.

'Ask when his relief is due,' I told Mark.

'Relief aircraft already scrambled and on their way,' the pilot's voice boomed.

Mark's tacbe had a volume control somewhere, but it seemed

95

to be permanently jammed on max. Before I could say anything, the pair of F16s rolled out of the heavens and screamed down low into the valley, passing over the Iraqi troops, who dived for cover. We got up and ran as fast as we could in the direction of the ERV. The Iraqis opened up on us, but fortunately their fire was wildly inaccurate.

As we pushed on towards the ERV my chest was burning horrendously and I kept spitting blood. John had his head down and was tabbing as hard as he could, determined to keep going. Ian stayed in the rear, pushing one or other of the mini-gunners along – fatigue had set in. I was dizzy, but told myself it was the higher altitude we were now at. I was finding it more and more difficult to move my left arm as the swelling increased round my chest and shoulder. As we gained altitude the valley closed in still further: if there were any Iraqis ahead, we were well and truly fucked.

Our ERV was at the head of the valley, where the ground flattened out into a small plateau. It was exposed, but it would be easy for the CSAR pilot to identify. I stopped the group half a mile short: we were ahead of time and I didn't want to draw attention to the location. We lay down in all-round defence and Mark checked in with the pilots again. He tried to muffle the noise from his tacbe, but it was still stuck on maximam volume. Two relief aircraft were now in our immediate area, which might just be enough to save our skins. Mark began calling up the new pilots, as we watched the Iraqis edging up the valley towards us

We waited as long as we dared, then decided to move on to the plateau and towards the ERV. But as I tried to get to my feet a wave of pain ripped through me, and I all but collapsed on to the ground. John and Steve grabbed my arms and hauled me up.

'Jesus, boss, you OK?' Steve whispered as he tried to steady me. 'You look white as a sheet even in this bloody darkness.'

I nodded, but was unable to speak. For a moment I thought I

was going to keel over as black and white squares filled my vision and a rush of heat went to my head.

'Come on, boss, I'll get you out of this shit,' I heard John say, trying to reassure me now.

As I watched the approaching Iraqi force, now just a short distance below us, I finally found my voice. 'Mark, I hope your FAC's bloody good,' I rasped. 'I need you to call in whatever they have up there in a straight line, right across the enemy's approach and lead elements.'

Mark got back on the tacbe to two F18 Hornet pilots from the 'Gunslingers' of 105 Strike Fighter Squadron, who flew CAS (close air support) missions for coalition Special Operations. I checked the map with my red-light torch, confirmed where the Iraqi forces were in relationship to us, and relayed what I hoped were the exact co-ordinates to Mark. He radioed them to the pilots above us, and began to talk them down on to target. But the new F18 pilot came back on the net saying he couldn't understand the order, so Ian grabbed the tacbe and went through the whole fire-mission request again. Then the pilot came back with the confirmation we desperately needed to hear. All I could do now was pray I'd got the co-ordinates right, and that the bombs weren't about to drop on top of us.

Within thirty seconds, the aircraft screamed past overhead and I looked towards the bouncing vehicle lights, about eight hundred yards below us. I was holding my breath when, suddenly, a salvo of bombs rained down on the Iraqi troops, obliterating the lead element in a mass of dirt and smoke. As the massive explosions punched their way across the valley, echoing into the distant hills, we were up and running towards our final ERV. Within minutes we had reached it, and were looking out across a wide, empty, exposed plateau. Behind us we could see one set of vehicle lights still heading after us. You had to admire the bastards' courage and determination. As we knelt down in all-round defence, Mark received a call.

'Hello, India One Sunray, this is Foxtrot Sierra Alpha Romeo Three Three, do you copy? Over.'

Mark looked at me, and I took the tacbe. It was the CSAR chopper.

'India One Sunray, roger. Over,' I replied.

As I spoke I saw a huge CH53 Super Sea Stallion Pave Low helicopter ahead, skimming the ground fast. It carries a lot of firepower, and if they mistook us for Iraqis they could seriously upset our day. I stood up and waved, confirming on the tacbe that we were directly ahead of him. The pilot was flying using PNGs and pulled up close to us. A CH53 is more than seventy feet long, so for a few horrible seconds I thought he was going to land directly on top of us. As his mini-gunners scanned for enemy troops, I made sure that we hadn't left anyone on the ground this time, then gave the thumbs-up to the chief loadie.

As we lifted off I pulled John across to me. He was shuddering, his head buried in his hands. In the relative safety of the CH53 the shock of what had happened was now setting in. He fought to keep his act together, but I could tell he was in a bad way. I put my arm round him, which hurt like hell, as the wind buffeted us from the open forward side door. Our two mini-gunners were beaming at me – this little adventure would pay for their drinks for years to come. I was elated that we had escaped, but sad for John. His days of soldiering were over. I should have stopped him coming in the first place, but ultimately the decision had been his. He had thought he was OK, and I'd felt compelled to let him sort it out for himself.

The CH53 crew took us directly to our FOB where Tosh, Dianne and the others all awaited our return. News had gone ahead that John was in a bad way. They had assumed he was seriously wounded so had set up the emergency operating theatre, with Dianne and the SEAL surgeon good to go. They also believed that I was coming in ready for theatre, having been hit by a .50-cal round.

As we landed, the CH53 hadn't even stopped before Doug had jumped aboard and I was being manhandled on to a stretcher. Dianne's face shouted into mine while she tried to get a line into my arm. I was yelling that I was all right, but I was still bounced across to the medical tent. The same was happening to John, who lay perfectly still, arms across his chest, eyes shut. When Mark, the only one of us with an actual flesh wound, got down from the CH53 and tried to call attention to his painful backside, he was ignored.

As soon as we reached the medical tent, Doug was swearing at me. 'You fucking mental case,' he raged. 'I'd have been right in the shit if anything serious had happened to you.'

I tried to sit up, but he pushed me down hard on to the stretcher, until I was hoisted on to a gurney. Baby Steve was on a neighbouring one, with a large bandage over his left eye. He gave me a wave and, a grin.

As Dianne started to cut away my bootlaces and trousers I tried telling them again that I was all right. 'Fuck sake, will someone listen to me?' I yelled in frustration. 'I'm fine.'

But they continued to ignore me, and Doug practically tore open my dish-dash, chest webbing and body armour.

'Told you he was a faggot,' said Malcolm, as Doug bent over my near naked torso.

As Doug and Dianne helped me undress, the release of my body armour and chest webbing eased the pressure of the swelling, but the pain was intense. I could see the blackened, burnt hole from the impact of the .50-cal that ran through my kit. It looked nasty, all right. Baby Steve came over to have a look, and it turned out that several splinters of Perspex from the Black Hawk's windscreen had embedded in his face. One had cut his eye, hence the bandage. When I finally managed to get my T-shirt off, Dianne and Doug looked worried. I glanced down at my left side and saw why. I was bright purple from neck to navel, with severe bruising, and noticeably distended. Dianne forced me to lie down and keep still, as the SEAL surgeon got a line into my arm.

'I'm flying you out first thing and back to the UK,' Dianne told me sternly. 'I need detailed scans of the internal damage.'

I looked across at John, who was still lying perfectly still. Dianne followed my gaze. 'And he's going back with you,' she added. 'I'll sedate him in a moment to relax him and stop the effects of shock, but I suspect his nerves are shot.'

Eventually we put John into a private tented area as he wanted to be left alone for a while. Before I left him we had a brief chat about what had happened. It turned out he thought I'd told him not to get on Athansa's chopper, when in fact I'd told him the opposite. In all the noise and being half deaf in his right ear, he'd misheard. The fog of war, I thought, and the old mnemonic CLAP sprang to mind – Clear, Loud and Precise.

Tosh couldn't get over how apparently blasé I was about the whole sorry saga, and that we'd lost an expensive Black Hawk. As he saw it, I was irresponsible and had demonstrated a reckless lack of concern. He wasted no time in telling me so, but I didn't have the energy to deal with him.

I showered, splashed on all sorts of lotions Dianne had given me and contemplated my return home. No sooner had I got out of the shower than Ian arrived with new kit for me. When I was dressed I felt a lot better and could no longer taste blood in my mouth. But it then struck me what we had just survived. I'd come close to letting my children grow up fatherless. It would be devastating for them if I didn't come home, and for a few seconds I understood where John had been coming from. Tosh had been wrong on how I felt about it all, that was for sure.

At that moment Doug came in with a mug of tea for me and

we went to meet up with Tosh and the others in the ops tent to start preparing our notes for the formal inquiry we knew would follow after the loss of a helicopter. We wrote up our own descriptions of events, so that the investigators could see if the stories matched. It was bureaucratic bullshit, but part of the game nevertheless. Once it had been collated by some geek the paperwork would be destroyed anyway, as it was a deniable operation. But that would only happen after the inquiry had established that we had indeed lost the chopper, not sold it at a vast profit, which in the past some wayward lads actually had.

I finished my report before the others, except Doug, who wrote, 'See Niall's, and I concur.' He had even less tolerance for red tape than I did. As I got up, Dianne asked how I was feeling. I told her I was fine and had decided I would stay, not go home as she'd advised. A large part of me wanted to escape, but I had to finish what we'd started. Besides, I'd given my word to the Peshmerga that I would be back. Dianne flew into a rage, insisting I must go home, but eventually we agreed on a compromise: I would return to Konya with John and have a detailed X-ray session. If the results were OK, she would allow me to stay. If they were bad I would return to the UK. Dianne was still far from happy and insisted I should rest, as anything might rupture without warning.

An hour or so later John still hadn't joined us, so I went to check on him. The area where we'd left him was empty. I knew he shouldn't have been left alone in his present state, but he'd insisted we give him some space. He was being very hard on himself, repeatedly saying he'd let the side down. I checked the weapons rack for his Minimi and felt seriously alarmed that it was missing. Wherever he'd gone he'd taken it with him. Too many operators had suffered a breakdown and committed suicide.

I asked in the medical tent and one of the SEALs had seen John heading for the showers. I hurried over there and could hear someone groaning in a cubicle with the water running. I looked under the door and saw John crouched, still fully dressed, cradling his Minimi as water cascaded over him.

'John, mate, it's me,' I said. He didn't answer, so I went in to him.

I couldn't see his tears as the water was washing them away, but the groaning gave him away – an awful, empty, spine-chilling sound. His gaze was fixed and he wouldn't acknowledge me. I knelt down with him, trying to get his attention, but he looked right through me. It wasn't until I shook him gently that he registered my presence. Then he let go of the Minimi, grabbed my shirt and sobbed uncontrollably, clenching and unclenching his hands. I was close to tears myself – and I was getting soaked, but I couldn't lift him to his feet as he was a dead weight. Finally, Big Matt peered in and saw my predicament. 'I'll go get Doc,' he remarked, reached over and turned off the shower.

'I can't, I can't, I can't,' John cried. 'I can't even protect my family no more.'

All I could do was hold him and wait for Dianne to arrive. When she did, she injected John with a relaxant, without him even knowing it. Doug, Matt and Baby Steve were close on her heels, but Doug soon took the hint and ushered them away. John, Dianne and I were left sitting in the shower, as we waited for John to come out of whatever horrible place he was in. Just as we were getting him back to something like normal, Malcolm came in. 'I hear there's a gang bang,' he joked, before covering his mouth as he saw the situation.

John stretched out his free hand to him. Without a word Malcolm grasped it and helped lift him to his feet. Together, Malcolm and I walked John back to a quiet room. My chest was hurting again, big-time, and Malcolm offered to get John dry and into a warm sleeping-bag as the jab began to take effect.

We had all lost track of time, and as the sun came up we

gathered for some food. The mood was sombre. Malcolm took his meal to John's room, so he could keep an eye on him, as the rest of us discussed how best to inform John's wife of his collapse. Doug suggested we get Sara or Victoria to contact her, but that didn't seem fair to them. I called her direct. As soon as she heard my voice she burst into tears, fearing the worst – she'd had really bad feelings for the past three days. Quickly I set her mind at rest: physically he was fine, but he had suffered what Dianne called a 'stress breakdown'.

'Just get him home to me, please,' she cried. 'Just get him home. I don't care what he's had, we'll be fine. Just please, please, get him home safely.'

I promised he would soon be on his way, and that she should be ready to collect him within a few days. As I spoke I could hear their two little girls in the background shouting, 'Yippee,' because their daddy was coming home. I had a lump in my throat.

Eight hours later Malcolm and I boarded a Black Hawk chopper with John for the ride out to Konya. The entire FOB turned out to see him off as he climbed aboard staring ahead, eyes wide but unseeing. Doug helped strap him in tightly – he was seriously concerned that he might try to jump out. As the Black Hawk powered up, it felt as if we were going to a funeral.

We arrived at Konya to be met by two officious USAF personnel asking for me. They demanded I follow them to a waiting vehicle. As we helped John out of his seat I told them they could fucking wait, and I was more than ready to kick off if they argued. But Malcolm didn't want any unnecessary shit in front of John, and told me I should go quietly. He was right, of course. I left John in his care and was driven to a hangar on the far side of the base, without a word spoken.

I was taken into a small room and immediately confronted by two geeks. They went over and over every detail of the helicopter crash. I was tired, in pain and emotionally raw, in no mood to take that kind of crap. I stopped answering their questions and demanded to know who exactly they were, which pissed them off. They were aircraft-crash investigators – so just doing their job – from AFOSI (Air Force Office of Special Investigation), but assigned to Seaspray, the clandestine US Army/CIA aviation unit, which our chopper had been part of, but they demanded to see my body armour and chest webbing, as well as the bruising. If they had asked politely I would have had no issue with them, but they were condescending and arrogant. Eventually my patience ran out. 'You want my gear, you come and get it,' I said. 'You want to know about my injuries, you file for my medical records. Treat people like shit, you get shit in return.' I stood up to leave.

'Just where the hell d'you think you're going—' one started.

I slammed the door on them before he could finish. Fucking arseholes, I told myself as I strode off.

I hurried to the apron area through melting snow, hoping to find John before he left for the UK. I was in time to see Malcolm helping him board his flight, with an RAF pilot as his personal escort. It was the last time I saw him as a Special Forces soldier.

5

UNHOLY BLOOD

After John's departure I flew back to Cizre with Malcolm. I hadn't bothered to get the X-rays done, so I was probably in for a bollocking from Dianne. To make matters worse, the two crash investigators had decided to come with us. Malcolm stared at them all the way, and after half an hour it really got to them. As soon as we landed at Cizre, Dianne was demanding my X-rays. I tried waffling about how they'd be on the next flight, but Dianne was having none of it. She stormed off, ranting – how on earth could she do her job properly if no one took her seriously? I shrugged my shoulders guiltily and headed for the mess tent.

Within the hour the investigators had collected my damaged kit and all our reports about the Black Hawk. I couldn't help laughing when I spotted Malcolm's, complete with a cartoon showing his Black Hawk flying away, arms waving out of it to our chopper, and laughter bubbles coming from inside. Needless to say, the investigators didn't find it amusing. As they lifted off to return to their base, two lone figures in the back of their helicopter, we waved them off, feigning tears.

I took myself off to my tent to read and digest the latest intel. I lay down on my green maggot and made a start, but I was tired so

I asked Tosh to check my emails and respond on my behalf, which he kindly did. When I woke up it was dark outside and I was cold, aching like hell. I must have been asleep for several hours. Soon Doug appeared with a welcome mug of tea. 'Good news, boss,' he announced, with heavy sarcasm. 'Dan's paying us a visit. Appears we've pissed off his buddies somehow.'

Just what I didn't need. I grabbed a quick wash and shave, then headed to the ops tent. Alone, I read through the latest intel. A report that dealt with the urgent confirmation and location of Iraq's WMDs caught my eye, but it was the attached comments from MI6 that really grabbed my attention. It stated that in their opinion there was no threat from Iraq as the country didn't have WMD capability. How had this 'top secret' document ended up in front of me? There was also a message from Patrick, my UK controller, on an encrypted CD. It warned me of the showdown between various Labour ministers, their spin doctor Alastair Campbell, MI6 and JIC (Joint Intelligence Committee) about Iraqi WMD. Patrick advised caution at our end and asked me to let him know immediately if we heard anything relating to WMD on our sorties. I'd just started to write a secure response to him when Dan Meany arrived. Tosh welcomed him off the chopper and brought him across to me.

'Glad to see you're busy,' Dan announced as he entered the ops tent.

'Keeping up to date on all the latest,' I replied, as I shook his hand.

We got straight down to business. Dan told me it was imperative we get back out in the field, embed ourselves with the Peshmerga and find out exactly what their plans were. If they insisted on entering Kirkuk, he would have them stopped. Turkey wouldn't allow them to stay there. It would look bad if American troops had to face off Turkish soldiers, so we had to follow Dan's lead. I let him say his piece until he was suddenly banging on about how I was answerable only to him while in theatre.

'Excuse me, Dan, I don't think so,' I interrupted. He laughed and sat back. 'What makes you say that, and why say it at all?' I enquired, somewhat puzzled. So was Tosh.

'Shit, man, when are you guys going to wake up and smell the coffee?' Dan clapped his hands together. 'You guys are only here 'cause we asked for you. Why d'you think all of your support is US supplied? Why the camp in Konya? Why Navy SEALs from our Delta attachment, and Delta boys?'

Tosh and I exchanged a glance. Neither of us could believe our ears.

'Come again?' Tosh asked.

'Wake up and smell the coffee, guys,' Dan repeated. 'It was us who fixed to have you guys out here. You did well before and I remembered that. And our mutual buddy, Patrick, he agreed with me you were perfect for the job, so it was a quick call from our government boys to your government. I mean, Jack Straw's department are so giving, wouldn't you agree? This is our show, run by us for us. No insult intended, but it was your country that fucked up in the first place. If you Brits hadn't screwed up after World War One, we wouldn't be in this shit. And now it's us running the show.'

'We're here at the instruction and request of our MoD and government,' Tosh responded stiffly.

'You fucking believe that?' Dan barked. 'Well, let me tell ya, you're here for one reason only – 'cause we requested you guys to work with and for us. Hell, shit, I bet half your MI6 buddies ain't even gotta clue you boys are here. Fuck, they ain't even gotta clue what the other half of their own office gets up to. You're here 'cause the Kurds sure as hell don't trust us. But they do you guys – the good ol' honourable Brits.'

After that the ops tent was silent until Doug walked in. 'I heard what you were saying. So, what else is new? No reason we should have a problem with that,' he said calmly as he sat down. The grin disappeared from the CIA man's face. 'But let's get one thing fucking clear,' Doug continued. 'If you're setting us up, or if you fuck us over, I'll hunt you down. Personally. I'll make it my fucking life mission to find you. And when I do you'll wish to fuck I hadn't. Now, am I making myself clear?'

'Guys, guys, come on, we're all on the same side here,' said Dan, trying to placate Doug. 'But you guys gotta realise—'

'You didn't fucking answer me. Am I making myself clear?' said Doug, as his fist smashed into the table.

'Sure, sure you are, buddy,' Dan answered hurriedly. 'But you gotta realise where the buck stops on this one, and who's yanking the chain. I need to know I can depend on you to ensure your Pesh friends toe the line. This is bigger than just anti-terrorism operations, or oil, or removing Saddam. Believe me, guys, it is, and we're driving it.' Dan paused. 'And when this is all put to bed, I can promise you some interesting, lucrative jobs based in Maryland.'

'Dan, you only had to ask and we'd deliver. You know me well enough by now to be confident of that. I've already given you my word we'll have the Pesh on board and playing the game. You don't need to come all heavy with us. But we need to know who else you have operating in the region. I don't want any confusion or overlap on this one. Nor do I want to hear any of your shit about need-to-know-only basis. If we are, as you say, under your direct control on this one, which I'll need to confirm with Head Shed, then you'd better keep us well and truly in the loop.'

'That's fine and dandy with me. You guys are the only operators in your area and, trust me, I personally guarantee if any other operators get involved you'll be second to know after me. Believe me, I need this operation to work. There's a much bigger picture here, and before you say it, this ain't a case of me doing the need-to-know-only bit on you,' Dan replied, grinning again.

'Then give me the bigger picture, Dan,' I said.

'Well, that I can't tell you, as I don't really know the full details myself yet.'

'Balls,' snapped Tosh, and threw his pen down on the table. Dan's performance was getting to him. 'And my orders certainly came from our Head Shed direct. There's no confusion on that score.'

'Don't I know it,' Dan retorted. 'I counter-signed them. Like I said, your government is just an extension of ours, buddy.'

Part of me suspected that Dan was just playing the same old mind games I'd witnessed before, and was now trying to provoke a reaction. That meant it was probably best to wrap up the meeting and get him out of there before Doug killed him.

'OK, whatever. Leave us to get on with the job in hand,' I said. 'As far as I see it we'll carry out our operational remit, regardless of where the orders come from.'

Doug was staring at Dan with a chilling look in his eyes. Dan was usually a cool player, but something in Doug's manner ruffled him. You knew with Doug that if you messed with him you'd be in serious shit, regardless of who or where you were.

Dan left the three of us sitting round the ops table. We were all wondering the same thing: how much of Dan's speech had been true? We all knew that within Special Forces and intelligence communities there were many wheels within wheels. It had to be that way to maintain security on operations. But Dan's boast that we were only there at his request and ultimately under his command was disconcerting. And it was possibly true.

The three of us talked through what might be the 'bigger picture' that Dan had mentioned. Doug suggested, joking, that it was about finishing unfinished business between the Bush family and Saddam Hussein, but we knew it was more than that. We also knew it was bigger than just getting hold of Iraq's oil – there were far easier ways for the West to do that. Tosh was very annoyed that Dan had blamed the present Iraq situation on the British. Doug said he couldn't care less whose fault it was, so long as we weren't stitched up.

I took myself off to think alone for a while and lay on my green maggot. Unlike Doug, I was incapable of blindly following orders. I had to grasp the reasoning behind them. Dan's opinion that it was all Britain's fault kept coming into my mind. I understood what he had been driving at. The Kurds have a proverb that is particularly appropriate to their situation: 'No friends but the mountains.' Throughout history they have been deserted and sold out by those they had considered friends, but the mountains have endured, giving them sanctuary and a place to hide. But with the advent of modern machines of war – tanks, trucks and aircraft – they can no longer rely on them.

Britain had indeed played a pivotal role in selling them out. She had presided over the division of their homeland, Kurdistan, between Turkey, Iran, Iraq and Syria. In 1916, the British diplomat Sir Mark Sykes negotiated the secret Sykes–Picot Agreement for the division of the territories of the Ottoman Empire, signalling the death knell for Kurdistan. 'A consolidated Kurdistan is an impossibility,' Sykes stated. 'There is no reason why the distribution of the Kurdish people should dictate frontiers, or why Kurds should be regarded as a people who require consolidation.' I wondered if he had ever considered the dire long-term consequences of what he had written or the agreement he negotiated.

Kurdish scholars do not deny that the Kurds are a people with a tradition of identity and a homeland. There is confusion concerning their origins – whether they are the descendants of the Medes, Gutis, Harrians or other ancient tribes who first inhabited the Zagros mountains – and debate over the origins of their language, and whether they ever constituted a 'nation'. But there is clear evidence of continuous occupation of the Kurdish homelands by Kurds from at least 400 BC, when the Greek Xenophon wrote about them in his Anabasis text.

For decades after the Sykes-Picot Agreement the world ignored the 'Kurdish problem'. Iraq, Iran, Syria and Turkey had been given free rein to 'ethnically cleanse' the Kurdish homeland, torturing, killing, massacring and even gassing the people. It was only the mountains that offered Kurds a respite from the atrocities. And it was only after the failure of the West to support them during the first Gulf War that the world started to take notice of them.

The next morning I sorted out my new chest webbing, body armour and dish-dash. We'd been back at Cizre for three days now and I'd been unable to get a replacement Diemaco C7, so I had to sign out an M16A3 assault rifle, with a 40mm M203 grenade-launcher slung beneath it, plus a Glock 36 pistol. I spent a few hours on the ranges with Doug, zeroing my new weapons. He'd managed to grab an M240B, a US 7.62mm GPMG off the SEAL team, his weapon of choice. It weighed in on the heavy side at twenty-six pounds, but it was a devastating weapon with an effective range of 1500 metres. He was like a kid with a new toy as he fired it on the ranges.

I went to find Tosh. He was in the ops tent, and still in a serious sulk that he wasn't coming in theatre with us. He'd been trying every conceivable trick to get into the field, but his role as base liaison back to Head Shed was crucial. Should the shit hit the fan, as it had once already, we would be 100 per cent reliant on him getting a CSAR chopper into the air for us. He'd done superbly well when we'd needed it before, and I told him that that was a major reassuring factor for us. But that didn't do much to improve his mood.

Tosh's main area of expertise was psychological warfare and

profiling, and he'd bragged that he could get any woman he chose to fall for him, given enough time. He was a good-looking bloke too. As I got up to leave, he said he'd keep Victoria posted for me and might just sweet-talk her while I was away. I knew he was only saying it to get at me, but it niggled. She was image- and status-obsessed, Tosh continued, and would be easy to sway with promises of love, security and money.

'Show me a woman who fucking isn't,' bellowed Doug, as he barged in.

'You don't know Victoria,' I told Tosh, as calmly as I could, ignoring Doug. 'She's far too smart to fall for the likes of you. Besides, she loves me. Or doesn't that count for anything in your book?'

'We'll see then, shall we, Niall?' Tosh retorted.

I outranked him, but he was from a moneyed, upper-class background and spoke with a plum in his mouth, which I didn't – probably one of the main reasons I got on well with the likes of Doug. As I moved towards the door, Tosh joked that as he was my friend and knew me well, he could press all the right psychological buttons with Victoria. If she responded to him, he continued, she didn't love me, and he'd be doing me a favour. I thought he was joking, but as I walked away Doug caught up and warned me it was a bad idea to let him have such free contact with her.

Before I had time to call my children or Victoria, I was climbing aboard another Black Hawk. Dr Dianne was still furious with me for not listening to her advice, and she made it clear I was in the dog-house. Baby Steve's eye had healed well enough for him to go back in theatre, so he and Layla hopped aboard – she was keen to return to the mountains. She and the two Peshmerga guides had kept a low profile at the base – I'd thought the Turks wouldn't appreciate us bringing them on to Turkish soil. Five more SEAL lads joined us and we were complete.

The flight was uneventful, and we touched down in early-evening darkness at the LZ. Romero was on the ground to meet us, having chosen the location. Guss, Big Matt and three other SEALs were on hand to help offload the extra kit and ammo we'd brought. It was a six-mile tab from the LZ to the cave complex with the gear, and as I was still sore I felt every inch of it.

We were greeted almost as conquering heroes. Wajy was excited to see us, and even more so when we showed him the boxes of kit we'd brought for them. Layla was surrounded by a gaggle of female Peshmerga, all eager to hear about her travels in the Black Hawk and her other adventures.

I was just arranging my gear and sleeping kit in one of the caves when I glanced up to see a familiar face from previous operations. I wasn't too pleased: its owner was one of Dan's boys, working with Grey Fox. He had his back to me, and was walking away, evidently hoping I hadn't recognised him.

'Stop him!' I yelled at Doug.

In a few strides Doug had blocked his exit. I walked over and forced him to look at me.

'Phil,' I said.

'Hi, Moses, how're you doin'? Just passing through,' he replied, using my old nickname. In Saudi Arabia I had managed to navigate the desert, and en route I gave my usual history lesson about how Mount Sinai was where Moses received the Ten Commandments. From then on my troop nicknamed me Moses.

Phil was renowned as a 'lone player'. An ex-member of Delta Force, he was fluent in many Arabic dialects and a natural survivor. With Doug as escort we ushered him to a secluded area for a chat. I wasn't impressed when I learnt that Dan had ordered him to the area to mingle with all parties on the ground. I knew Phil was only doing his job, but I was still pretty angry to find that he'd been sent without my knowledge. Wajy spotted us, and came over to join us. He took me to one side and explained that Phil was one of the operators who had insulted and belittled him and Kosrat Rassul before our arrival. Wajy had only allowed him back into the area because he had been under the impression that he was with us.

I was annoyed, but I couldn't show it. If I denied that Phil was with us, it would look unprofessional. If I agreed he was, I'd be aligning myself with Grey Fox, and I already knew what Wajy thought of that lot. I had to fudge it so that I could retain our credibility and keep Wajy on-side.

'Phil's here with my knowledge and permission, but only so I can establish clear lines of operational conduct and areas of responsibility to avoid conflict further down the line,' I explained.

Wajy was clearly trying to fathom whether I was feeding him bullshit. 'I'm glad,' he said finally, 'very glad that this is the case. When he arrived I was not pleased, but if that is all he is here for, then very good, and he can leave soonest now.'

'Phil, do us all a favour. Keep us updated and in the loop and I'll guarantee likewise,' I said, as I reached over to shake his hand.

Phil hesitated, then guessed I was trying to convince Wajy we were all on the same side so he shook my hand. He stayed out of sight, and later we had a personal chat away from everyone else. In one sense I was glad it was Phil that Dan had sent to snoop on us. He was a nice guy, and even he didn't trust Dan completely. It transpired that he had several other Grey Fox men, plus a SEAL team, with another faction of Kurds, in a not too distant valley. I was far from comfortable about them being there, with the potential for confusion and overlap, but we parted on good terms, agreeing to stay in touch and support each other should the need arise.

Just after we'd said goodbye, two more men arrived. They sported beards but were clearly Europeans.

'You seen a guy around here, an American named Phil?' the

taller one asked, without a hint of warmth. His accent was British, but both men were dressed in full Arab gear and carrying AK47s.

'Who are you?' I asked him. I wasn't about to give them Phil's whereabouts before I knew the answer.

'Fuck off, and who the hell are you?' he retorted aggressively.

I was stunned by their outright hostility, but Wajy was approaching again, and a second showdown with our own kind wouldn't look good. I ushered the new arrivals towards Malcolm and Big Matt, who were sitting at a nearby table, but the taller guy tore his arm away from me with a cold stare. My patience was running out. This was supposed to be a covert operation at a secret location hidden deep within the mountains, yet it was more like Piccadilly Circus. Who the hell *wasn't* aware of our presence? Luckily, at that moment Doug appeared cradling his GPMG. With a few choice words he managed to persuade the pair that I was the boss and not to fuck around any more than they had already.

We sat them down at the table double quick and I got Malcolm and Big Matt to distract Wajy by opening some of the boxes of high-specification RDX explosives we'd brought for him. RDX is an aluminised explosive manufactured in the US as penetration-augmented munition (PAM). It is easier to handle and has more explosive potential than any of its predecessors. Just fifteen kilos has the same explosive power as ninety of the previous generation C4 plastic explosives. With RDX the Kurds would be able to cause even greater damage to bridges, roads, vehicles and communication masts.

Wajy knew that something was not right between my team and our two new arrivals. Also, several of his sharp young fighters were eyeing up the new arrivals, and could see the tension between us and them. I was relieved when Layla joined us, which made things look a little more relaxed.

'OK, you may not have noticed, but we run the show around

here,' I said quietly, as I took a seat. 'We've got a bigger bunch of guys and a bigger bunch of guns, and the Pesh are our very good friends. So, you'll appreciate that we're not fucking around. I want to know who you are and what the fuck you're doing here. You tell me, and I might not have to upset your day.'

'We're FO,' the shorter of the two guys said.

'So what the fuck're you doing here?' Doug demanded.

'We've been sent out to link up with the Peshmerga,' the taller guy cut in. 'Now why don't you tell us who you lot are?'

I told the guy to shut up, as I was doing the questioning. It turned out that although the Foreign Office had sent them out, they'd had no idea we were already in the region. I was aware that the FO had its field agents, almost paramilitary, which was where these guys were from, but I didn't like their manner or attitude. I got Doug to search them, which really put their noses out of joint. They were both person sterile, but they had blood chits – pieces of material printed in various languages stating that if anyone helps the person presenting the chit, they will be highly rewarded. The eight-digit number was unique to the person to whom it had been assigned.

I got Guss to radio Tosh and tell him to run a check on the blood chits and find out what was going on, then informed the FO lads they were staying until we'd checked them out, and were now under my direct command, whether they liked it or not. If we couldn't establish positively who they were, I would put them on the next chopper back to our FOB and have them arrested. I'd rarely, if ever, pulled rank, but now the situation warranted it. I was running these guys out of town, but after their behaviour, they deserved it.

Eventually, when Guss had had confirmation of their credentials, I allowed them to leave and returned their weapons. As they did so, they demanded to know who we were, but I was telling them nothing.

'You're fucking loose cannons, that's what you are. Increment, I bet,' one said accusingly, as Doug escorted them away.

I could see Layla watching us closely, with several Peshmerga lads. I couldn't afford public bad feeling between us, even though I could have smacked them both quite cheerfully. 'Listen, we know who you are. The fact we know your real names should prove we have the right contacts, and that's all you need to know. As for Increment, I thought that was all bullshit stuff for black-flag operations,' I said, trying to defuse the situation now that they were leaving. 'Look, we got off on the wrong foot so why don't you come back tomorrow and we'll see how best we can work it out.'

One of the FO men decided that enough was enough, and reached out to shake my hand. He apologised somewhat sheepishly for the earlier debacle. They'd been told they were the only British operators in the area and when they'd spotted me, they'd assumed I was a journalist, trying to get an exclusive story, like several others they'd already encountered in theatre. It was an understandable mistake, and we all agreed to meet the following day.

That evening, I joined Wajy and his commanders for a meal in one of the largest caves. Guss and Big Matt took sentry duty outside, with some of the Peshmerga lads. Layla sat next to me and Malcolm was opposite. There was no escaping the fact that she was a striking girl, but Victoria was always in my mind. It soon became stiflingly hot so I stripped down to my shirtsleeves, as did the others. The women tied up their shirts, revealing light brown skin. Malcolm's eyes lit up.

'Boss, I thought they weren't allowed to show any flesh,' Doug murmured.

Layla overheard him, laughed and whispered to the woman next to her.

As the night drew on, I found myself in a far corner with Layla,

Doug and an older woman, who turned out to be Shams Mahmoud, the overall commander of the women in the region. 'There is barely a Kurdish woman in Iraq whose husband, brother or son has not suffered or been killed at the hands of this regime. My job is to teach them how to look after themselves, and how to fight to liberate this country. It doesn't matter how long it takes,' she told us.

'Do you think those here can ever return to civilian life, and the conventional role of a Muslim woman?' I asked her, as I glanced round at the heavily armed women.

'The Peshmerga love the Kalashnikov and an outdoor life too much. Even when the cause is gone, they will remain,' she replied. Layla nodded in agreement.

Shams called over another of her team. I'd noticed her already, as she was beautiful and charismatic. Shaima Sami never went anywhere without her Kalashnikov. She was just twenty. Saddam Hussein's Ba'athist party had executed her father and brother, she explained. Her mother had immediately joined the Peshmerga with her three daughters when Shaima was just fourteen.

When we finally managed to escape the Kurds' hospitality I lay tired but unable to sleep. My side was agony and my lung was burning, but I managed to doze off eventually to the sounds of Doug starting to strip and clean his GPMG. A short while later I woke with a jolt: Guss was trying to thrust a handful of intel briefings into my hand. As I got up and went to collect some breakfast, Doug leafed through it all, immediately picking up on the reports from Carne Ross, Britain's Iraq expert at the United Nations: he was urging extreme caution about going to war. In his opinion any war against Iraq without the full support of the UN would be illegal.

Ross was making no bones about his growing disillusionment with the British government's desire to escalate the conflict. He was responsible for drawing up resolutions on behalf of Blair and

Bush to prepare the case for war to be put to the UN. Lord Goldsmith, the attorney general, had also intimated his concerns over the legality of conflict and was under enormous pressure, especially from senior MoD planners, to give a definitive yes or no so that they could plan accordingly. Ross was arguing that the evidence was unambiguous that Iraq posed little or no threat in terms of WMD, so any legal case for war was flawed. He was backed by Elizabeth Wilmhurst, then deputy head of the Foreign Office legal department.

'Surely our government wouldn't send us to war on a lie?' said Baby Steve. At his age, he was the least disillusioned of us all.

'From what these guys are saying it's an illegal war, and there's no justification for it,' Romero pointed out.

'Who cares?' Doug grunted. 'It's good nosh, the weather's great, and the money's fucking lovely.'

'You really don't give a shit, mate?' Malcolm had been silent until now, but he had looked decidedly worried since the discussion had begun.

Debate ensued as to whether we would or wouldn't go to war. I had to stop it as our Kurdish friends were picking up on it and becoming more than a little concerned as cancellation of the show would have a direct bearing on them. I told Guss to dispose of all the printouts, still bemused as to why we'd been sent the information. Half an hour later he could explain. Head Shed had cover-copied the wrong intel to us. They would send the right material at 17.00 hours.

I was about to disappear for a discussion with Wajy when Guss handed me yet more intel. There wa a report from John Morrison, then deputy chief of Defence Intelligence, complaining that intelligence was increasingly being used as a PR tool by the Blair administration. Intelligence analysts were being pressured to come up with information that would help ministers defend the notion of war in Iraq. A memo was attached, detailing how stunned he had been when Blair warned of the 'serious and current threat' posed by Iraqi WMD. In short, Morrison was accusing Tony Blair of misusing intelligence to back up his claim that Iraq posed a serious threat when in reality no such threat existed.

Another memo was attached to the intelligence reports, this one from Sir Richard Dearlove, chief of MI6. It was addressed to Mark Allen, MI6 director for the Middle East and Africa. Why on earth had I got it? The memo outlined Sir Richard's serious concern about his intelligence officers being badgered by ministers to beef up the evidence for Iraqi WMD. I was still reading through the memo when I walked into the room where Wajy and his deputies were waiting for me.

I had barely sat down when one of the Peshmerga leaders, Mam Rostam, stood up and waved a newspaper cutting. 'What is this?' he demanded, clearly angry.

Mam was a highly respected Peshmerga veteran, who was eager for the attack on Iraq to begin. He handed me the newspaper cutting. It was dated 10 February 2003, and detailed Washington's proposals to allow Turkey to take control of some disputed Kurdish areas in north-western Iraq. Wajy and I had already been over this ground. I looked Mam in the eye and told him that the news reports were not true. It was media hype, and we had absolute guarantees that the Turks would not be allowed to send their troops into disputed Kurdish areas. I promised that I would stay with them and be at their side, should Turkey decide to try it.

'On my family's lives, I swear it,' I told Mam emphatically.

'I'm so fucking glad I'm not related to you,' I heard Doug mutter under his breath.

I was lying through my back teeth. I knew that Washington had made such an agreement with Turkey. The rest of the meeting focused upon the actual intel we had on several key

Iraqi players, including the general who was intimating that he would defect with his Special Republican Guards. The Peshmerga had no quarrel with the average Iraqi: it was the oppressive and brutal henchmen of Saddam's regime they hated. When the women served lunch, the atmosphere relaxed considerably. I could sense Mam still wasn't convinced, so I sat with him to try to get to know him and build a bond of trust. He told me he had been born in Kirkuk in 1955, and become a Peshmerga at twenty. He was proud that he'd been one of the first to join the PUK and had fought the Iraqis in 1976 after the collapse of the previous revolution in 1975. He was now one of the PUK's senior commanders co-ordinating the liaison between PUK and KDP.

Christ, I thought. In 1976 I was a teenager living in Cyprus. From 1976 to 1991, Mam had lived in the hills, fighting Iraqi government forces. Romero was sitting opposite us, quietly attentive. In 1991 Mam had come down from the mountains with the other Peshmerga, having heard President Bush Senior state that it was time for the Kurds to take matters into their own hands and liberate Iraq. They attacked Iraqi government forces in the Kurdish cities of Sulaymaniyah, Arbil and Dohuk, and chased them out of the Kurdish homeland.

'The most memorable day of my life was when we liberated my city, Kirkuk, on the twenty-first of March 1991. Our national day of Nawrož,' [National day of celebration] Mam continued, 'we attacked the Iraqi military, security and intelligence offices. The surprise was spectacular. They didn't know what to do. The people of Kirkuk joined us. We liberated more than half of the city.'

He paused, and Layla placed a comforting hand on his. Then he looked up at me. 'As you can imagine, our people, especially those whose relatives were killed by the government, were very angry. They killed all the security and intelligence personnel and other figures of Baghdad's repression. We could not stop them.

They were hysterical. But while all this violence was taking place, about a hundred thousand soldiers of the Iraqi Army who surrendered to us were shown respect. I remember sharing my meal with two throughout the time they were with us. We became good friends. This was a clear example that the peoples of Iraq have nothing against each other. We handed them over to the Red Cross to give back to the Iraqi government.'

'Toxic Texan,' Layla laughed, then prodded me and Mam in the ribs playfully.

'Yes, the Toxic Texan,' Mam echoed. 'That's what we named Bush, when we'd thought he would protect us from Saddam Hussein and he didn't. To our surprise, when Saddam Hussein flew his helicopters to crush us, Mr Bush turned his back on us and went fishing. I hope his son is not going to do the same.'

No. Bush Junior will probably be playing golf, I thought bitterly. 'I promise you, Mam, that this time things will be different,' I assured him, and felt like a complete shit.

Layla gave such a beautiful smile that I was consumed by guilt. I couldn't give any promises that I could keep, yet I felt a real empathy with these people. I told myself that if all else failed, I'd fight as a Peshmerga to honour my word to them. My sense of honour meant a lot to me, as it clearly did to them, and I was becoming personally involved with them and their struggle, which we are always told never to do – but how the hell could you not get involved if you had a heart?

Romero shrugged his shoulders apologetically. 'Don't tar all us Americans with the same brush,' he said, with a smile.

Mam sat up straight. 'When Saddam attacked, our situation was desperate,' he continued. 'Millions of us had to flee to the cold mountains. People were dying in thousands every day. When the Allies came and the safe haven was established, we returned to our homes and regained control over the majority of our region. Apart from Kirkuk.

'Now, with all this talk of war against Saddam,' he went on, 'all my relatives and every other Kirkuki I know are very excited. All have joined the Peshmerga army to take part in liberating their homes. But my fighters fear that if Saddam is attacked he will again retaliate with chemical weapons. We Kurds fear we might be left to his brutality again. Look around you. The Israelis have protection. The Kuwaitis have protection. The Iranians, the Turks, everyone has protection apart from us, and we were the only victims of Saddam's chemical weapons. We need protection too. We need protection against chemical weapons.'

Mam paused as I nodded sympathetically. If Dan had his way they'd get disposable masks, which would be next to useless against most chemical agents. I felt even worse than I had at the start of the discussion.

'Yet despite all this, and that our weapons are basic, our morale is high,' Mam continued, his mood lightening. 'The Iraqi Army's morale is low. They contact us on a daily basis from the front lines, Iraqi soldiers and officers. They tell us they have no intention of fighting against us. In fact, they sell us their weapons all the time. We can buy anything from them. If we can get decent weapons and have some protection against the chemicals, we will do wonders.'

This last information was marvellous humint – in just a few minutes I'd got a shedload of intel from Mam. Romero raised an eyebrow and half winked. It had not escaped him either. Again I assured Mam that we would be with them all the way, and told him that the respirators were coming among an airdrop of supplies. I didn't know how they would react when they saw what they'd been given. So, rather than build up their expectations of effective protective clothing, I thought I'd do better to play down the threat posed by Saddam's WMDs.

'Remember the British airstrike that took place in 1998, codenamed Desert Fox?' I told Mam. 'Several of Saddam's key WMD sites were attacked and destroyed. The threat of him using chemical weapons against the Kurds is far less than before.'

'If that is true, why are Mr Bush and Mr Blair making so much of Iraq's WMD capabilities now?' Mam asked, as he pushed back his chair to leave.

I couldn't think of an answer, and he left me with the impression that he knew I was bullshitting. I immediately set about compiling a report for Tosh to forward to Head Shed in the UK and JIC, asking for proper respirators, and chemical and biological detector kits. If we couldn't deliver on our promise to equip the Kurds so that they could defend themselves against a chemical attack, how could I carry them with us into the war? We could never convince them that Saddam had no usable chemical weapons. Their people had been gassed before.

I thought back over my conversation with Mam. I had spent my life trying to live by a code of honour, chivalry and ethics, which I didn't see as being at odds with the code of the warrior. Quite the opposite, in fact, as long as I was fighting on the side of right. But now I was lying to and deceiving a people whom I respected, and who trusted me, and preparing them to fight in a war that was probably wrong. My parents had sent my brother and me to a private school run by Catholic nuns, the only two Protestants. My father believed it was character-building and it was, but it left me also with a burning desire to know all I could about religion. I studied Catholicism, Judaism, Hinduism, Buddhism, Mormonism, Jehovah's witnesses and Islam. As I had grown up in a military household, I knew that I was expected to go into the Army, but I felt torn. My religious studies had made me wonder how it could be right to kill. Imagine my delight when I first came across a Knights Templar castle while we were living in Cyprus, and discovered the ancient chivalric order who had fought in the Crusades. I was hooked. I studied other orders of chivalric warriors, became fascinated by the Samurai and studied 'the way of the warrior'.

I wanted to belong to something similar and when I discovered the SAS, in my mid-teens, and that the SAS 'dagger' is supposed to represent King Arthur's Excalibur, I knew I had found my calling. I learned the Regimental prayer – 'O Lord, who didst call on thy disciples to venture all to win all men to thee, grant that we, the chosen members of the Special Air Service Regiment, may by our works and our ways dare all to win all . . .' I learnt that SAS members were known as Pilgrims, to whom self-discipline and dedication, to duty and each other, was everything. This, I decided, was my future path.

When I passed SAS selection, I joined to become a soldier who was always on the good guy's side. I would help avert major conflicts by stopping them before they started and taking out the bad guys – potentially saving thousands of lives. Many men join the SAS with a similar aim to mine, and I'd managed principally to uphold that philosophy throughout my military career. I felt I could justify to myself each and every conflict I had fought in, but not any longer. With this operation, I felt like I had sold out. I went to bed early that night: I was not in the mood for company.

The following morning Romero and I went through intel reports complete with photos of some Iraqi generals who might be willing to defect. We were laughing over a picture of Jack Straw that some joker had put in when Kosrat Rassul turned up with Phil and the two FO lads. At first I thought they'd linked up with Kosrat and were now working on him, the sneaky bastards – and, indeed, they had tracked him down, but he'd refused to have any dealings with them unless I was present. I felt honoured by Kosrat, and deceived by Phil and the FO lads. As we all sat down to talk, Kosrat invited several other Peshmerga commanders to join us. Then he asked us to explain how much we knew about their 'long and distinguished history'. There was a few seconds' silence as everyone, myself included, wondered what to say.

'Tell me everything you think you know about us, especially our history,' Kosrat repeated.

'Please start,' he urged, smiling. 'Tell me about what you know of Sharafnama, or Ahmadi Khani, whichever. Either will do.'

The FO lads' faces told me they hadn't a clue what he was on about, but I did. However, I didn't jump in straight away.

'Well, er, first, it's not our area of expertise to know all the details. We, er, rely on our specialist analysts to keep us updated and informed on such matters,' Phil stammered.

'Is that so?' Kosrat asked, clearly unimpressed.

'Sort of,' I interjected, before Phil could make matters worse. I'd let him and the FO lads roast for long enough. 'But on this operation, I'm here in that capacity also. Isn't that right, Phil?'

Phil, the two FO lads and Doug obviously thought I'd lost the plot.

'Isn't that right, Phil?' I repeated, a little more forcefully this time.

'Yes, that's right. It's, er, his area,' Phil replied. 'So he can explain.'

Phil and the FO lads stared at me in amazement as I reeled off just about everything I knew on the subjects that Kosrat had mentioned.

'Sharafnama was the name given to the Kurds' national project establishing their identity and history as written down by the scholar Sharafkhan,' I said. 'Sharafkhan narrated their general origins and character, tribal classification, and the geography of Kurdistan. Ahmadi Khani did so too, but to a lesser degree. Sharafkhan noted the demonising of Kurdish origins by Arab and Persian historians, who said that Kurds were the offspring of the devil or of cohabitation between human beings and monsters. He divided the Kurds into four groups according to variations in dialect and some of their customs, the Khmanji, Lur, Kalhur and Goran.'

I paused for breath. I was enjoying this.

'Sharafkhan described the Kurds as proud, independent, re-spectful, honest, generous, loyal to their leaders and gallant,' I continued. 'A Kurd eschews begging and helplessness, and would prefer to rob.' This last comment brought smiles from the Peshmerga leaders. 'Sharafkhan knew that although Kurdistan was poor compared with other countries and most Kurds led a simple life, poverty never made them lose their self-esteem and national pride. The most defining characteristic of the Kurds, he said, was courage.' This brought even bigger smiles.

'Continue, please,' Kosrat enthused. 'Who among you knows about Rostami Zal in the times of Kaiqubad Pasha, Darami Gurgin and the famous lover Farhad?'

I felt like I was on *Who Wants To Be A Millionaire?* I deliberately delayed answering – let the others sweat a bit – as I studied their faces. As the seconds ticked by even Doug looked uncomfortable. The two FO lads appeared to be shitting bricks.

'Am I the only one who knows that Rostami Zal was the man who dug through the mountain of Destoon for his love of Sheerin?' I asked.

As I sat back the room erupted with clapping and laughter. Doug sighed, with relief, as if we had just pulled off some major coup. Food was called for, and Phil and the two FO lads looked as if they were about to throw up. I got up to fetch some coffee and Doug followed me. 'We're Destooned, we're all Destooned,' he joked, in a mock-Scottish accent. 'I hate you, you mad smart bastard.'

Phil tapped my shoulder. 'Jeez, you strung us out there big-time, buddy.' His heavily tanned face creased up as he smiled. 'I mean, I thought I'd seen some scamming in my time, but that was pretty fucking impressive.'

I hadn't been scamming, just using what knowledge I had to gain the Peshmerga commanders' trust. If I hadn't done my homework, I was convinced we'd have been in a totally different ballgame now. Sure enough, that afternoon Kosrat informed me that he and his people would indeed work with us in the forthcoming invasion of Iraq. Phase one of our mission was complete. Now the stage was truly set.

6

H HOUR

Phil and the two FO lads joined us for the evening meal, over which we agreed to bury the hatchet and work together. Phil offered to organise the delivery of several armoured Humvees so that we could move about faster and more efficiently. The two FO lads said they could get hold of two former UN Land Rovers, which would have to be dirtied up as they were still painted in UN white. As all the vehicles were in Turkey, we'd task some of the SEAL lads held in reserve there to drive them down, using some of the lesser-known back roads that criss-crossed the Kurdish highlands.

Just as we were 'enjoying' our after-dinner Kurdish coffee – very much an acquired taste – Guss rushed in with an intel report. He'd received a warning order that the full-scale invasion of Iraq was about to start, and we would have exact timings the following day. It was mid-March, and as the initial invasion had been set for some time in January, we didn't doubt that the conflict was now almost upon us. He'd also received confirmation that Turkey had refused permission for the US 4th Armoured Division to advance into Iraq from Turkish territory. This meant that our operation, and the role of the Peshmerga forces, was now more important

than ever as no Allied ground forces would be invading northern
Iraq other than the lightly armed 173rd Airborne direct from
Italy, if they were ready on time. I told the Peshmerga leaders our
news, and in all their euphoria over the imminent start of
hostilities they seemed oblivious to the fact that Turkey was
turning against the war, which had grave implications for them.

I needed space to think so I went outside and sat under the
starlit sky. We were on the edge of a major conflict, yet all I could
feel was sadness and deep foreboding. After a quarter of an hour or
so, Layla came out with a blanket, a skewer of lamb and some tar-
thick coffee. She put down her Dragunov sniper rifle and sat close
to me.

'Bastard,' came Malcolm's voice. (Jokingly.)

I ignored him, and the only sound we could hear was a flag
flapping above us. It was bright yellow, with an orange circle in
the centre and the letters KDP emblazoned across it. Layla fell
asleep, her head on my shoulder. I could smell the scent of her
dark hair against my face, and drifted into a pleasant daydream in
which I married her, joined the Peshmerga and never went back
to my life as a soldier-spy. I was tired of the bullshit and lies. I was
tired of deceiving people who didn't deserve to be deceived.

'Fucking bastard.' It was Malcolm again, bringing me back to
the present.

Early the following morning Guss received urgent intel that
TV news crews were en route to our location. One was a CNN
crew fronted by a female reporter, and the other was the BBC's
John Simpson and his crew. I decided to unleash Doug on any
journalists who turned up, and maybe send them toward's Dan's
Grey Fox lot. I laughed to myself. It would seriously upset Dan's
day.

By midday there was no sign of the TV crews, and we'd
received more intel: a warning order with priority targets along a
huge stretch of Iraqi front-line positions. Trench systems, bun-

kers, fuel depots, communications lines, transmitter masts, vehicle checkpoints: we, and the Peshmerga, were supposed to deal with all of this across several hundred miles of Iraqi front line. We'd been promised full air support from both land and carrier-based aircraft, which would help, as well as a carpet-bombing campaign by giant B52 bombers on the eve of war. But I wanted more time to engage with the local Iraqi commanders with whom the Peshmerga were already in contact. They might agree to stay in their positions, as so many were suggesting, which would free us to concentrate on the units that did put up a fight. It would save countless Iraqi lives, and help to prove that Saddam was the main enemy here.

I got Guss to fire off a request that we negotiate 'surrender' deals with specific Iraqi units, which would enable them to be left out of the carpet-bombing. Later we got a negative response. The bombing of Iraqi positions was scheduled, and it was too late to change the game plan now. Bollocks, I thought. All war plans were subject to the changing nature of a combat situation. Unless you were able to adapt and change a battle plan at the last moment, you would fail to keep an edge over your enemy. Either the planners didn't give a shit about saving Iraqi lives, or they didn't believe we had the wherewithal to ensure specific surrenders.

Later I met Wajy, Kosrat, Mam and several other Peshmerga commanders, who all told me confidently that they'd more than enough fighters to take out the targets we'd been given. They would start to move their forces immediately into nearby locations. As communications between different Peshmerga groups and us would be patchy at best, they would all take the start of the B52 carpet-bombing as their signal to attack. Wherever they were, every Peshmerga unit would see the bombardment start, so it would be a good marker. 'Keep it simple' had always been my mantra, and there was no simpler start signal than this one. The first Peshmerga units would depart that night en route to the more distant Iraqi targets, with the remainder on standby, good to go at a moment's notice.

As we began to work out target allocation, it became increasingly clear that the Peshmerga would be stretched over a vast expanse of terrain. It was obvious that we didn't have enough US and British Special Forces to co-ordinate things properly, and that we were painfully short of weapons. Improvisation would be key to the success of our war. We decided to stagger small groups of SEAL lads along the front line. That way we hoped we could call down enough co-ordinated air assaults on to targets to create chaos and panic among the enemy. We knew the Iraqis' morale was low, as was their determination to fight, but we couldn't take it for granted. As the attack was pressed home, we would use the main roads for fast transit, plugging any gaps in our assault. Then Guss rushed in with the reassuring news that the US 173rd Airborne would be flying from Italy and parachuting directly into northern Iraq in support of all operations there.

He called Tosh to organise extra supplies of weaponry as a priority. Due to our location and the amount we required, it would have to be delivered by airdrop from a C130 Hercules. He was confused when Tosh asked him to confirm what method of airdrop we wanted.

Dan came up over the net requesting that we link up with his lot as one combined force when the operation finally kicked off. Doug, Romero and I were uncomfortable with this, and I replied that we'd get back to him shortly, then went outside for some fresh air. I walked straight into a female news reporter, with her cameraman in tow. He started filming as Doug came out behind me. 'FUCKING WELL TURN THAT OFF!' he roared.

'You can't stop us! Excuse me, excuse me,' the journalist yelled, as the cameraman tried to back away from Doug and keep filming.

Doug overtook the man, grabbed the camera unit in one hand and half wrestled its operator to the ground. 'I said STOP, NOW,' Doug yelled, voice laced with murder.

'You can't stop us!' the woman shrieked.

Doug swung his gaze to her and stared at her as if he'd like nothing better than to rip her throat out. I'd never seen him so enraged. 'But – but we're allowed to be here,' she argued weakly.

Doug ignored her and turned back to her colleague, who was struggling upright. Doug was still holding the camera unit. Now he flipped it on its side, opened the cartridge release and took out the tape. He turned to the woman, holding the tape, walked up to her and stood with his face inches away from her. 'Take one more of these and I'll do this to you,' he stated. He took a pace backwards, dropped the cartridge on the ground and trod on it heavily with his left boot. 'One more tape, and that's what fucking happens to you,' he repeated, as he ground the tape into the earth.

He turned away, walked past me and disappeared into the cave complex. The cameraman and reporter looked at me hesitantly. 'I'd heed his advice if I was you,' I said. 'I won't stop him.'

The reporter walked up to me as her cameraman rubbed his neck. 'This is outrageous—'

'Don't,' I snapped. 'Don't even go there. I don't want to have to call him out again . . .'

It did the trick. She finally shut up.

'Look, come in for a brew, if you like,' I told them, as politely as I could in the circumstances, 'but you're not staying. I want you away from here as soon as practicable today, and you're not doing any more filming. Do you understand?'

They nodded, so I led them into the nearest cave. I got Big Matt and Athansa to check them over and temporarily confiscate their camera and sound-recording equipment. As I made them some tea, I asked them what the hell they were doing there.

It turned out that the cameraman, Ben, was British and a former Royal Marine. She was a reporter with CNN. They told me they'd been given our location by 'a senior US military adviser' in Turkey, who'd told them to come and 'embed' themselves with us for the duration of the conflict. I strongly suspected that the 'senior military adviser' was Dan, who'd sent them our way just to fuck with us. Originally they'd had a sound engineer with them, but he'd got cold feet and headed back to Turkey. I told Guss to get on the net, chase up Dan and find out if he'd sent them, and if so what the hell he was playing at. Doug's intimidation had worked to a certain extent, but that didn't stop the woman, Heather Smyth, asking questions, most of which I declined to answer. I assured her the 'senior military adviser' had been mistaken in sending them to us, and that we'd arrange an escort to get them out of our area later that day. Part of me had to admire their bravery and tenacity: they'd got to us overland by themselves with no protection. Heather told me that John Simpson was also on his way, not many hours behind them. This was fine by me – we'd send him away too.

'So why're you working with the Kurds?' she asked me spikily. 'You know that Turkey views them as a bunch of terrorists willing to do anything to achieve their blood-drenched dream?'

'Well, you know how the old saying goes,' I replied, with a forced smile. 'One man's terrorist is another's freedom-fighter.'

I had neither the time nor the inclination to get into this debate with her, and while I knew she was only trying to do her job, I didn't like her attitude to our Kurdish hosts. I told her nothing about who we were or what we were up to, although I presumed she knew we were British Special Forces. I had Guss arrange for them to be collected as soon as possible by helicopter and escorted back to Turkey. I asked Big Matt and Athansa to stay with them until the helicopter landed, and when I left, I made sure Doug came with me. That had been no act he'd put on earlier, and I knew now that he had a real issue with the press. If he caught them trying to film again, there was no telling what he might do to them.

Doug, Romero and I headed off to sort out a suitable drop zone (DZ) for the weapons airdrop. We were getting lots of advice from the Peshmerga lads but it wasn't as simple as finding an open field and having the kit parachuted on to you. Up here in the mountains, with Iraqis probing the area, we had to take great care. Any potential site had to be looked at from the pilot's point of view: it had to be free from aerial hazards, such as prominent hills, towns or other areas of habitation, anti-aircraft batteries and potential sites for the launch of hidden surface-to-air missiles (SAMs). As the drop would take place at night, any easily identifiable navigational features had to be noted.

The number of supplies we required was too much for even a fleet of helicopters to deliver, so it was going to have to be a C130 or nothing. A C130 Hercules is far less versatile than a helicopter, further restricting our choice of DZs. We had to explain all this to the sceptical Peshmerga, and the discussion went back and forth over the maps. As we were deep in the hills I favoured the HAARS (high altitude airdrop resupply) system, particularly well suited to areas where there was a high risk of air defences or ground obstacles. Pressurised containers are dropped from an altitude of 800 metres by a C130 flying at 150 knots. After several minutes of freefall, a BOD (barometric opening device) triggers a blasting cap that releases the parachute. As long as we gave accurate bearings for the pilot to come in on and correctly judged wind strength and direction, he should be able to release the containers at the correct point, enabling them to land in our desired DZ.

We already had an emergency resupply DZ, but we could not reveal that to our Peshmerga friends. That was set up purely for us in the event that it all went belly-up. If the Turks sent in their army, who was to say that the Peshmerga wouldn't turn on us? I didn't reckon this was likely, but it worried Doug and Romero, and I had to balance my instincts with their detached logic. We had chosen the emergency DZ before we flew in theatre, and if we missed a prescribed number of scheduled radio calls, the emergency resupply procedures would kick in: Head Shed would consider that we had been compromised and were evading the enemy. Any of our team who made it to the emergency DZ would be able to use the equipment and stores.

At dusk the following day, Ian, Big Matt, Athansa and several Peshmerga escorted Heather and Ben to the LZ. But when the chopper touched down, Athansa came over the net saying that Tosh had arrived and would be coming back with them. I was appalled: Tosh had deliberately ignored everything I'd told him, and had disobeyed orders that he was not to come in theatre. I immediately got back on the net and told Athansa that under no circumstances was he to let Tosh stay.

No sooner had I sent the message than Tosh came back, using Athansa's radio, asking me what was the big deal, and why did we have to steal all the glory? I ordered him back on the helicopter, and repeated my instructions to Athansa. Not only was Tosh acting like a complete twat, but he was keeping the helicopter on the deck far longer than was acceptable. He tried to object, but was forced eventually to reboard – after he had let cameraman Ben take footage of him posing 'in theatre'. I was seething and sent a message to Cizre, telling Tosh to do exactly as told or he'd be on the next plane home to the UK.

As soon as I'd sent the message I went outside to cool off a little. I was met by a Kurdish woman carrying a baby, which was screaming its head off, followed by a stream of old men, women and children stretching off down the winding track. What the fuck was going on? Peshmerga lads were everywhere, helping the refugees – for that was what they clearly were. Suddenly Layla emerged from the crowd. 'They are seeking protection,' she blurted out, as she laid a hand on my arm.

I shouldered my weapon – some children were looking at it nervously. Doug came out of the cave to see what all the commotion was about, closely followed by Guss. It turned out that most of the civilians were related to the Peshmerga fighters who were with us, and they'd fled from their villages and towns as they'd heard that war was about to start. Panic had set in and they'd headed for their faithful friend, the hills. What the fuck was I going to do? Layla clutched my arm as I tried to think. We couldn't keep them with us – we were cramped for space as it was in the cave complex, and I knew from long experience that weapons, explosives and kids didn't mix. But it was rapidly getting dark so there was no way we could send them back. Mam, Phil and Doug joined me.

I gazed at the dishevelled throng, which stretched away to the turn in the track beneath us and out of sight. Faces etched with fatigue and worry stared back as they waited for me to make a decision. It started to rain. A frail old woman immediately in front of me went down on her knees, clasped her hands together and raised them in prayer. She said nothing, just knelt there, praying. Then the crowd behind her did likewise.

'Boss, you'd better do something,' Doug whispered. 'You ain't the real fucking Moses yet.'

'Best move 'em on or we can't operate,' Phil said, all too loudly.

The scene was surreal to say the least. The rain fell harder as I clocked Maberley and Matt walking up the track.

The Peshmerga started to lift the crowd to their feet, but they were clearly exhausted.

'Layla, tell them to get up and go inside, please,' I said. She squeezed my arm, kissed the side of my face, then turned to pick up the old lady in front of me.

'And your next piece of genius is?' Doug asked, with a raised eyebrow and a smile.

'Hi, boss bastard,' said Malcolm, referring to Layla's kiss, and went to help the refugees inside.

Just then two Peshmerga lads approached me. What now? I groaned inwardly. We'd nicknamed them the Terrible Twins as they were so alike, always together, never said much and wore constant scowls. Neither had a decent tooth between them and they looked positively rough. The twins started to jabber away in their native tongue. I raised my hands to let them know that I couldn't understand.

'Boss, boss man, we – er, how you say? – thanking you no send away peoples,' Twin Two began. 'Very good peoples. Family, family.' His eyes welled uncharacteristically with tears.

'Not a problem,' I replied, though it was one big fucking problem.

'You, you part of family also,' Twin One said, placing his hand on his chest then on mine. 'Trust you, trust, yes, trust you.'

I felt almost embarrassed and went into the cave complex, where people were being ushered into every available space. Now would be a good time for Dr Dianne's services, I thought. Some of them were in clear need of medical treatment. Doug walked with me as we checked all of our more secure areas.

'Fucking open house it is then, boss,' he remarked quietly. 'You know it's either them or us? One of us is going to have to leave.'

He was right, of course. But where could I have sent them? They were terrified of being gassed, bombed or simply bulldozed alive into the ground by Saddam's forces. They'd trekked for two days through the mountains to seek sanctuary, even though we probably couldn't give them the protection they needed. I waited until I knew Tosh would be back at the FOB and called him. He started moaning about being sent back. I told him to pick up his kit, all of Dr Dianne's medical gear, the two journalists and get back to our location as soon as he could. Tosh couldn't believe his ears, and probably thought I'd gone mad. But desperate circumstances required desperate measures. Tosh wanted time in theatre and he was about to get it.

I told Athansa and Big Matt to quick-time it back to the LZ to collect Tosh and the rest, then called an immediate orders group. Soon everyone was waiting for me in the large dining area, which doubled as the command centre. Wajy and Mam stood at the back; Doug, Guss, Phil and Layla sat at the biggest table.

'Ladies, gentlemen, our position here is untenable with the arrival of our guests,' I started. 'We cannot move them so we have no choice other than to leave.'

'Does that mean we let them all stay here?' Layla asked.

'Absolutely – unless anyone has a better idea?'

Layla sighed with relief, and immediately all the Peshmerga lads and women were talking excitedly. They had feared I would send the refugees back to their villages but, purely from a humanitarian perspective, I could have made no other choice. Here we had protective shelter. It was guarded and easily defended with minimal force. So long as we could get some extra food supplies, we could feed them adequately during the conflict.

'Why can we not all stay here?' Mam asked, once the hubbub had died down. 'We are used to having our families with us in such circumstances.'

'Sorry, not possible, Mam. There are simply too many of them and, if anything, we increase their chances of exposure to danger by staying with them. I'm suggesting we move to another location, in the field if required. We can leave several of our men, plus Tosh and Dianne when they arrive, to supervise this place temporarily. Dianne's a good doctor. Also, I'll be leaving the news reporter and her cameraman. They can record all that's happening and, if necessary, highlight the people's plight on the international news circuit. That may afford them the best protection possible.'

There were no more questions and I took Guss with me to get on the net. I made us some coffee and stole five minutes' silence in the radio room to gather my thoughts. As soon as Guss patched in, we received streams of coded teletype messages. Dan was telling us to move the Kurd refugees out of the area immediately and back to their homes, forcibly if necessary. What fucking planet was he on? Our resupply was delayed by forty-eight hours as other priorities had taken precedence. We fired off a response that we needed the resupply on schedule and a lot more besides. To Dan I sent a personal message that if he wanted the Kurdish refugees sent back, he could come and carry out his orders in person as we sure as hell weren't going to do that. Then we received another message that our dedicated air cover was being diverted for twenty-four hours. Something big was happening and, alarmingly, we weren't being kept in the loop, whatever it was.

'Get on to Konya, Cent Com, and your NSA buddies, whoever, Guss, and find out what the fuck's going on,' I told him.

'Is something wrong, boss?' he asked, as Doug put his head round the curtain that shielded the radio room.

'Something's cooking, Doug, and it's big,' I told him. 'I can sense it.'

'Well, in that case I'd better get some scoff down my neck,' he said calmly. 'Never know when you might get your next feed.'

My mind was racing. Either the political shit had hit the fan with the UN, China and Russia, or the war proper would start within the next forty-eight hours. My instincts told me it was the latter, but why, then, were we being left in the dark? We were far from ready, but given the green light, we could still get into gear and improvise. As I sat down to dinner that evening, I was still trying to work out what was going on. I'd barely taken my first mouthful when Mam tapped my shoulder and asked if I would go outside with him: an Iraqi officer had turned up in the camp and was waiting to see me. Sure enough, sheltering in the cave entrance from the rain, an Iraqi colonel and two of his soldiers were carrying white flags. Not to surrender but to indicate a truce to talk, obviously.

The colonel and I greeted each other formally in Arabic, then waited for the other to speak. I was alarmed that they had known our location, but curious as to why they had come. I wondered if they were going to demand our surrender.

'State your purpose,' I heard myself say.

'We have come to talk terms of surrender,' the colonel replied, in almost perfect English.

'Sorry, no can do,' I told him.

The colonel lowered his head, saddened. 'Then a lot of good people will surely die needlessly,' he said.

My mind raced as I contemplated an Iraqi attack on the base. How would we defend our position and the people with us? And how the hell had this Iraqi colonel discovered our location? The colonel moved slowly towards me and stretched out his hand with a note. I took it and unfolded an A5 sheet of paper. It was a leaflet produced by the Americans, proclaiming freedom and liberty from Saddam Hussein. It urged the Iraqi military not to fight but to stay in their barracks when the war started where they would be safe. I was amazed at myself for having been so narrow-minded in thinking they could only be asking for our surrender. It had never entered my head that they'd come to discuss their own. I asked the colonel how he had known where to find us, expecting him to tell me they'd followed the refugees up here.

'We have known of this location for many months,' he replied. 'We have our own informants, and they told us about it.'

I tried to remain expressionless. War was practically upon us and they knew that, this time, Saddam would fall. Not surprisingly, they all wanted to be a part of the new Iraq. What the colonel was now asking for was exactly what I'd been hoping would happen. Better late than never, I thought. At least it meant we could avoid engaging in major combat operations against his forces. Overstretched as we were, it was a welcome proposition. I ushered them to the only secure room in the cave complex, and had Guss get on the net to inform Head Shed that the leaflet-dropping campaign had yielded one positive result. Then the colonel and I made polite chat and he seemed positively chirpy that we were discussing how he could ensure the safety of his section of troops.

He gave us grid references for his bunkers, lookout points and trench systems. Guss forwarded them on to the CIA in Langley, and to JIC in London, with a simple message: 'Do not target. Non-hostile troop deployments in this region. Co-ordinates follow from Iraqi colonel.'

As we led the Iraqis towards the cave exit I was aware that some of the Peshmerga lads were eyeing them with suspicion, but when I made it clear that they were here to agree not to fight, they were pleased. They started shaking hands with the Iraqis, which confirmed what Mam had told me of how the Peshmerga felt about the Iraqi peoples. If we could do this here, we stood a good chance of doing the same further along the line.

Removing Saddam Hussein and his regime by using high-tech weapons systems would guarantee the coalition's success in taking over the country. But maintaining control of it afterwards was where the problems would start. Any chance we had at this stage of gaining the Iraqis' trust and support was essential to the long-term outcome of the war. This was common sense, as far as I was concerned, and something that the planners must realise. Or so I believed and hoped. After the Iraqi colonel had thanked me many times, Romero and Athansa escorted him and his men away with a large band of Peshmerga in support.

Later, I grabbed some much-needed sleep, only to be woken by Layla lying down beside me. She put an arm round me, her hair untied and hanging loose, I sat up quickly and looked at her. She smiled and motioned me to lie down again. Just five minutes of comfort could do no harm, I told myself . . . But it would open up a whole new can of worms. War was all but upon us, the base was full of refugees, and I had Iraqi troops coming in to surrender. I couldn't deal with this as well. And I had Victoria to think of. I stood up, smiled and said I'd much to do, but she should stay and rest.

We were all sharing each other's sleeping-bags so it was no major issue her being there. If you found one empty you dived into it.

I left Layla and headed for the radio room. As I approached, I could hear Tosh before I saw him, talking loudly. He was with Heather, Ben and Guss, having arrived an hour previously while I'd been asleep. Heather was asking all manner of questions, which he was all too eager to answer. Not good. As I walked in she stood up, smiling from ear to ear, and Tosh fell silent.

'Thanks for letting us return so quickly,' she said. 'Not quite sure what the deal is, but thanks.'

'Don't thank me, thank him,' I replied, pointing at Tosh. 'He'll be staying here with overall responsibility when we head off to do our stuff. That leaves you free to file whatever reports you see fit from here.'

Tosh looked confused, so I thought I should elucidate. 'When he heard about you two he volunteered to come in theatre as your mentor, and co-ordinate from here,' I explained. 'Isn't that right, Tosh?' I raised an eyebrow at him.

'Oh, er, yes. Absolutely. I did, yes,' he stammered.

I asked Guss to follow me. Out of earshot, I asked for the latest on the resupply. Pilot Steve was dealing with it back at Cizre, Guss explained, and trying to get a CH47-H2 Chinook to do the job. Although it is a big helicopter, there was no way it could do the sort of resupply we required, especially at our altitude where the air was thinner so the rotors produce less lift. I set off to find Doug, but Tosh rushed after me in full combats and body armour, no local gear.

'Niall, what's the bloody game here?' he demanded, as he shouldered his rifle.

'You wanted in-theatre time, you got it. And don't use my first name here,' I replied.

'What – I get to nursemaid bloody reporters, women and children?' he snapped, his face reddening.

'This was the only way you were ever going to get in theatre, so don't knock it.' I squared up to him. 'And, quite frankly, that "nursemaiding" is essential to this operation right now. It's too delicate to leave in just anyone's hands, so I thought of you. You saying you're not up to the job?'

Tosh stood back a pace, his mind working overtime.

From nowhere Doug appeared behind him. 'If you can't handle the responsibility, I suggest you fuck off back to Cizre,' he stated.

'I need someone utterly reliable here to keep it all going, Tosh. I need the Pesh to know their family members are well protected. Your presence alone will help foster that impression,' I cut in.

'Fucking scare me more,' Doug said sarcastically.

There was silence, apart from the distant cry of a baby. I was disappointed in Tosh – I'd expected better of him. He was keen to get in theatre and eager to prove himself, but at the expense of others.

'Would you rather I stay here and you go out into the field and lead it?' I asked him.

He thought about it for a moment. 'No, that's OK,' he replied finally. 'So long as I know exactly what is required of me here, I'm happy.'

'You need to dirty yourself up then,' Doug said, and wiped his hands on his dish-dash. Tosh nodded.

That afternoon we discussed the resupply and other issues. Wajy and Mam joined us, with what seemed almost every other Peshmerga commander in the area. Phil and the two FO lads also squeezed in. Within minutes it was hot, the air stale. A couple of the Peshmerga women came in with a coffee pot and some incense burners. As the Iraqis seemed to have known of our location all along and done nothing about it, we agreed to leave the refugees where they were with light protection. Tosh would stay with six SEALs, who would liaise with the round-the-clock air cover and support.

When all the Peshmerga started talking loudly among themselves Tosh stood up in speak-and-be-heard mode. He was desperate to say something but realised he wouldn't be heard over the rising chatter and noise. He sheepishly sat down again. I actually felt sorry for him. As I turned for my coffee, I found Layla behind me holding my cup. I was glad to see her – she had been avoiding me since I'd left her alone in my sleeping quarters.

Guss came in with confirmation of the DZ location for the resupply drop, which would take place at 02.00 hours. It was about ten miles north-east of our location, on a high plateau. The final decision had been made by the C130 pilot after careful consideration of the terrain and weather.

As I left the meeting, Tosh came hurrying after me. 'Niall, Niall, mate,' I heard him calling, 'can I at least come on the resupply recovery?'

He was still pushing the issue about getting out on ops, and I looked at him in bewilderment. He was certainly persistent, but so irritating that I felt like telling him to grow up, this wasn't some fucking game. I bit my tongue. 'OK, sure, if you really want it. And *stop* using my first name so loudly.' I continued walking.

I checked in on Dianne, who had been working non-stop

since she'd arrived, administering medical aid in a makeshift surgery. Big Matt had taken a shine to her. He was a qualified field surgeon and combat medic, and they made a good team. But when I found her, Dianne was alone, taking deep breaths to control herself. She was looking decidedly weepy. When I asked what was wrong, she started to shake.

'I'm fine, honestly. Just a little edgy and apprehensive about being here. I'm fine when I'm busy and concentrating, but as soon as I stop it's reality–check time and my nerves go a bit. Go on, tell me I have to get a grip, pull myself together. Be professional.'

'Why would I say that? Come on, sit down and take five.' Clearly, she was close to exhaustion.

Big Matt stuck his head round the corner.

'Come in, Matt,' I said, as he glanced at Dianne with evident concern. 'Matt will give you whatever help and support you need,' I told her, 'and as for being apprehensive, it's only natural. Tell you the truth, I'd be seriously concerned if you weren't. Sure as hell we all are. Just don't have the guts to show it, that's all.'

'You're softsoaping me to make me feel better,' she replied, trying hard to regain her composure. 'I just had no idea it would feel like this.'

Matt sat next to her and put an arm round her. 'Hey, we all get it, honest, all the time. But you manage it and it becomes easier to control. Believe me, I should know – I'm the biggest coward here,' he told her.

'You're big, granted, but I don't believe the coward bit,' she said, with a sniffle.

'No, that's my speciality,' I joked. She let out a little laugh and wiped her nose.

On cue Layla walked in and, seeing Dianne upset, immediately sat on the other side of her and offered her a bright orange hankie. Then Doug appeared. He just stood in the doorway quietly, waiting for someone to say something.

'I feel really silly now,' Dianne said.

'What happened, then? Break a nail?' Doug asked, with his classic delicate humour.

Fortunately, Dianne laughed.

Outside in the corridor section of the cave I could see masses of people all waiting for her to see them.

'Di, do whatever you can in your own time, OK?' I told her. 'And Matt here can be your right arm until further notice. I'm sure he won't mind.'

With that I was off to round up the resupply reception party. I ran into Baby Steve and Malcolm, both with opened 58-pattern water bottles. Malcolm raised his bottle, putting it to his groin.

'Only fucking hole I'm going to get into here, boss!' he said, grinning broadly and thrusting his pelvis back and forth on the bottle opening.

'He's had enough of Pammy Palm so it's on to Betty Bottle,' Baby Steve added. They carried on walking and discussing the merits of using the water bottle for sexual pleasures. I had to smile. I was sure they weren't joking, either.

At 23.00 hours we set off into the mountains on a high, winding track. One section of the path traversed a ledge barely three feet wide. It ran across a sheer rockface that fell away vertically some several hundred feet. I was glad it was dark – it made things feel a lot safer than they were. My right shoulder was pressed firmly against the rock as I made my way across. Two Peshmerga lads up front acted as guides, followed by Athansa, Maberley, Malcolm, Ian, SEAL Ian, Tosh, several Peshmerga, then me, Doug, Baby Steve and eleven more Peshmerga. The rear was covered by Romero and Phil. Gusts of wind hit us, forcing us to hug the rockface. Once we were across I checked our position and timing. Tosh took a photo of us using his NVG image-intensifier. We all stared at him and he put away his camera rather quickly.

'Twat,' Doug remarked.

We were falling behind schedule to make the DZ on time, so I told Athansa to open up the pace, which he did, practically running with the Peshmerga guides. We jogged and speed-marched across the terrain, huffing and puffing, and ascended the plateau as we heard the C130 on its approach run, although we couldn't see it. Rapidly the parties fanned out into their respective groups, with Romero setting up our outer defences as Malcolm prepared to send a radio check to the pilot, confirming our authentication code. At that moment, Tosh stepped forward to ask if he could call in the airdrop. 'I know my FAC and RSVP [rhythm, speed, voice, pitch] better than most,' he whispered, 'and it'd be great practice.'

'Fine,' I said. 'Let's get on with it.'

Malcolm passed the handset to Tosh, who grinned with delight. 'Hello, Foxtrot Romeo Sierra, this is India Three Three, message. Over,' he intoned, clearly loving it.

'This is Foxtrot Romeo Sierra, send. Over.'

'India Three Three, authenticate Delta Zulu Table four,' Tosh continued, giving the code word for the DZ. Next he gave the location of the DZ in batco (battalion system for giving out coded co-ordinates) and open quadrant co-ordinates. 'Location is three two Tango Papa Tango six four one two four three. Open one three zero degrees to two two zero degrees and three three zero degrees to zero one two degrees. Track three six zero degrees. One hilltop, zero eight six degrees six KM (notice and distance of any obstacles). Over,' Tosh confirmed.

'Foxtrot Romeo Sierra, roger. Out,' came the pilot's reply.

Two minutes later, we saw the parachutes open high above us. It looked to me as though they were drifting far too fast and would land over the edge of the plateau in a ravine. But the fly boys had checked the wind speed and judged it exactly: the containers fell bang on target. We never even saw the C130 and only faintly heard its engines high above us. Within fifteen minutes we had secured the area and 'policed up' the newly arrived kit. The Peshmerga lads commandeered the parachutes, which were 'ripstop' silk and would be used to make underwear.

If the journey in had been precarious, the return was a noisy cluster-fuck as we struggled back with the heavy kit. The ledge around the cliff face proved interesting, and once we hit a wider section of open track Tosh ran up beside me. He asked what I'd thought of his radio work earlier and told me to be critical. I told him he'd done well, kept calm and spoken using the correct procedure. My only criticism was that he had not needed to detail obstacles – like the raised hill section – as the C130 was flying at 800 metres. Unless there was an undiscovered Mount Everest in the Kurdish mountains, none of the hills around there would have caused the pilot any concern.

He seemed somewhat taken aback, and sloped off into line without a word. I gathered that he was the sort of person who needed constant praise and reassurance. As we started our descent towards the cave complex Guss came on the radio. The Iraqi colonel we'd met earlier was asking for an urgent meeting. He had heard rumours that their positions were about to be targeted by Allied air strikes. I agreed to meet him at a bridge midway between the cave complex and the Iraqi front line. There, we would have the cover of the hills immediately behind us, but the Iraqis would have to come across open ground to meet us.

I called our party to a halt. It was around 03.00 hours, and we were about half-way back to the cave complex. We decided to split the party in two, with Romero and Phil taking the resupply back to the caves, while Doug, Baby Steve, Malcolm, Maberley, the two Ians and I would press on to the meeting-point. I could feel Tosh looking at me pleadingly as we dumped the ammo and other gear with the Peshmerga lads. I relented and let him join us. We were now back to being a bit more tactical in our movements, but we still had to be fast on our feet if we were to make the intended rendezvous. Guss came over the net asking if we could see any aerial activity – he was picking up masses of air traffic, as well as a lot of electronic jamming counter-measures. We looked and listened but detected nothing untoward. Yet if Guss was picking all that up, something must be happening.

We arrived at the bridge to find the Iraqi colonel already there, his Soviet-era Gaz jeep parked up as he paced up and down with two soldiers. He must have trusted us to be there to leave himself so exposed. Either that or he was desperate. We studied the area from the safety of some high ground until we were fairly certain it wasn't a set-up.

'Boss, I'll go check him out,' Doug whispered.

'Nope, you cover me with the Gimpy (7.62m general purpose machine-gun) and I'll go,' I whispered back at him. The colonel knew me so it made sense for me to go. I shouldered my weapon and started to walk down towards the bridge. I felt vulnerable and alone as I approached the figures on the bridge in the dark. I was almost there when one of the soldiers saw me and pointed. The colonel hesitated for a moment then walked towards me.

'Assalamuh allacam,' I said quietly, greeting him in regional Arabic.

'Wa allacam assalam,' he replied, and shook my hand vigor-ously.

He explained that he'd received intel from his contacts among the Peshmerga that his positions had been targeted for an assault that night. He pleaded to know if it was true and kept referring to the leaflet the Americans had dropped, promising them their safety if they stayed in their barracks. I told him his details had been passed on, but only to ensure that his positions weren't targeted by Allied airstrikes. He changed visibly, as if a mighty weight had been lifted from his shoulders. I assured him that all was well, that we'd keep to our side of the bargain and that his men would be safe as long as they stayed in their positions.

Then I was distracted by a noise behind me, and turned to see Tosh and Malcolm running up to join us. Tosh had his rifle in his left hand – and a digital camera in the other. I stared at it in disbelief.

'Boss, Guss thinks there may be a problem,' Malcolm whispered, drawing me aside. 'He just got a warning order – we're to stand by for immediate orders. Like we suspected, something big's cooking.'

The Iraqi colonel saw the radio antennae on Malcolm's back and came over to me. 'Is there a problem, please?' he asked politely, but I could tell that he was nervous still.

'No, not at all,' I replied. There should be no problem, I told myself. We'd passed on the correct co-ordinates of the Iraqi colonel's positions. The US leaflet had assured all Iraqi military forces who chose to remain in their barracks that they would be safe . . .

A series of massive flashes erupted on the distant horizon. My face was lit up, as was the colonel's. The rolling thunder of explosions reached us. The colonel stared at me in horror. I met his gaze, and then he turned back to face the destruction being unleashed as, with perfect precision, B52s pounded the area where his men were.

The detonations rolled on as more B52s dumped their munitions on target, and the colonel turned back to me, the anger and pain in his eyes clearly visible in the light of the explosions. Doug arrived at my side, weapon at the ready and raised towards the colonel, who looked at the GPMG and shrugged.

'No!' I yelled at Doug, and pushed away the barrel.

The other two Iraqi soldiers jumped into the Gaz jeep, fired it up and sped off into the distance. Tosh opened fire on the vehicle, but it sped into the distance without being hit.

'What a fucking twat,' Malcolm snorted, as Tosh lowered his weapon.

I couldn't shake my gaze from the colonel, his eyes filled now with tears of frustration and rage. There was nothing I could say. I felt utterly wretched, consumed by guilt, and as if I'd been personally violated. Then, quick as a flash, the colonel whipped out his pistol and raised it to his temple. As Doug's GPMG barrel rose to drop him, I lunged forward and knocked away the colonel's hand as he fired, the bullet just missing his head. I grabbed his wrist and forced him to drop the pistol. He stared deep into my eyes, tears streaming down his face. I pulled away from him. He turned and ran, but tripped, and somehow his ankle boots fell off. He started to run from the bridge in his socks towards the bombs raining down across the horizon and certain death.

'Find out what the fucking hell's going on, will you, Malc?' I demanded, trying to keep my composure as I hurried back towards the LUP (lying-up position).

Tosh was grinning from ear to ear, happy to have had 'trigger time' in country. Big bad Tosh had fired his weapon in anger, and I hoped he was pleased with himself. What was happening now was an indefensible war crime, as far as I was concerned, yet this idiot was enjoying himself. I felt an almost irresistible urge to punch him, although I knew that this massive betrayal was none of his doing.

As I trudged back up the hill I knew that there would be many survivors of this bombardment, and that now they'd hate us for eternity. They had believed in and trusted us by giving us their positions, and we'd betrayed them. They would become the new insurgents, the new 'terrorists', whom we would have to deal with. And how many more Iraqis, who had been eager for the US-led invasion to free them from Saddam's clutches, would turn against the US in consequence? What the hell were the fucking planners playing at? How could they be so short-sighted and stupid?

'Boss, H hour was just then, with that first B52 airstrike. Full operations to proceed,' Malcolm announced breathlessly as he caught me up. 'Guss is getting shitloads of intel and orders so we need to head back.'

As Malcolm was speaking, Tosh had taken out his camera and started to film the continuing explosions on the horizon. We watched him until he turned and saw the contempt on our faces. Then he put away the camera hastily, evidently embarrassed.

The tab back to the cave complex took nearly two hours, by which time the sun was climbing over the hills to the east. My chest hurt and I was wheezing. Once again I could taste blood.

We arrived to be met by a scene of mayhem. Peshmerga soldiers were milling about all over the place. Equipment and stores were being issued and vehicles loaded. Every now and then a pick-up would leave, crammed with Peshmerga heading for Iraqi positions.

Guss came out with Romero and Athansa to greet us.

'It's all kicking off,' he bellowed, excited.

I looked at Romero. 'H hour was early hours of this morning,' he confirmed.

So, the war had started. And we had been some of the last to know about it.

PART TWO

MOUNTAINS OF FIRE

7
PROXY WARRIORS

I glanced around at the chaos. 'What the hell's going on with this lot?' I asked.

'Well, boss, they saw the flashes and heard the explosions,' Romero explained. 'That was their cue for taking up positions so they were off, no stopping them.'

Wajy and Mam were walking towards me. Both were smiling, Wajy now dressed in a smart camouflage suit and forage cap with an embroidered KDP Special Forces badge. We were all scruffy in dish-dashes. 'It's a good day today, very good day. Today we take back what is ours,' Wajy proclaimed. He greeted me with open arms and a bear-hug. Mam was more subdued, but still smiling. I noticed that the female Peshmerga had already gone, thought of Layla and said a quick prayer for her safety. I could see that the refugees were still with us, now working their way through the food containers from the air-drop. Wajy went to climb aboard a Toyota Hi-lux, waving to his men as they formed up in several other vehicles behind him. By now all of his Special Forces had donned military-style uniform and red berets.

As Wajy placed a camouflage cap upon his head, a photographer snapped his photo as he pulled a serious look. I had to smile.

'Come, you don't want to miss the show,' Wajy shouted at me.

'Boss – look.' Doug nudged me in the ribs and nodded at the track below us.

I looked, and spotted the two FO lads, each driving a white ex-UN Land Rover, followed by four desert-painted Humvees. Here was our transport. Nice colours up here in the green hillsides, I thought. Dianne and Matt came out of the caves. Dianne looked exhausted – she had been up all night treating the Peshmerga families.

'We meet you at the bridge, my friends,' Wajy shouted, as his vehicle convoy pulled away. As it did so, I saw Ben and Heather filming them.

Now the refugee children were crowding around us, jumping up and down and shouting. Athansa took out a handful of sweets, threw them some distance away and the children ran off to find them. 'Little trick we picked up in the Balkans,' he said. 'Only way to get kids away from your wagons and stop them getting hurt.'

Doug followed suit, but only after having taken out his favourite flavour sweets first.

It was the morning of 20 March 2003. British troops were first into southern Iraq, landing as an amphibious assault force on the Al Faw peninsula. Sadly a US Navy CH-46 Sea Knight helicopter had taken a nosedive into the desert, killing the British Marines and American crew on board. I'd seen the reality of this war already, down at the bridge, and felt deeply troubled by it. But we were committed now and I'd given the Peshmerga my word that we'd be with them all the way. During the night forty Tomahawk Cruise missiles had been launched from US Navy ships in the Persian Gulf as well as PGM (precision guided munitions) 2000-pound bombs from F-117A Nighthawk Stealth planes against Baghdad.

I told the lads to dirty up the white Land Rovers by rubbing mud all over them. When they started to load them with kit and supplies, I had a quick breakfast – I'd not eaten since lunch the day before. As I tucked into some cold lamb kebabs, unleavened bread and olives, Heather ran over to me. The BBC's John Simpson was nearby, she told me. She wanted to take Ben and link up with him.

'If you can find him, go for it,' I said.

I got Guss to bring me all the intel and orders he'd received while we were away – I wanted to know why we'd been kept out of the loop until the last minute. But our orders told me little that I hadn't known already: they simply stated that we had to move to our pre-identified positions and await further instructions. I took my food and sat with Guss in the radio shack. We received a congratulatory message for being so quick off the mark. I double-checked on the map where our Peshmerga troops were heading, copied the details on to my own and hurried out to get our lot under way.

I called all the lads together and told them that we were now in invasion mode. I checked that we were all happy with what we were tasked to do, that we had the correct radio frequencies and enough ammo to start our own personal war. Dan came over the net on Malcolm's radio confirming that his team was heading to their locations. I sent him a terse reply: when I saw him next, I wanted a full explanation as to why the Iraqi colonel's positions had been targeted by our warplanes. I was just about to climb into the lead Land Rover when I spotted Tosh getting into a Humvee.

'Tosh, what're you playing at?' I asked.

'Aren't I coming on this one, then?' he replied, as Matt hauled some medical kit aboard the Humvee. 'I noticed Matt was coming, and he was supposed to stay with Dianne so I assumed we were all going.'

'Hey, bud, I'm just loading some extra gear for the guys.' Matt turned back to the cave complex.

I indicated the caves with a nod and Tosh slung his weapon, then walked off towards them.

It was more than an hour of slow, rough road driving before we were at the bridge where the meeting with the Iraqi colonel had taken place. Heather and Ben were already there, filming.

'There is little belief here that the Iraqi soldiers have the stomach for this war and will stand and fight,' Heather announced theatrically. 'As further evidence of deserting Iraqi troops, a pair of boots, left abandoned by the roadside.'

Those boots had belonged to the Iraqi colonel who'd tried to save his men's lives and whom we had betrayed. I wondered whether I should tell Heather the real story behind the 'deserter's' boots. Just then Doug jumped down from our vehicle and strode towards her and Ben. Ben stood back, but Doug walked past him, picked up the boots and slung them over the side of the bridge. 'Fucking parasites,' he said icily as he passed them on the way back.

I had to find out what Doug's problem was with reporters. Clearly he hated them.

We took the main road east towards the ancient city of Mosul to link up with our first group of Peshmerga. A cold wind was blowing through the front of the Land Rover: the FO lads had taken out the windscreen so that we could fire forward if we needed to. Guss had managed to cram his large frame and radio set into the back, as Malcolm had in the second wagon. We reached a road junction where the Peshmerga unit was supposed to be, but no one was there. This did not bode well. We had no choice but to push on, and as we continued along the road, Guss was checking in with Allied aircraft in our immediate area, confirming who we were.

We arrived at the next location, relieved to find Wajy and several vehicles of Peshmerga in place as agreed. Several women Peshmerga were there, but no Layla. Good, I thought. I didn't need her as a distraction. Several pick-ups screeched to a halt behind us. Mam appeared from the lead vehicle and hurried across to us. He'd been waiting for us at the first junction, his men and vehicles concealed in the gullies, and we had sped past. Oops! My mistake for not trusting Mam to be where we had agreed.

We left two SEAL lads, experienced FAC experts, with Wajy's group to call in airstrikes, and put Ian and Athansa with Mam's convoy to do the same and they headed to their locations to await further orders. Kosrat Rassul and his men headed off to link up with other PUK groups further east around Mosul. As Mam's convoy disappeared, I felt the distant percussion as another B52 bombardment hit Iraqi positions some three miles to the west of us. The horizon erupted in huge blasts of dirt and debris, throwing dense clouds of dust into the sky. I took out my binoculars and saw tiny figures running everywhere on the skyline.

One bunker system suffered a direct hit, but even as the dust was settling survivors ran out, heading for the cover of the next. I watched three men disappear into the second bunker, only for that to be hit. I refocused my binos and was half pleased to see the same three emerge alive again. This time they didn't run for the next bunker, but jumped down the emplacement and began to run our way. Then Peshmerga noticed the three Iraqis. Some took pot-shots at them.

'No! No! No!' I shouted.

They looked at me as if I was cracked, but Wajy intervened: taking out those three men would achieve nothing tactically or strategically. In any case, they had survived the bombardment and deserved a chance. As they got nearer they glanced behind them at the hell they had just lived through. Then they raised their arms high in surrender.

Suddenly a rifle shot rang out across the valley. The nearest Iraqi dropped as the bullet struck him in the chest. I glanced round to see who had fired. A Peshmerga lad of no more than fifteen was lowering a smoking AK47. Not one of Wajy's Special Forces, he was shaking, half laughing and half crying, all at the same time.

'What are you doing?' I yelled.

Several older Peshmerga slapped him and one took away his rifle as he shielded his face. But it was more for effect than anything. The two surviving Iraqis stood frozen with terror. Malcolm hurried down to the wounded man and administered first aid, managing to insert a chest drain to stabilise his condition.

The young Pesh lad was led away in tears. It turned out that his parents had been killed by Saddam's forces when he was a baby, and he had sought his revenge. But it was not as sweet as he'd imagined it would be.

We put the wounded Iraqi on to a Humvee with the two prisoners, then sent it back to the cave complex with a Land Rover as escort and instruction to pick up Athansa from Mam's location to keep an eye on the casualty. We radioed Tosh that we had a wounded Iraqi soldier on the way, and for Dianne to be ready. He might not survive the journey but it was worth a try. Also, we'd get valuable humint from the captives.

For the remainder of the day we watched wave after wave of B52 strikes. Midnight came and went, and I was about to brew up when a convoy of Humvees appeared out of the darkness, their drivers using PNGs. Out stepped my nemesis, Dan Meany. His unit were all in army combats, no Arab dress. As Dan approached he was smiling and held out his hand for me to shake. I ushered him away from the Peshmerga so that we could talk privately.

'What the fuck's going on?' I asked him. 'I gave the co-ordinates for those Iraqi positions so they would *not* be targeted. I gave my word to the Iraqi colonel. Why the fuck were they obliterated?'

Dan took off his hat and rubbed his hands through his hair. 'As I said before, buddy, there's a bigger picture here.' He was choosing his words carefully. 'We had an informer within the Iraqi units, and he told us it was a trap. The Iraqis had their élite Republican Guards units holed up in that bunker system. They were gambling on us playing fair, as per the flyers we dropped. They were waiting for us to pass them by so they could hit us hard from behind. Your Iraqi colonel was a fraud, and you fell for it. But our intel showed it was a trick so the order to waste them went ahead.'

The expression of betrayal on the colonel's face flashed through my mind. If it had been a trick he had not been in on it. His shock had been genuine.

'If that's so, Dan, how come all the Iraqi soldiers running and deserting are conscripts?' I asked. 'I've seen dozens of them and not one Republican Guard.'

'I sense you don't believe me.'

'You sense correctly.' There was a moment's silence, during which I felt Doug come to stand by me.

'Well, if you have a problem with it I suggest you take it up with Quigly later. It was his call,' said Dan. 'Don't go gettin' all high and mighty and takin' the moral high ground with me now, ya hear?'

I stared at him in silence. I would indeed take up the matter with Quigly. Lieutenant Colonel R. G. Quigly II, Quick Quig to his friends, was in overall command of all CIA, NSA and other covert ops in the area. I'd worked with him before, and had a lot more faith in him than I had in Dan.

'Anyways, you have a more immediate problem, buddy,' Dan continued. 'Turkey is sending troops across the border later today into the disputed Kurdish areas. You need to ensure your Peshmerga lot don't kick off about it. Make sure you do.'

Before I could think of a suitable response, he had turned on his heel and walked away. I wanted to pursue him and kick off myself, but I knew it wouldn't help. Dan was fucking Dan, and if you showed him he was getting to you, he'd exploit that weakness. But I was now in a horrible position. I was convinced the Iraqi soldiers had been killed as short-term expediency, and I now had to keep my Peshmerga friends in check, when I knew that if I were them and the Turks were streaming into my country, I'd want to kick them right back out.

No sooner had Dan left for Mosul than Tosh contacted me. Sure enough, intel was coming in that Turkish troops were crossing into the Kurdish disputed territory. I compiled an urgent radio message to send directly to Quigly. First, I told him we'd had reliable humint from the Iraqi colonel that their surrender had been genuine, and that the bombing of their positions was indefensible. I told him bluntly that the story about the Iraqi Republican Guards units was not credible. I wanted it on record that I believed the bombing to be a disaster and a war crime, and that I should be warned if anything similar was mooted at any stage during the conflict. I also pointed out that it had been a wasted opportunity to bring the Iraqis on-side.

I informed him then that if any Turkish troops were allowed to cross into Kurdish lands, he'd better prepare himself for another battle. The Peshmerga would not accept it. The Turkish troops should be stopped, fast, because as soon as the Peshmerga got wind of their arrival they would kick off big-time. And there was nothing I could do to stop them.

Fifteen minutes after he'd sent the message, Tosh relayed Quigly's response. If the opportunity arose again to take the surrender of Iraqi troops, he would personally authorise me to deal directly with any Iraqi commander on the ground. Cheers, Quigly. If ever there was a poisoned chalice that was it. He continued that my priority must be to keep the Peshmerga on track for the coming operations. He assured me that he would deal with the Turkey issue.

For the best part of Friday the twenty-first we kicked our heels, waiting to proceed to our designated targets as briefed. It was a beautiful, moonlit night and we stayed awake, listening on the radio to the assault by 3 Commando Brigade unfold on the Al Faw peninsula. I knew that in the morning Victoria would hear about it on the news, so I got Tosh to email her that I was fine.

The following day, the twenty-second, some of the Peshmerga lads became highly agitated at news reports of Turkish incursions into Kurdish areas. I prayed that Quigly would come good on his promise to deal with it. But my greatest worry was that we were doing nothing while Dan and his lot were doing heaven only knew what.

Finally, late that evening, we received the signal to start attacking our targets. Just as we were pulling out, we received an urgent message: Doug, Romero, Athansa, Ian and I were to return to the cave complex immediately. The SEAL lads were to press on with the Peshmerga to their objectives. I double-checked the order, but it was confirmed. We left Heather and Ben with the Peshmerga, as they wanted to film some action.

Two hours later we were at the caves. I'd hardly stepped down from the vehicle when Tosh hurried me into the signals room to speak to Quigly direct.

He thanked me for my earlier signal and the frank expression of my views, then said that a problem was brewing: Turkish tanks had arrived on the borders of Kurdish lands in the north. Tension was running high and many Kurds were now aware of their presence. Quigly assured me that they would use the media to play down the affair while frantic negotiations went on between the US and Ankara. He needed my confirmation that the Kurds would take up arms against the Turkish military. I confirmed that if Turkish tanks crossed into Kurdish areas the Peshmerga would turn on them and I was powerless to stop them: I knew how strongly they felt about Turkish aggression. Quigly asked me to stay put and await further orders from him direct.

As time progressed, Tosh couldn't understand why I wasn't climbing the walls or eager to get back out there. I was, just not making a song and dance about it. Tension was increasing by the hour: the Peshmerga reacted angrily to news reports of more Turkish tanks moving into their area and I understood why. Officially, the Turkish government admits to having killed some 23,000 Kurds over the past two decades, although the real figure may be far higher – which puts the Turks up there with Saddam Hussein. Of course, Turkey claims the people it killed were 'terrorists', but the Kurds say the majority were women and children. And this was a country that was negotiating to join the EU. As more and more of the Peshmerga heard about the Turkish troop movements, they wanted to abandon their Iraqi targets and head off to engage the Turks.

I fired off an urgent warning to Quigly that our northern operation was threatening to unravel. Quigly replied that diplomatic pressure was being brought to bear on Turkey. They'd better get a move on, I told him, as the Peshmerga were about to take matters into their own hands. Then Quigly warned that if the Peshmerga moved to engage the Turks, we were to use all means at our disposal to delay or stop them. The phrase 'all means' ran through my head. What a load of bollocks! If we attacked the Kurds, how were we supposed to hold together the fragile coalition between our Special Forces and the Peshmerga who were deployed to fight Iraqis? Many were already attacking Iraqi bunkers overlooking the Kurdish-held town of Chamchamal, with warplanes in support.

I needed some caffeine fast and a good feed. Dianne was still working with Matt and looked very tired, but she'd stabilised the wounded Iraqi. Over dinner, Romero finally opened up and talked about his private life, explaining that he was married with a wife of eight years. They had met at high school and were childhood sweethearts. They had a five-year-old daughter. In response, Doug got into an uncharacteristically deep conversation. He asked Romero how he'd managed to maintain a relationship that worked for so long whilst being a Special Forces soldier.

It was Monday, 24 March, 03.45 hours. I'd fallen asleep with my head on the table when Guss came in with a signal from Quigly. Their efforts with the Turks had paid off: the Turkish government had been told that unless they withdrew their troops, entry into the EU was off. I breathed a major sigh of relief. To save face, Turkey announced that it had sent only a token force to help stabilise the Kurdish area. In reality, some three thousand troops had gone in.

I looked at Quigly's second message. Apparently the commander of an Iraqi Republican Guards unit from Mosul had read the US leaflets and wanted to discuss terms for his men to remain out of the conflict. True to his word, Quigly asked me to go in and negotiate with him. My team and I would be dropped in open desert near the Iraqi forces. From there we were to observe the Republican Guards unit and report accordingly. When the time came, I was to meet the commander and negotiate an agreement. Quigly mentioned something about dragging out the 'crossover time', but I hadn't a clue what he was on about so ignored it.

Quigly had promised I'd have the location of the Republican Guards unit by morning. I needed sleep badly and now had the chance to grab a few hours. Doug and I found Dianne, who looked like the walking dead, and dragged her off with us for some rest. She was out cold before I had time to take off my dish-dash. Doug sat in the only chair and closed his eyes while I lay down on the floor on Tosh's sleeping system. As soon as my head hit the dirt I was out like a light. While I slept, Heather and Ben returned to the cave complex, after feeling increasingly uncomfortable alone so far out in the field.

8

BEHIND ENEMY LINES

I hadn't been asleep long before Tosh was shaking me awake. Dan was demanding to speak with me urgently. I went to the radio shack and listened to him rave about how the Peshmerga were refusing to do as he was ordering because it was not what I had said would happen. They wanted to strike on to Mosul and Kirkuk, but Dan wanted them in the hills to attack the Iraqi positions there first. Wajy had told Dan that he would do whatever I recommended, which was why Dan was yelling at me to tell Wajy to do as he ordered. Then Wajy came on the net and I told him he shouldn't rush headlong into Mosul or Kirkuk until our ground forces and air power were committed to the offensive. I assured him that, if he could wait, I'd be back out there to join him shortly. Wajy said he would, but only for a few days, and that Mam was now en route to link up with PUK Peshmerga on the outskirts of Kirkuk via Chamchamal.

I chased up Pilot Steve as we would need his services. He told me his new Black Hawk was already out for maintenance so he was on the scrounge for a Sea Hawk from the US Navy. At this point Doug came in and kicked us all out so he could send an email to Sara.

That morning, news came in that Turkey was threatening to send its troops back into the disputed Kurdish areas. The political brinkmanship to force them to back down was not working. Quigly was aware of the predicament this left us in, so sent a message that all non-essential personnel should return to Cizre immediately: he couldn't risk us being taken hostage by the Peshmerga, should the Turks do what they were now threatening. I told Tosh and Dianne they had to go back to base, which immediately sent Tosh off on one. I had to draw him aside and tell him why. Then he realised the danger, felt rather stupid and apologised sheepishly.

'He's a fucking liability, boss, and I don't trust the twat,' Doug said, as Tosh walked away. 'We'll be better off without him.' He seemed more vitriolic than the situation warranted, and I wondered why.

Clearly Tosh had heard that, but he didn't respond. He knew he was no physical match for Doug, so feigning deafness was wise. Heather and Ben were waiting for confirmation of John Simpsons's whereabouts, so opted to stay with us, knowing it was at their own risk, and sat nearby as I waited for confirmation of our new orders to go in and link up with the Republican Guards unit. I checked the latest news on the internet – headlines about immense public protest against the war in the UK and US. The conflict I was involved in had attracted very bad press and it was unnerving to read that so many people thought we were fighting an immoral, illegal war.

I had just one short email from Victoria, in which she moaned about our finances. I knew she had emailed Tosh several times, so I felt a bit pissed off. I tried to ignore it, but alarm bells rang. I also had an email from Sara, asking me to keep an eye on Doug, and make sure I got him home safely. Intel was streaming in regarding 3 Commando Brigade's advance towards Basra in the South, so I logged off to allow him time on the net, although he was texting Sara with all manner of lewd suggestions.

I had just sat down to breakfast when Guss ran in with our new orders. Pilot Steve was going to pick us up at 21.00 hours and fly us out to a vast open area west of Mosul. There, we would hide up during the day and await confirmation of our meeting with the Iraqi commander. I studied a map of the area: open, flat terrain with a few wadis and depressions to lie up in. If there was any trouble we would be exposed with no real escape route, so going in on foot was not on. Pilot Steve now had a CH47-H2 Chinook, a big enough chopper to carry a vehicle. I asked Doug to strip down one of the UN Land Rovers – we'd take it with us.

Quigly called up with specific orders for the mission: get guarantees from the Iraqi commander that his unit would stay put, and their exact co-ordinates, then relay them to him. I was worried that this meeting would end up like the last one, when the Iraqi soldiers had been bombed anyway, but Quigly said there was no danger of that: humint indicated that the commander in question genuinely wanted to negotiate his unit's safety, with the proviso that he remained in charge of it once Saddam Hussein was gone. If the commander couldn't give us the guarantees we needed, we were to get out fast, Quigly warned, because MOABs would be used against him.

'What the hell are Moabs?' I asked Romero once I'd signed off the radio.

They were the new version of the daisy-cutter bomb (the BLU-82) that had been used so effectively in Vietnam and Afghanistan. MOAB stood for Massive Ordnance Air Blast, but it was more popularly known as the Mother Of All Bombs. The daisy-cutter had weighed 15,000 pounds, and was dropped out of the rear of a C130 cargo plane. The MOAB weighs a massive 21,700 pounds and carries 18,700 pounds of high explosives; it was developed in just nine weeks, specifically for the Iraq campaign, and uses a slurry of ammonium nitrate and powdered aluminium explosives. It had been tested on 11 March at Eglin Air Force Base by the 46th Test Wing as an air-force research lab technology demonstration and now it was in theatre. Quigly told me that an air-force C130 Combat Talon II in Turkey was primed and ready with one, should the need arise to use it. Napalm was banned under the Geneva Convention, but MOABs were slightly different, and legal.

As we were now at war it was no longer necessary to land the helicopters in out-of-the-way LZs, so I checked the frequencies and call signs of the AC130 Spectre gunship and the C130 with the BLU 82s, then went to see how Doug was getting on with the vehicle.

Outside I found him with Matt and the two Ians. The Land Rover was now a shell, its main bodywork and cab gone.

'Will that do, boss?' Doug asked, smiling at his handiwork.

'Hope it's still got an engine.'

Doug, Romero, Athansa, Baby Steve, Malcolm, our Ian and I would go on this job, I'd decided. Phil had asked to come too but I'd said no. Instead he would link up with Wajy. Our two FO lads went to link up with Dan and many new SEAL team members being flown directly in from Turkey and naval vessels out in the Mediterranean along with the remainder of US 173rd Airborne Division from Italy. Around 20.00 hours we boarded the Chinook. My information on the Iraqi unit we were to link up with was sketchy. We didn't have any indication of its designation, or the name of the commander we were to meet. It was a job tailor-made for the SAS: suck it and see.

Just before we took off, news came in that two Royal Navy Sea Kings had collided, killing both crews, and I said a prayer that our bird would stay in the air. We'd only been going ten minutes when I noticed what looked like a small boot sticking out from under the Land Rover's front end. I did a double-take and Romero, who was closest, moved over and pulled it. A little

Kurdish girl crawled out, looking sleepy and scared. How had she got in there without us noticing?

Romero sat her on his knee, stroked her forehead and offered her some chocolate, which she started to eat. I made my way up front where Pilot Steve and I agreed we couldn't turn back. The little girl would have to endure the flight and return with the aircrew.

Suddenly Steve threw the aircraft hard left as Mark feverishly pressed buttons. Bright flashes exploded all around us – the helicopter was letting off 'chaff', hundreds of flares to confuse any heat-seeking missile that might be targeting it. My stomach dropped as Steve pulled the Chinook violently upwards, then dived, finally levelling out again. As quickly as it had started, the roller-coaster flight was over.

'Sorry about that.' His voice came over the intercom. 'We had radar lock-on from a SAM.'

The little girl was clinging to Romero as if her life depended on it. The loadie (a nickname for aircrew who work in Aircraft Cargo Areas) was pulling faces to make her smile, but not having much success. The poor kid would certainly remember this trip, I thought. She was no older than my youngest daughter. Who were her parents? Did she even have any now?

'ETA two,' Steve announced.

I took off my headset and started to get ready. The others had all been sitting quiet, contemplating the job in hand, weapons pointed down. You can't afford to have an ND (negligent discharge) inside a helicopter going up, as the bullet may hit the working parts. The Chinook banked steeply, levelled out and stopped, hovering just above the ground. The loadie lowered the tailgate and moved the minigun aside, so that we could get the Land Rover out.

Doug had the vehicle free within a matter of seconds and drove out to take up position shielded by a large natural sand berm. We piled out after him, all except Romero, who was having trouble with the child. Eventually the loadie pulled her away from him, screaming. As soon as he was out, the chopper lifted off and disappeared into the night.

I checked our position on the map and with the GPS. Good. Steve had put us exactly on target. I crept up to the brow of the berm on my stomach. We were inside a sand and stone-type 'crater', with the berm running away from us in either direction. Our little hole was one among many dotted along the surface. Below, flat, featureless desert stretched as far as the eye could see, dotted with the odd bush. I could just make out the mountainous terrain of the Kurdish lands to the east. Ian sent a sitrep that we were in position, and now all we had to do was wait for confirmation of a time and place to link up with the Iraqi commander on the plain. We set up all-round defensive positions with some claymores in case any unwanted guests arrived.

The next morning, around 1100 hours we saw a convoy of four vehicles heading directly towards us in full view. Through the haze and dust thrown up we couldn't make out who they were so Romero and Doug quickly broke out two LAW 66s (light anti-armour weapons, 66mm) ready to fire, and Malcolm readied a LAW 80 (94mm anti-armour weapon). I got Ian to radio in and check if any of our lot were in the area. We received a negative, which meant they were Iraqis, or Pesh lads doing their own thing. When I broke out my mini-binos to take a closer look they were closing fast. They were six-wheeled Land Rovers, fully armed, and one six-wheeled quad-type buggy. The only people I knew who used those were our counterparts in the Australian SAS, but none of their lot was supposed to be in the area.

I told Doug and Romero to hold their fire as the vehicles came ever closer. About three hundred yards from us the convoy stopped. A figure got down from the lead vehicle and walked back to the second. I refocused my binos.

'Australians,' I told the others. I stood up in full view and raised my arms to wave at the vehicles. The lead-vehicle gunner immediately swung an M19 40mm grenade-launcher in my direction. As I started to walk down the slope towards them, I took off my *shemagh* so that they could see I was European. Seconds later, the quad-type buggy was powering towards me. It stopped in front of me.

'English,' I said, and grinned.

'Fuck, mate, you lost or something?' he asked.

Within minutes we'd established who was who and the Australians moved their Land Rovers into the shielded area with us. They had had no idea we were in the area, and vice versa, which was worrying: we could easily have had a blue-on-blue with each other. I was impressed by their six-wheeled Land Rovers, as was Romero. Blue deck-chairs were strapped to the rear of the vehicles with lots of other goodies, including many items stamped 'Platypus Supplies'. I'd known Ben Cox, the proprietor, years before, and he must have made a killing with that lot.

Mike, the Aussie commander, radioed in his location and that he'd met up with us, and we did likewise with Head Shed. There was an Iraqi air base not far from our position, and that was the Australians' mission objective. They'd decided to drive during daylight as their intel people had assured them there were no Iraqi forces in the area. Doug and I told him there was an entire Republican Guards unit out there somewhere, and that we were ordered to negotiate their surrender. Mike got straight on his radio, furious at the bad intel they'd been given, but I wondered if perhaps there was no Republican Guards unit and that we'd been sent here to get us out of the picture.

'Is someone yanking our fucking chain, boss?' Doug asked,

reading my mind. 'Maybe it's just a fucking ruse to keep us out of the way.'

Mike and I agreed that we'd stay put until we had clarification from both our headquarters as to what the hell was going on. As the day dragged by, the frustration of our Aussie friends became more apparent. Eventually Mike came over and told me that his lot weren't hanging around any longer, regardless of what Head Shed came back with. Just then we received a warning order, telling us to remain in our present location for at least another twenty-four hours. So, we were going nowhere. Mike agreed to wait until nightfall, so that they would not attract attention as they drove off.

Just after sundown, when the Aussies had gone, Quigly came on the net to tell us that our Republican Guards unit would be in our area that night; they had been delayed by heavy and sustained Allied bombings.

Then Tosh said, also on the net, that he was having a lovely conversation on-line with Victoria, and would I like him to pass on any message.

'You should stop him now, mate, having so much contact with your girl,' Doug told me. 'That fucker'll stir you a whole pile of shit, otherwise.'

I knew he was right, but I had to concentrate on what I was doing, rather than worry about my love life.

As we were settling in for the night, Ian pointed out a large hole near to where he'd set up his stag position, certain it was the entrance to the home of at least one camel spider. They were huge arachnids, some twenty inches across, that looked more like something out of *Alien* than anything that occurs naturally on earth. They can run at ten miles an hour, jump up to five feet, and inject you with a numbing substance. You wouldn't necessarily realise you'd been attacked until you saw the thing eating your flesh. It also injects a solution that dissolves soft tissue, then laps it up like soup. Scorpions were bad enough, but those things were a nightmare. I hate spiders, so I kept an eye in the general direction while Ian set up a barricade with mess tins all around the hole. That way, if it came out it would collide with the tins and the noise would alert us.

Romero nudged me in the ribs. In the distance vehicles were coming up from the south, a lot of them, heading in our direction. They had no lights on and were driving across the open ground, keeping clear of the roads. As they got closer we could see they were Iraqi military: an assortment of Soviet-bloc vehicles, including Maz-200 seven-tonne canvas-backed trucks, Kraz-214 seven-tonne 6 × 6 wagons, BM-21 122mm rocket-launchers, several BTR-60s (a small armoured car with a weapon mounted on top) and an assortment of BDRM-2s (six-wheeled armoured personnel carriers). Ian was convinced he saw a glimpse of a Scud missile-launcher before it vanished behind a wall of other vehicles. I knew they were Republican Guards, all right – as some of that kit was bang up to date, and only élite Iraqi units had it.

I sent a sitrep to Quigly, reporting that the Iraqi unit was right on top of us. Then Ian tapped my shoulder and beckoned me to the other side of the berm. From there I could see more approaching Iraqi vehicles. Now we were effectively surrounded. If the Iraqi commander decided not to play ball, we couldn't fight our way out. Quigly came back on the net, telling us to stay put. They had an informer within the Iraqi unit, and he'd just confirmed that their commander had no intention of doing a deal but would rather die in the service of his great master, Saddam Hussein. He was well aware that we were somewhere in the area, and determined to hunt us down.

As the vehicles approached, I briefed the lads as best I could. No doubt about it, we'd been stitched up good and proper, although I was still unsure as to who was really behind it.

Doug half cocked his GPMG and checked it had rounds in the feed tray. 'Game on, then, boss,' he whispered.

Game on indeed, I reflected ruefully.

Quigly came back on the net in voice mode, informing me that 'crossover' had not happened with this Iraqi commander so he was calling in the Hercules C130 Talon to drop a MOAB on the entire unit. I wondered how on earth he thought we'd be able to get our heads down effectively. I was just about to ask, when he told me we'd have to make a break for it just before the MOAB fell out of the sky.

'What if we're compromised before then?' I asked.

'Better make sure you ain't, bud, or you're gonna need a fireproof suit, fast.'

I went back to the berm and checked the vehicles pulling up below us. Sure enough, one was a mobile Scud launcher. The vehicles had been spaced out across a large area, to make them less vulnerable to air-attack. We watched as they camouflaged them until they blended into the surrounding terrain. Several Iraqi soldiers began walking towards our position, and I was certain they would see us or our badly brushed tyre tracks. Some fifty yards short they stopped, and one urinated. We could hear the others chatting. Romero spoke excellent Arabic: he told us they were planning to dig themselves into the side of the berm – to go higher would mean skylighting themselves on the horizon.

'We've got to get out of here. Come daybreak, they'll see us. And Quigly's sending a MOAB to waste them – with us in the middle,' I told him.

His tanned face turned white. 'You're fucking with me, aren't you? You gotta be kidding me.'

'That's what he said.'

Romero took off his hat and rubbed his hands through his short hair. 'We have to leave now, then.'

I could see he was concerned, which was out of character for Romero. 'That bad, is it?' I asked him.

'The MOAB? Fuckin' evil,' Romero replied quietly. 'If we're still here when it goes down, we're toast.'

I sent Quigly a typed message that we'd be bugging out of there at the first opportunity. But there was only one way to do it. We'd have to drive at full speed straight through the Iraqi lines, firing as we went, and praying we could create enough confusion to escape.

Quigly came straight back reiterating that we had to wait until the C130 Talon was in the area, or we'd risk alerting the Iraqis, who would run. At present, their commander thought he was safe there, because he believed Allied forces still thought he was ready to discuss terms of surrender. At least, that was what Quigly was telling me.

But from where I was sitting it didn't make sense. What if the Iraqi commander was there because he *did* want to negotiate? He was already taking one hell of a risk by turning up with all his troops at a predesignated position where Allied air power could easily target him. It was a major tactical risk if his only aim was to capture six Special Forces soldiers and one ex-UN Land Rover. The episode with the Iraqi colonel was in my mind. Was this going to be a repeat performance? Did this Iraqi commander really have no intention to negotiate? Had we been used as pawns to draw him out simply to allow Allied air power to blow him and his men away?

We all lay perfectly still as the Iraqis dug into the side of the berm, and I racked my brains for a workable escape plan. Suddenly a barely audible yet somehow screaming hiss sounded out of the darkness. We all jumped out of our skins and I looked around wildly. Ian was on his feet, jumping about like a madman, trying to stamp on something. Whatever it was kept screaming at him as he tried to beat it down with his hands as it jumped at him.

It was one of the biggest camel spiders I'd ever seen and, as quietly as we could, we all started to kick at it.

If we hadn't been in such a dire situation it would have been funny. Malcolm took a classic cricket-bat swipe at it with his rifle butt, knocking it straight back to Ian. Then Doug appeared with a shovel off the Land Rover, and came down hard on it. We all froze as the clang echoed across the landscape. Doug looked up from where he had the shovel pressed down hard on the giant spider, now silent, as we strained our ears for any reaction from the Iraqis, but they were still digging and talking.

Suddenly I was laughing, which set Ian off. There we were, surrounded by enemy troops, laughing silently fit to burst, with tears running down our faces. Ian's mess-tin ambush hadn't worked, so England and America's finest Special Forces had been terrified by a screeching spider. Ian joked it was probably a mutant from Iraqi chemical experiments that had gone wrong.

When we'd recovered, Romero whispered to me that we needed to get out of the area *now*. He gave me a brief outline of what happens when a daisy-cutter bomb goes off. He didn't want to be incinerated or have his lungs turn inside-out as all the oxygen was sucked out of the area before the fireball engulfed our position. Doug suggested we should try driving past the enemy lines quite slowly, pretending we were just another Iraqi vehicle passing through.

Tosh forwarded a teletype signal direct from Head Shed, in Northwood, to the silent KP-43 unit – part of the OTP (one-touch pad) attachment for our main radio. It backed up Quigly's order to stay put so that the Iraqis weren't provoked into changing position. 'Imperative you maintain position until de-livery of MOABs,' the message concluded. So, more than one. But the fact that the Iraqi commander was staying put still suggested to me that he wanted to negotiate his surrender. If he was trying to hunt us down he'd have had patrols out all over the place.

I grabbed the EMU (electronic module unit) and sent an urgent message to Quigly, asking why we couldn't talk terms with the Iraqi commander. I waited over an hour for the response, and when it came I gathered the lads round me: we were being told we couldn't negotiate but neither could we do a runner. Instead, we were supposed to sit there and wait for the MOAB. It was an insane set of orders, if ever there was one.

'Well, I'm seriously fucked off now,' Doug whispered to me, as he lay on his back, the first faint streaks of dawn in the sky above us.

'Why's that, mate?' I asked.

'Well, looks like I won't get Sara on me boat.' After the conflict, Doug and Sara had planned to cruise around the Caribbean or the Andaman Islands for a few months. Briefly we discussed walking out on foot – it was still dark enough. Realistically, though, there was no alternative but to stay put and wait for developments.

As dawn was almost upon us, Ian and Doug draped the Land Rover with our desert camouflage nets, and we crawled in under the cover. I could have murdered a cup of tea, but brewing up in these conditions would have been tantamount to suicide.

As the desert sun rose above the horizon, Doug edged himself up the berm to take a look at our situation in the harsh light of day. 'Think of fucking Zulu Dawn,' he whispered, as he edged himself down to us.

All day we stayed in our hole, listening to the Iraqi soldiers in the vehicles parked up close by. A radio played Arabic music, then American rap, then more Arabic music, with news reports constantly interrupting it. All day Tosh kept coming on the net telling us we had to stay put. There had been a technical delay with the delivery of the MOAB.

We'd all had a bellyful of this shit by now. If we were still alive by nightfall, I decided that we would drive out of there, come what may. We would head for an ERV and get Pilot Steve to evacuate us. I teletyped this in a message to Tosh, but Quigly replied that we had to stay put for as long as possible. Pilot Steve was needed elsewhere, he added, so no one could extricate us. When the MOAB had been deployed we could get the hell out of there.

I repeatedly requested confirmation of the MOAB delivery time, only to be told to 'wait out'. Bollocks to this, I thought. I wasn't going to sit around and wait to be fried, especially if they couldn't give us sensible updates or any reassurance. Romero was desperate to get out: his sixth sense was kicking in big-time. The rest of the lads were equally keen to move.

Around midday, Tosh came on-line in voice mode even though he had been told to use teletype only: he'd had a message from Phil, who was deploying with Wajy and the Peshmerga lads, but Dan was muscling in. Wajy was asking whether I'd honour my word to join and stay with them. I sent Phil a message for Wajy that I'd be there as soon as I could. I dispatched it encrypted in burst mode, which meant it could basically hang about like a text does until the recipient picks it up.

Tosh came back with a second message from Phil: we should get out of the area without delay, regardless of our orders. He was obviously privy to something we didn't know, and it was pretty damn serious for him to have sent that message. Now I was certain we were being used as bait. Our presence was a ruse to convince the Iraqi commander that we were there to accept his surrender, while in reality he and his men were being targeted by the MOABs. With us there he would have the confidence to bring in his troops, thus offering the Americans the perfect opportunity to take out his entire unit.

Over the years I'd learnt to trust my instincts, as most SAS did.

Serving in Malaya and Borneo, back in the 1960s and 1970s, SAS operators had spent weeks living in the jungle and had become so attuned to the environment that their natural instincts were heightened – when a sixth sense told them something was wrong, in nine out of ten cases it was correct. Now, deep down, I felt we were going to get out of this one, but how eluded me. The rest of the lads weren't so sure, and Romero was increasingly agitated. He confided in me that, from the start of our operation, he'd felt he wouldn't get out of the conflict alive.

'We'll be fine, mate,' I whispered to him.

'Yeah, you may be right, but that don't mean I will.'

Doug and I eased ourselves up to take another look over the berm. More Iraqi vehicles were pulling in now and spreading out into defensive positions. Getting out would be even more difficult.

As dusk approached fast, we could see vapour trails of B52s and other aircraft high in the sky. I decided that when the next group of Iraqi vehicles pulled in we'd fire up the Land Rover and make a break for it. There was half an hour or less to go until dark, and we'd just have to pray that the MOAB wasn't dropped before then. Just as we were preparing to bug out, an Iraqi soldier walked up the berm towards our position, carrying a small shovel. He made for a secluded section no more than twenty feet from our vehicle and squatted.

Romero took out his pistol, which had a silencer, and made clear he would drop the Iraqi if he noticed us. By now the soldier had lit a cigarette. Baby Steve crawled closer to him, with a knife in his hand, in case Romero failed to get him. If the Iraqi stood up and turned to face us, he'd see our vehicle, regardless of the cam netting. He finished his cigarette, stood up and pulled up his trousers. Then he shovelled sand, and paused momentarily. I thought he was about to turn round. Finally, he clambered over the rim of the berm and headed back to his mates.

As we all breathed a sigh of relief, a message came in from Tosh that the MOAB was about to leave on the C130 Talon so we'd better move sharpish. Within ten minutes we'd cleared the camouflage from the vehicle and climbed aboard. Baby Steve was keeping an eye open for the next set of Iraqi vehicles to arrive, which might offer us some cover as we drove out. The night was already cold and I was shivering as I sat in the passenger seat, with Doug behind the wheel, his GPMG wedged between the central spar of the now absent windscreen and the wiper element. Romero had offered to stay behind and cause a diversion because he was convinced he was going to die, but we all told him to get in as we weren't leaving without him.

Fifteen minutes passed and no more Iraqi vehicles turned up. We waited another fifteen, and still none. All day as regular as clock-work, and now when we needed them there weren't any. It was now completely dark and the Iraqis weren't showing any lights.

'Fuck it, Doug, let's just go for it, full throttle,' I whispered finally.

I glanced back to check that everyone was on the wagon, to see Romero and Ian propping up four poles, then draping cam nets and sacking between them to create an almost box shape at the rear of the vehicle. It was supposed to make us look more like the Gaz jeeps the Iraqis drove.

All of a sudden there was pandemonium. Engines fired into life, and within seconds the Iraqi vehicles were heading away from us at speed in all directions. Had they got wind that the MOAB was on its way?

'Hit it,' I told Doug, not wanting to hang around either.

The engine caught and Doug hit the gas, sending us forwards and on to the ridge of the berm. As we raced over the top, Baby Steve flew off the back.

'Stop!' Romero yelled, and Doug hit the brakes as we careered down the slope.

We slewed to a standstill as Baby Steve ran after us and dived on. 'Go! Go! Go!' he shouted.

Doug didn't need telling twice and we accelerated away, weaving through the remaining Iraqi vehicles.

9

DEATH RUN

No one was paying much attention to us – a good thing too, as Romero and Ian's disguise was flying off the back of the Land Rover in all directions. We bounced and raced past the Iraqis' slower vehicles, heading north-east as Quigly had recommended. We passed a six-wheeler Zil-157 truck with a solid boxed body, used only by specialist units. I wondered if it was a mobile chemical laboratory. Then we overtook a Gaz-66 4 × 4 truck full of Iraqi soldiers, and a BDRM-2 armoured personnel carrier complete with a 122mm recoilless anti-tank gun sticking up at the rear.

As we edged past, Iraqi soldiers looked down at us. The moon just cresting was now bright enough for them to see us quite clearly. The driver had his foot to the floor, and as we passed he turned to stare at us. He pointed at us, then said something to his co-driver, who leant forward to look. I nodded and waved my right hand (in Arab tradition it is insulting to use the left), hoping they'd think we were friendly forces. A 12.7mm Degtyarev-Shpagin, or Dushka, heavy machine-gun graced the roof of the truck. A figure now clambered into position and began to cock it. The Dushka can penetrate 17mm of armour at 500 metres, so I knew it could totally mince our vehicle. He started to swing it round to bring it in line with us.

'More speed would be good,' I yelled at Doug, who glanced across and saw what was happening.

Without hesitation, he swerved across and smashed hard into the side of the Iraqi truck. As we bounced off, I looked up straight into the face of the Iraqi driver who evidently couldn't believe what was happening. The roof gunner couldn't depress the Dushka low enough, as we were now side by side with the truck, grinding into each other. But the Iraqi driver in the vehicle following put his foot down, one of its crew firing his AK47 in our direction. The Iraqi soldiers in the back of the truck began yelling at the others to cease fire, as the rounds were hitting them. I raised my rifle and swung it round to take out the truck driver, but as I did so he slammed on the brakes and the truck skidded to a halt behind us, the soldiers in the back flying in all directions.

Doug had his foot to the floor now as we sped away, Romero, Steve and Malcolm firing out of the back as we went. We were going so fast and bouncing all over the place that I feared we'd turn over. But Doug was laughing, and obviously having a great time. He swung the rear of the vehicle from side to side, kicking up more dust and dirt to act as a shield. It must have worked, because the Iraqis only fired off a few more rounds in our direction and we disappeared into our own little dust storm. I'd forgotten how fast Doug likes to drive, and after we'd put enough distance between us I urged him to slow down a little.

Malcolm gave a sitrep and identified our position to friendly forces, especially aircraft. Tosh came back with 'Well done getting out of there', then advised us to hide up for the remainder of the night and await new instructions.

We drove for a couple of hours and, with the map, I navigated us to a gully nearer the mountains that afforded some cover and was isolated enough for us to see anyone approaching from any direction. Baby Steve and Malcolm took on the first sentry duty, so I prepared a brew. Then we waited for the MOAB delivery.

The night sky was criss-crossed with aircraft trails and I could hear the odd whine of jet engines. In the distance I saw flashes from explosions and shortly afterwards heard the rumble of detonations. I was tired and desperately needed to sleep, but I was also curious to see the awesome MOAB go off. When 03.00 hours came and there was still nothing I requested an update. Quigly came back with news that the MOAB drop had been cancelled, and that many more members of the US 173rd Airborne Division had been parachuted en masse nearby.

I was pretty damn angry now, although I didn't have the energy to show it. Not because the MOAB hadn't been dropped, but because I now knew we'd been used as bait – in a plan that had fucked up anyway. OK, in war game plans changed constantly, but why hadn't we been told from the start our main purpose in going there? If Quigly had shared his intel with us, we would have accepted it as part of the job, but instead we'd been duped into going. Would our 'leaders' ever learn to trust the motivation and abilities of men on the ground? I wondered bitterly. The time had come to let him know that we weren't fools, and that he'd get a lot more out of us if he treated us with a little respect.

'Ask, and we will do,' my tersely worded message began. 'Level with us about what you want and we can deal with it. Keep us in the picture and we can be fluid and get there every time. But don't feed us any more bullshit.'

As the sun came up Phil came on the net. He was pleased we'd got out OK, and keen to link up. We agreed a rendezvous for midday with him, Wajy and his group of Peshmerga. I'd just sent confirmation when Baby Steve pointed to a group of Iraqi vehicles on the horizon, heading in our direction, most likely following our tracks. We packed away our gear and Malcolm called Tosh, requesting some CAS (Close air support). We didn't have the fire power to take on this little lot, especially the armoured vehicles. We had several LAWs and two LAW 80s, but our position was not ideal, and we'd have to move back into the more rugged landscape to our rear if we were to mount a successful defence. As soon as we broke cover the Iraqis were bound to spot us, so speed was the key.

As we pulled out of the gully into the wider wadi, we were taking incoming from the 122mm recoilless gun on one of the Iraqi BRDM-2s. Malcolm called for CAS, only to be told there was a four-hour delay due to massive commitment to coalition troops. We weren't a priority. So, we were on our own. Doug floored the accelerator and we sped away, but as fast as we were going the Iraqi gunners compensated: 122mm shells exploded behind us as if they were following our tracks, and each time they were closer. Anyone who thinks that the Iraqi armed forces are pretty useless should come and sit where we were.

'Come on, you fucking heap of shit!' Doug bellowed at the vehicle.

Baby Steve readied a 66mm LAW, but with the vehicle's bouncing he couldn't hold one position long enough to aim it. The only viable option would be to stop, rapidly aim the LAWs and fire them, but with more than a dozen Iraqi vehicles in pursuit we weren't about to do that. Besides, we were almost at a metalled road, which meant we could put some serious distance between us and our pursuers.

Romero fired at the Iraqi vehicles but they were too far away for his 5.56mm Diameco assault rifle, so he switched to his Heckler & Koch AG-360 40mm grenade-launcher and fired off several smoke rounds. The result obscured the Iraqis but only for a short time. Their BRDM stopped briefly, as it re-aimed, but the next shell exploded close to our rear and showered us with dirt.

Suddenly Doug slammed on the brakes without warning.

Romero rolled forwards into Malcolm, as Steve and Ian grabbed a side rail and I hit the dashboard.

A shell exploded right in front of us, in exactly the spot we would have been had we carried on driving. Doug jumped up on to his seat with the GPMG, swung it across what was left of the internal roll bar, cocked it, pulled it into the aim and fired in a continuous stream at the BRDM. The Iraqis were not out of range of the 7.62 mm rounds from the GPMG, and as the belt of ammo fed itself into the weapon he maintained his fire. I stood up to see the other vehicles veer off and stop as rounds slammed into the BRDM. The lie of the land as it rose gently towards the mountains meant that we were looking down into the BDRM and Doug kept pumping away.

Then one of the BRDM's tyres burst into flames as tracer rounds ploughed into it. Doug concentrated his aim into the open rear where the 122mm cannon was located. Black smoke rose in a plume as a figure jumped into view and was hit in the legs, falling back into the stricken vehicle. Two more rushed out from the back, as the black smoke turned into gouts of flame. A small explosion blew out the door on the right side, and Doug kept firing. Finally, the belt ran out and he stood up straight with a fixed stare. Suddenly, the BRDM erupted in a huge ball of flame and flying debris. At that Doug looked at me, blue eyes wide, nodded, and sat down in the driver's seat. He wedged his now steaming GPMG back into position and fired up the engine, slammed the Land Rover into gear, and we were off again, Romero trying to refix the end caps on to a LAW 80 that he'd readied to fire. When we finally hit Tarmac, Doug stopped, looked left, then right, and pulled up on to the side. 'Directions would be good,' he remarked, his voice deep from adrenaline.

I checked the map and indicated right. The smooth road surface was a joy to travel on, but after our hair-raising getaway, we didn't have enough fuel to take us to the RV with Wajy and

Phil. I identified another location where they could come to us. It was situated up a long valley, with a single dirt track leading into it. It resembled an old volcano crater, and with our people round the rim, we would have excellent security. Doug drove on, almost mesmerised. It was only when we drove up the dirt track and reached the RV that he relaxed. He let out a sigh, closed his eyes for a moment, then looked at me. 'Sorry, boss, I was in fight mode,' he said.

We hid the Land Rover and set up our LUP to await Phil and Wajy's arrival. When we were settled in, I asked Doug what had happened earlier, when he'd taken out the BRDM.

'I'd been counting the time between each shell, trying to work out how quickly they could stop, load and fire, move on again, stop reload and fire. Then I judged how close the shells were landing, and tried to work out which one had our names written on it. It was like I'd gone into some state of heightened awareness. I was thinking incredibly fast, like I could do anything. When I threw out the anchors I just knew that shell was coming for us. And that was when I turned the Gimpy on the fuckers. I knew we had to stop that BRDM, boss, or we'd all have been in the shit.'

Doug had described a sensation that is not uncommon in soldiers. I'd felt it myself – it's as if you're on autopilot, concentrating with ease and pace on the problem to the exclusion of everything else. The adrenaline's pumping and you find you can do things you wouldn't consider in normal circumstances. I was glad Doug had had a 'zombie moment' when he did – undoubtedly it had saved our skins.

As we settled into our new position, Romero took off his dishdash to freshen up and noticed a hole in the back of it. He slung off his webbing and discovered he'd been shot. His body armour had stopped the round, but in all the chaos of our escape he hadn't even noticed it. 'See? I was right.' He glanced at me. 'Told you I was going to get it.'

In the distance we could see a tiny plume of smoke from the burning BRDM. As I looked east down the main road, I saw more vehicles approaching. Were they the Iraqis or Wajy's convoy of Peshmerga? When I looked west, I saw even more vehicles heading our way. We were playing cat-and-mouse with the Iraqis, and I didn't want to mess with them again just yet. Malcolm tried to raise Phil on the net, but Tosh confirmed that one group was Phil with Mam's Peshmerga, while the others were Wajy and his lot. They'd split up during the night to check on separate targets. Then we received a message that we now had our air cover. Typical! I thought. Just when we didn't bloody need it any more.

The scenery was lush and quite green where we were now, at the foot of the Zagros mountains. Mosul lay to the east and Phil had been on the outskirts helping to co-ordinate and designate targets in the city. Wajy and Mam had moved into position and simply awaited orders, true to their word.

Within minutes Phil and Mam's convoy pulled in, complete with several Humvees and US SEALs newly arrived in theatre, then Wajy's group appeared behind them, accompanied by Pathfinders from the 173rd Airborne. Athansa was chuffed to be back with us again, as was Guss. I saw Ben and Heather emerge from Wajy's convoy, and go straight into filming mode. As I approached Heather was saying, 'And here, on the front lines, Kurdish fighters celebrate control of the area as they link up with US paratroopers.'

She turned to face the west as another B52 carpet-bombing run rumbled out across the open plain, and Ben filmed the huge clouds of dust thrown up on the horizon. The Kurds punched their fists into the air.

'And, as you can see, the Kurds are celebrating the strikes against the Iraqi military,' Heather continued.

What bollocks, I thought. Don't the images alone say enough? But she was doing her job.

When Wajy spotted us, he rushed over and gave me one of his bear-hugs. He was bursting with enthusiasm and excitement. Phil looked rough, his black hair long and unkempt, and he was sporting several days of facial growth. He told me I looked like shit, so I thanked him and told him he did too. He grinned, face creasing as always. We had a quick heads-up, and it was reassuring to learn that the Peshmerga were sticking to the plan and not rushing off at the first opportunity to liberate Kirkuk.

After a break for lunch, we went over the Iraqi targets, starting with the ones marked as a priority – trenches, bunkers and communication posts. Saddam had fortified all the areas bordering the Kurdish territory, and we were about to dismantle some of the key fortifications, helped by rapid progress of other coalition advances and the six hundred Cruise missiles that had already been fired during the 'Shock and Awe' campaign. Also, several locations had been identified as bases for Islamic fanatics, and we wanted to hit those hard, but as they were mainly in villages and towns they couldn't be bombed – innocent civilians would be killed. I learnt that Kosrat Rassul, the Kurds' intelligence chief, was busy on the other side of Mosul and had already achieved many of the objectives he had been set. Layla was with him. I felt guilty for having asked about her – my mind should have been on the job and, when the mission allowed for it, Victoria.

We started planning the next series of strikes on Iraqi positions, which had to take place over the next night. We'd arranged a four-hour window during which there would be no US bombing, allowing us to make our attack runs on key targets. Excitement grew when confirmation came that the strategic airbase at Tallil was now in US hands and that the entire US 173rd Airborne Brigade, some thousand troops, had successfully completed their deployment in northern Iraq, officially opening a new front. Then Tosh called me to deal with an urgent radio call: another Iraqi commander was interested in negotiating the safety of his Special Republican Guards unit. The intel boys had no way of confirming if this was the same commander we'd tried to meet earlier, but might I be willing to attempt a meeting with him? I told them to fuck off and get some other monkey to act as their bait. This brought an immediate, outraged response from all levels.

Shortly, Quigly came on the net stating that we had not been 'bait' and the original plan had been legitimate. He asked me whether I'd take a similar mission if this time it was confirmed beyond doubt, with full CAS and back-up. He was obviously playing mind tricks now, seeing if he could draw me back into his game. He knew I was still in favour of getting the Iraqi military on-side, a hearts-and-minds policy that would pay dividends later when the fighting had stopped and we needed them to maintain law and order, so I said I'd consider it, but only on our own terms.

We had several hours to kill before nightfall and the next stage of our mission, so after briefing the lads I thought I'd grab some sleep. Doug was cleaning his GPMG as I lay down – after looking for spiders – when a signal came in from Head Shed, apparently contradicting Quigly's request and asking me return to Cizre at the earliest opportunity. Talk about the fog of war, and the right hand not knowing what the left was doing. I ignored the message: I had a sneaking suspicion that it had been sent because they were worried I was showing too much loyalty to the Peshmerga and might run off the rails. But I was determined to stick with them as I'd promised, and there was no way I'd desert my team in theatre.

I woke several hours later when it was dark. Doug was sitting close by, texting Sara, and handed over a mess tin of cold chicken curry. I ate it, washed, using my mess tin, and looked over the blackened bruises still showing from the .50-cal round. Wajy, Mam, Phil, Doug and I gathered round the radio with our maps showing the target locations. We planned to do a sweeping movement encircling Mosul and then, at 02.00 hours that night, hit all the targets at once, calling in airstrikes as required. Our orders for taking out the Islamic insurgents (whomever they turned out to be, Iraqi, Iranian, Syrian or otherwise) were specific: 'Do not arrest or capture – kill.' We didn't have the manpower to deal with these fanatics as prisoners and, besides, we knew how badly the Peshmerga wanted them dead. As we were discussing this, Wajy pointed out that in many of the targeted houses there would be women and children. There was a long silence.

'Shit happens,' Doug said, breaking the silence.

We moved on, discussing how to co-ordinate the strikes. Many of the Peshmerga were already in hidden positions, thanks to Phil and Wajy's busy schedule over the past two days. Radio contact was only possible with those groups that had SEALs with them. All Iraqi radios had been jammed by US AWACs, which swamped their signals and pumped out radio and TV propaganda. The electronic counter-measures were good in theory but played havoc with our radio sets too. At 02.00 hours we would head off in convoy as each team attacked its respective target. We would link up with the first group, pick them up, then move on to the next. Any groups in trouble could call on us for back-up and support when we reached them. Once we had rounded up the Peshmerga groups, we would RV at a location just short of the first major bridge that spanned the Great Zab river.

When we were across the bridge we would leave several SEALs with thirty Peshmerga to secure it until they were relieved by the 173rd US Airborne Brigade, or other elements heading that way, and the rest of the convoy would proceed towards Kirkuk. Once that city had been effectively surrounded and contained, we would press on south to Tikrit and central Iraq, eventually linking up with US 3rd Infantry Division coming up from there. Naturally everything was subject to change.

As we talked, calls came in from Quigly, Dan and others, asking for assurances that the Peshmerga were sticking to the game plan. The Turkish government was concerned that they would seize Mosul and Kirkuk, and was again threatening military action. Why the hell our people couldn't get the Turks to wind their necks in I didn't know; there was little I could do about it from my end.

At around 23.00 hours the SEAL team commanded by Maberley informed us that his Peshmerga group had brought forward the start time for their attack as their target was packing vehicles to leave. They'd engaged them already, and a fierce fire-fight had broken out. News of this would rapidly filter out to the other Iraqi targets, so I told everyone we were setting off in ten minutes' time. Fluid programme, eh? Wajy led our convoy out of our hidden position in his Toyota pick-up. Baby Steve, Ian and Phil had the stripped-down Land Rover, while I jumped into a cosy Humvee with Doug, Malcolm and Romero. We hit the main road south and picked up speed.

As we drove through the night, Doug and Romero were deep in conversation – about Zen Buddhism, of all things. Romero was well into Buddhist philosophy and, to my amazement, Doug maintained that many years earlier he had been too. But he'd got so irritated and impatient with his master that he'd given it up.

Doug was usually a man of few words, so I was amazed when he came out with the history of Zen philosophy, how it had spread from India to China and on to Japan – now the only place where it is a living religion. I had studied it during my years of religious searching, and because I wanted to understand the way of the Samurai. Romero mentioned the twenty-six patriarchs of Zen philosophy, the gurus and masters, and Doug reeled off their names.

Even Malcolm was listening now. 'Hey, you named twenty-seven,' he said, when Doug had finished.

'That's because there's twenty-seven patriarchs,' Doug replied. 'You got it wrong, mate.'

'Bullshit,' Romero retorted. 'It's twenty-six.'

'Twenty-seven, mate,' Doug shot back. 'The twenty-seven patriarchs. Any true disciple knows that.'

'It's twenty-six,' Romero replied stubbornly. 'Ain't no doubt about it.'

'All right, then, mate, put your money where your mouth is,' said Doug. 'What'll you bet on it?'

'Anything you want,' Romero said.

'Well, how about your Land Rover against my Shogun?' Doug challenged him.

'Sure, no problem,' Romero replied, with a grin. 'I'd hate you to lose it, knowing how fond of it you are.'

'All right! Malc, Niall, you make sure the fucker pays up when he loses.'

'No problem,' I said. 'Anyway, you're both wrong. There's twenty-eight patriarchs.'

At that moment Maberley came up on the net, requesting support or guidance. The attack they had started early at Makhmur had run into problems, and one of the Peshmerga had been taken hostage by a group of Islamists. It was an hour's drive to the location of the hostage-taking, so I signalled to Wajy that we'd move on ahead and try to sort it out, then link up with him later.

Mam Rostam, the senior Kurdish leader, was already busy in the southern Kurdish town of Chamchamal, otherwise he could have supported Maberley as he was nearest, so I also took two Peshmerga, Phil and SEAL Ian in the vehicle with us, then raced ahead of the main convoy, Doug driving dangerously fast again, with no lights. The road was littered with abandoned vehicles and we could see explosions ahead, as airstrikes over Mosul hit their targets. People were being killed, most likely women and children too. Terrified little ones would be clutching their parents right now. And I was part of the war machine that was raining down death and destruction. I thought of my own children, safe at home in England.

It seemed bizarre to be driving along a dual carriageway, passing road signs just as you would on any British road. Malcolm thrust a mug of coffee at me, and I was thankful he never went far without his Thermos. I glanced up at a sign that pointed to Mosul, and saw the after-burners of a jet in the distance; it had just delivered its ordnance on target.

'Get on to Tosh to alert the FACs and the AWACs to our presence,' I told Malcolm.

To any bomb jockey in the sky we'd look like any other target racing along the road in the dark. Apache helicopters were prowling all over the area and they would pick us up on their thermal-imaging systems. It took barely thirty minutes to race round the main ring road, which brought us to the bridge over the Great Zab. Malcolm raised one of Dan's lot, who were located on the opposite side of the bridge, and we waited until they confirmed we were cleared to cross. Doug put his foot to the floor and we went over at speed.

On the other side we were flagged down by several heavily armed Peshmerga, each with a bandolier of bullets wrapped round his shoulders. They came close to the vehicle for a quick check inside. Then one of Dan's SEAL lads rushed over, complete with knee and elbow pads, and hockey hat, as we called it, though it was really a tight-fitting, all black type of crash helmet, waving us on to keep moving. For once it appeared that our radios and relay of messages were working, and we sped off again. Doug pushed the vehicle as fast as it would go, and Malcolm had just started pouring me some more coffee when Doug stamped on the brakes. There was a screech, the smell of burning rubber and spilled coffee. We all stared at him as he slammed the vehicle into reverse and backed up the way we'd come.

'You fucking amateurs.' He waved a hand out of the window. 'Told you to yell out when we hit the sign for the turn-off.'

I glanced at the map on my knees. By my reckoning the junction that would take us to Makhmur should have been ten minutes away, but Doug had been driving faster than I'd realised.

'If we burst a tyre now you can fucking change it,' Doug continued, and elbowed me in the ribs. He floored the pedal again and we bounced on to the Makhmur road.

Twenty minutes later we reached the brow of a hill, and houses appeared on either side of the road. This had to be the outskirts of Makhmur. Romero and Doug hid the vehicle behind a mud-brick wall and we made radio contact with the SEAL lads up ahead of us. We agreed a rendezvous point, left the Peshmerga to guard the truck and set off into town on foot. Dirt tracks branched off the main road to either side of us, and the houses looked large and imposing. This was clearly the affluent side of Makhmur. A curtain flicked back, as someone watched us pass, but then there was the clank of shutters across the window. Other than that, there was no sign of life and the streets were deserted.

Within ten minutes we had linked up with Maberley. Small fires were burning round a plush-looking house, and a Toyota Hi-lux was ablaze, the flames sending shadows dancing across the walls. I knelt in some cover, put my hand down to steady myself and made contact with a soggy mess. I glanced down – and saw that I had inadvertently plonked my hand on the bloodied chest of a Peshmerga. His face was covered and he was dead.

Maberley brought me up to speed on what had happened. As his team had gone in to recce the target, they'd come under immediate and effective fire. Two Peshmerga had been killed, three seriously wounded, and one had gone down just outside the door of the target house. The enemy had dragged him inside. The intel on the occupants read like a *Who's Who* of the local crime mob, but they were members of Saddam Hussein's feared secret police. I asked who the captured Peshmerga was, and discovered it was Twin Two.

Many other residential buildings surrounded the one in front of us, and I was worried that some might offer an escape route to the enemy. Maberley said that the other properties had been cleared and that Peshmerga lads were now in position in all of them. I sent Romero and Doug to skirt the building anyway, to check the lie of the land. Phil, Maberley and I lay in a roadside gully opposite the building, with twelve Peshmerga, who were eager to rush the building, take out the Iraqis and rescue Twin Two.

The silence was punctuated by the coming and going of jet engines, and the staccato percussion of explosions lit up the dark horizon. Suddenly I heard a voice call in heavily accented English from the direction of the building: 'We want vehicle now or we kill hostage!'

Just then Malcolm rushed over to me on all fours. 'Boss, Tosh's just been on the net,' he whispered. 'We can't hang around as Wajy's lot're on the move again and making rapid progress. Seems as soon as they heard this one had kicked off they all went for it. Guss says they're pressing on to Kirkuk. Dan's thrown a wobbly and says you've got to stop them at the main junction.'

Bollocks to Dan, I thought angrily. He was sticking his nose in where it wasn't welcome and putting me under unbearable pressure. Even if we worked miracles here, I still didn't know if we'd be in time to stop Wajy.

'Tell those fuckers they've got ten minutes to come out or we're coming in regardless,' I told Phil.

He shouted our ultimatum at the building in Arabic. But some of the Peshmerga who understood English overheard my order, and stared at me in horror. I knew why: if we were forced to assault the building, Twin Two was as good as dead. 'We can't hang about here,' I told them, 'we've got to press on,' but I felt shitty about it.

The Peshmerga lads started talking among themselves, fast. Phil listened in, then told them to be quiet as we waited for the Iraqis to respond. The people in that house had been guilty of brutal atrocities and knew that they could expect harsh treatment if captured. Finally, one shouted that they would rather die than surrender. We knew they stood a good chance of fighting their way out and surviving, should we attack, so they had nothing to lose.

Malcolm received another urgent message from Dan: either we had to stop Wajy, or he would use extreme measures to do so at the earliest opportunity. He was cranking up the pressure and I didn't like it. 'Tell Dan to back the fuck off and give us a chance,' I snapped, and tried to work out how the hell we were going to break the siege.

Just then, Romero and Doug scrambled back into our position. 'Not good, boss,' Doug reported. 'There's no way in. They have the place pretty well wired up and covered.'

'If we storm it, we'll take casualties big-time,' Romero added, confirming what I'd suspected.

My mind was racing. We couldn't pussyfoot around any longer: we had to move out to check the progress of Wajy's convoy. It was one man's life inside the building against saving God knew how many of Wajy's lot from Dan. I had no doubt Dan would take them out if he thought it would help pacify the Turks. My ten-minute deadline was fast running out. Phil scurried off, saying he'd be back in a minute. The Peshmerga were all staring at me, waiting for me to say something. Then the front door of the building crashed open. An Iraqi appeared, using Twin Two as a shield and holding a handgun to his head. I could see the Peshmerga was bleeding badly from a thigh wound.

'If you don't give them a vehicle within five minutes they'll kill me,' shouted Twin Two.

Then the Iraqi dragged him back inside and slammed the heavy door. I was fast running out of options, and torn between the fate of Twin Two and that of Wajy and his men. Another five minutes went past, and I was certain that my deadline was up. Then Phil crawled back into view, carrying one of our LAW 80s. He took off the end caps and started to arm it. 'Sorry, bud, but we ain't got time to fanny around here any longer,' he stated. He raised the weapon to his shoulder and brought it to the aim.

This brought a frantic response from the Peshmerga sharing the gully with us. Phil hesitated.

A voice rang out from the besieged building: 'Sharafnama! Remember Sharafkhan! Allah Akbar! Allah Akbar!' It was Twin Two. His voice was defiant and insistent, as if he knew what was coming. He continued to shout 'Sharafkhan', and there was a stream of abuse from the Iraqis as they tried to shut him up. Suddenly two shots rang out and he was silent. The Peshmerga lowered their heads and closed their eyes as Phil took aim with the LAW 80. The front door to the building swung open again. One of the Iraqis appeared, kicking Twin Two's body into view as he fired his AK47 from the hip.

There was a click-whoosh from beside me as Phil fired the LAW. The rocket streaked towards the man, whose eyes widened in terror as he saw it. As he dived back inside, the LAW shot through the doorway and a massive explosion ripped through the building. Clouds of debris flew out of the door and windows, followed by flames. The roof seemed to lift off and stop in mid-air, then collapsed in on itself. There was no way anyone was alive in there now.

'Problem solved,' said Phil matter-of-factly as he discarded the empty LAW tube.

We rushed over to the building to give it the once-over, and one of the Peshmerga found Twin Two's body, one arm raised stiff and blackened from the heat of the explosion, the skin still sizzling. He knelt down next to it and removed the ring from the index finger, sobbing his heart out. When I suggested he could stay and recover his friend's body, I was told he could not: there was more fighting to be done. He stood up, wiped his face, feigned a brave smile and composed himself.

Malcolm sent a sitrep confirming to Dan that we were en route to meet Wajy, then got on the net to Guss, who, with Ian and Athansa, was with Wajy's column, and asked him to make sure Wajy waited for us at the main junction.

As we headed back to our vehicle, the local Peshmerga commander explained to me what Twin Two had meant when he had shouted, 'Remember Sharafkhan.' The Peshmerga had agreed that if any one of them was captured, they must not let themselves be used as hostages. They must remember the words of Sharafkhan: that a Peshmerga is always 'ready to die'. As soon as Twin Two had shouted his name, they had all known what he meant.

10

MURDER INC

We made a sharp exit, and were soon passing abandoned border-type posts between free Kurdistan and Baghdad-controlled areas. Maberley met us on the main road just outside the town and we all raced to the junction with the road to Kirkuk, praying we'd arrive ahead of Wajy. We waited there for half an hour, but there was no sign of his convoy. It was only when Malcolm finally got through to Guss – we had lost radio contact for a while – that we learnt the lengths to which he had gone to stop Wajy proceeding without us. He had deliberately crashed his Humvee into Wajy's Toyota, claiming that his steering had locked. When the chips were down, Guss could do what was required. I was gaining a grudging respect for the American 'loaf'.

I asked Wajy to stay where he was so that we could meet up with him. Guss gave us their location and we were on our way. Tosh came through on the radio that we were to regroup at an RV point away from Mosul and await further orders. At all costs Wajy and his convoy must stay with us. Dan, too, would link up with us at the RV – he was bringing more US Special Forces teams as reinforcements.

Half an hour later we joined Wajy's convoy of eight vehicles and headed on towards the RV. I spotted a burning T72 tank blazing on the main highway. Most Iraqi tanks were the older T55s, so this one was from one of the better-equipped Republican Guards units. I hoped there weren't many more lurking around. As we approached the city of Mosul, half of it was in darkness. Airstrikes were degrading the power supply, knocking out electricity sub-stations.

We moved into a hidden LUP where a dirt track led up to a goat-marshalling point. It was a natural depression ringed by hills, with a small lake in the middle. We drew the vehicles into a circle, slung tarpaulins between them and put Peshmerga guards in vantage-spots in the hills. By then dawn was breaking. We posted several of our own sentries, just to be on the safe side, and set about preparing some hot food. Wajy was pleased with the way things were going – one good thing to have come out of the day.

Now we sat and waited for whatever Quigly, Head Shed and the rest would throw our way. Guss and Malcolm were having problems with the radio signal, so Guss volunteered to venture higher into the hills to set up a sky wave and, hopefully, get better reception. I told him to keep an eye open for any US 173rd Airborne Brigade personnel in convoy. Tosh had reminded us to be careful – he didn't want them hitting us by mistake as they filtered into the area. It was now 07.00 hours and after Guss, a couple of SEALs and some Peshmerga had gone, we sat down for a meal.

'So, Mosul is Iraq's third largest city,' I began, between mouthfuls, with one eye on Doug, 'and it sits on the border between the Kurds to the east and the Sunni Arabs to the west. It's got a long history of providing officers for Saddam's army and his intelligence services. We have intel that his two sons, Uday and Qusay, may be hiding there. Who knows? Maybe we'll be tasked with taking them out.'

'I'd fucking love to get my hands on those two,' said Doug. 'Give the fuckers a taste of their own medicine.'

'They're not very nice,' I agreed, 'renowned for horrible tortures. At one time Uday had an industrial plastics shredder and forced anyone who'd pissed him off through it, feet first. Sometimes, if he was feeling merciful, he'd push them through head first.'

'Jesus, boss, d'you have to?' Malcolm remarked. 'I'm trying to enjoy me dinner.'

'Mosul was founded by the Assyrians,' I went on. 'The region around it, which includes the ancient city of Nineveh, is thought to have been inhabited for at least eight thousand years. Mosul was an important trade town, famous for its marble and the fabric to which it gave its name, muslin. The city was occupied by one force after another – the Romans, Muslim Umayyad dynasty, the Abbasids and the Ottomans.'

I was driving Doug mad, I could see, with delving into Mosul's history – to the delight of Romero and Baby Steve, who knew what I was up to.

'After the First World War, Britain took charge and eventually made it part of the newly crafted kingdom of Iraq,' I continued. 'British forces returned after the first Gulf War, providing warplanes to police the skies above Mosul and enforce the no-fly zones over Kurdish territory. With its proximity to major oil reserves, the city remains important for whoever controls it today.'

By the time I'd finished my lecture, my side was hurting again – but more from laughing at Doug's reaction to it than from my injury. Once I'd fallen silent, he started to take the piss out of Tosh, who was back at Cizre and unable to defend himself.

Later Tosh was on the net, informing us that another forty Navy SEALs were coming up to us from the Al Faw peninsular; we would meet at an RV where Dan would link up with us. In

Baghdad two 4700-pound 'bunker-busters' had been dropped; reports were coming through that Iraqis there were strengthening their defensive cordon in the Red Zone, the ancient city, which, officials and intel feared, marked the 'trigger line' for Saddam to unleash chemical weapons.

When we'd heard this, we moved into a better-protected area that gave us access over the side of a natural rock wall to commanding views of Mosul. Guss had to take down and reset his sky wave. We stretched IR (infrared) covers and tarpaulin sheets between the vehicles and set up a semi-permanent FOB. Heather and Ben decided to try to link up with other US forces coming down from the north – they suspected they would find more action to film with them. They needed a vehicle, so we lent them the stripped-down Land Rover.

We all checked our email, and Baby Steve had received a surprise dear-John letter – two, in fact. He'd had a couple of girls on the go in Hereford, but they'd just found out about each other and busted his balls. More news came in that US and British forces were making steady progress north, and Dan radioed that he couldn't find the RV. Romero, Malcolm and two Peshmerga lads guided him in as we were pretty well off the track. When he arrived with several Humvees and a dozen pick-ups full of SEALs and Peshmerga, he looked very stressed. I shook his hand and ushered him in out of the wind. News came of humanitarian aid being offloaded from RFA (Royal Fleet Auxiliary) *Sir Galahad* at Umm Qasr, and convoys were crossing from Kuwait.

'All political showmanship,' Dan bellowed as he sat down. He introduced me to his new SEAL team commander, Ryan Zinke, who recognised Romero. The two men had done SEAL selection at the same time, then Romero had moved on to join Delta Force.

'Where's your side-kick – Athansa, isn't it?' Ryan asked.

'He did a runner when he saw your ugly mug coming up the hill.' Romero grinned.

As the wind slapped the tarpaulins, Dan detailed all the latest locations of Iraqi armour and units. Mam's lot had effectively chased most of them from the Chamchamal area to the oil hub of Kirkuk, and were now scouring territory in the hills between Dohuk, in Kurdish hands, and Mosul, still Iraqi. He told me that as I'd refused to return to Cizre, I was to stay where I was: the Kurds' intelligence chief, Kosrat Rassul, was coming to meet me within a couple of days. 'I'll leave you some Pesh lads and one or two of your own,' Dan continued, 'but I'll be taking the rest of yours with me.'

Romero and Doug looked up at him in disbelief.

'No way, buddy.' Romero shook his head.

'Amen to that,' Doug added. 'And fuck off too, mate.'

'Sorry, Dan, no can do on that score,' I added, trying to keep things civil. 'They're my team and we stay together.'

Dan stood up straight. 'That ain't no request, buddy. It was a direct order.'

I shrugged. 'Well, I suggest you reconsider it. We stay together as a team,' I replied.

'Jeez, what is it with you guys?' Dan spluttered, and slammed his helmet on the table. 'You got any idea – I mean, *any idea* – of the bigger picture here?'

We all shook our heads, and Baby Steve started to laugh.

'This ain't no fuckin' laughing matter, boy,' Dan said. He might have been a lieutenant colonel, but he had zero skills when it came to managing people like us. His attitude just got our backs up. 'You turned chicken shit on me or what?' he asked.

'Watch your fucking mouth,' Doug interjected, 'and I don't care who the fuck you think you are.'

'Dan, you want me to sit here alone with just a couple of Pesh lads, is that it? Well, you can forget it. I'm not arguing with you because there's nothing to argue about. You can try having me removed from in theatre if you want, but you'll find it difficult. I stay with my team and Wajy, as agreed,' I said emphatically.

I'd noticed Wajy standing at the entrance, listening intently. Dan looked at him, then at the rest of us, and realised he was alone. Even his SEAL commander, Ryan Zinke, raised his helmet as if to indicate to Dan he was way out of line. First, I would only ever consider splitting from my team if it was absolutely necessary, but, second, he didn't need most of my team. And we'd never had any written orders to the effect that we were under US forces' command. As far as I was concerned, Dan could say we were until he was blue in the face, but I wasn't changing my stance. He was trying to wield the big stick, and I wanted to tell him to fuck off – but I had to be diplomatic. After all, we were on the same side.

'Dan, as long as I stay here, my team stays with me. Give me a valid reason for splitting us up and maybe I'll consider it,' I said, as if I was explaining something to a child.

'Sheer fucking disobedience, that's what this is,' Dan snapped. 'Gross insubordination! I could have you all court-martialled.'

'Erm, 'scuse me – we ain't officially here,' Doug put in. 'I'd like to see you try. We don't exist, remember? Figments of our own imagination, we are.'

Baby Steve burst out laughing again, and Dan looked like he was about to burst a blood vessel.

'Steve, sort the coffee and some scoff for us, will you?' I asked, partly to get him out of the tent – Doug had been far more abusive towards Dan but Baby Steve's youth was getting to him most.

I ushered Dan towards a table. 'Dan, sit with me and talk, but don't throw your weight around, please,' I said quietly, as I tried to ease him into a seat. 'You want Wajy to see and hear all this and leg it with his lot?'

Dan hesitated, but my remark about Wajy must have got through because he sat down. He rubbed his hands through his hair. He was clearly very tired and under enormous pressure, but I had little sympathy for him. 'Maybe you'd be so kind as to tell us the bigger picture that we're all so out of the loop on,' I said, as I sat down opposite him.

'Ah, what's the fucking point?' He sighed and rested his head in his hands. 'You're right, I can't order you guys around. What the fuck was I thinking of?' He took his coffee and looked straight at me. 'Niall, I'm sorry,' he continued. 'I was running away with myself.'

Either he had seen the light, or he was trying a new ruse. If this was genuine it wasn't the Dan we knew, all bombastic and aggressive. This Dan was deflated and exhausted. Whatever, I wasn't about to be talked into splitting up my team. In these operations it was teamwork that mattered. It was what kept you going when things turned nasty. Breaking us up amounted to wasting a valuable asset. We were more capable of achieving any objectives or tasks given us if we stayed together. And, to be honest, I felt a damn sight safer surrounded by my team.

'Well, how about explaining all the references to "crossover"?' I suggested.

Dan stared at his coffee for an age. Eventually he looked up. 'It's that critical moment when a key Iraqi leader or figure finally makes up his mind that he'll no longer support Saddam but co-operate with us. It's not as simple as they-decide-and-we-say-howdy.' He paused. 'We have to judge it and orchestrate it just right so that Saddam doesn't twig his command structure and power base is crumbling as his key players desert him. If he does it may push him over the edge to unleash God only knows what. He may decide to attack Israel and drag them in, or use chemical weapons, as he's so often threatened. We're still keeping fingers crossed he ain't got no WMD because our boys will soon be entering Baghdad's Red Zone. Your last little trip you noted a Scud launcher. Well, our intel indicated it was an upgraded version carrying a long-range Scaleboard weapon, not a Scud, and we needed it confirmed. If it was, we would've had to take it out as Saddam could wreak havoc with one of them. But how he got hold of one is what we wanted to know.'

Now that he had started talking it was as if he couldn't stop. He and other operators, including many of Kosrat Rassul's people, had been playing this game of crossover with certain key players and Iraqi military commanders without Saddam knowing. Dan's other CIA group were having trouble tracking down Islamists and other insurgents they knew had come in from Syria but were apparently working on behalf of Saudi Arabia. They needed to confirm whether or not they were Saudi operators coming into the country to stir up trouble so that Iraq would not stabilise. We were all a little surprised to hear this.

'No way would the Saudis authorise, condone or back such a group. They're US allies,' Baby Steve stated.

'I hope you're right, kid,' Dan said.

The long-term prospects for the Saudi monarchy didn't appear promising, he told us. Despite their twenty-one-trillion-dollar investment in the US, a stable and prosperous Iraq wouldn't be good for them: a US victory in Iraq might lead to elected popular rule in Iraq, which might lead in its turn to regeneration of the country's oil production, the consequences of which could prove injurious to the Saudi monarchy – a substantial increase in Iraqi oil production would erode Riyadh's oil revenues, which would threaten the huge subsidies it provided to appease its own people and various terrorist organisations, like al-Qaeda, from taking action against them. Saudi Arabia would be caught between a rock and a hard place. If it was proved that Saudi insurgents were indeed coming into Iraq to carry out disruptive operations and attacks on oil wells and pipelines, the political fallout would be catastrophic for peace in the entire region.

'Glad I ain't no politician,' Baby Steve announced, as he brought us some fresh coffee.

Dan's lot were already discussing Iraq's oil production with Saudi agents and officials. A compromise, with a regulated output of oil from Iraq, especially Kirkuk, had to be agreed so that the Saudi position was not undermined. If that could be guaranteed, the Saudi insurgents, following whoever's instructions, would have no excuse or reason to carry out any activities. But when had that stopped anyone in the past? The Kurds had made it clear during previous meetings that once they had secured their former capital, Kirkuk, they'd institute a major increase in oil production. If they did, it would have the same effect on the Saudis as a stable Iraq.

'My fucking head's beginning to hurt,' Doug observed, as he got up and left the tent.

I could see now why Dan was so determined to stop the Peshmerga entering Kirkuk, and my mind raced as I reached for means to stop that happening. And I was concerned for Wajy: after what he'd just heard, he looked despondent. Dan and he gazed at each other wordlessly for a while.

Ever since I had accepted the job, I had questioned the morality and legality of the US and UK entering into this 'preventive war'. I knew Romero shared some of my anxiety, but Doug and Baby Steve did not: they loved their jobs and that was enough for them. So had I when I had started out years ago, but I had changed. My parents and friends had noticed it. I was quieter, more reserved and took life more seriously.

I believed that Saddam deserved to go for the horrible crimes he had committed against his people, regardless of whether he had WMD. Knowledge of his evil-doing had helped to keep motivation and morale high among my team, but it was the method of his removal and the way we were prosecuting the war that bothered me – and that many thousands would be killed. And as Dan and I discussed the 'bigger picture', the wider dangers of the war became ever clearer.

Saddam's best option right now was to hide his élite troops where US air power couldn't hit them, Dan continued, then carry out a protracted urban conflict. This would have major disadvantages for the US and coalition forces: if Iraqis and allied insurgents organised themselves to fight in urban areas, the technological advantages of US ground forces would be substantially reduced. Urban warfare was costly in lives, and mounting US casualties would damage the American military's morale. It would also foster an impression among the terrorists that the US could be defeated. If Israel saw that the US appeared to be losing Iraq, they might decide to take pre-emptive strikes. And if Israel waded in, the Islamic world would unite against the war.

Another nightmare scenario that Dan raised was the possibility that Saddam might use WMD against his own people again, in a desperate attempt to wipe out entire ethnic groups, such as the Kurds. If he could inflict enough casualties, the US might be forced to accept demands for a ceasefire. US and coalition forces would have to operate in full protective NBC gear, which would slow operations considerably. Part of me felt that Dan was explaining all of this to justify their attempts to wipe out huge numbers of Iraqi troops, using the MOABs. He seemed to think that the fewer survived, the less trouble they could cause.

But I saw things differently: it was one thing to win the war, but to win the peace would be more difficult. To achieve it, you had to bring the Iraqi people on-side. Some people seemed to have forgotten all too quickly the lessons learnt from the last Gulf War. Then, Iraqi Republican Guards units had withstood intense US bombing in the weeks before Desert Storm. If they could do so then, they could do so now – with the added knowledge that US forces had tricked them into giving out their co-ordinates, then betrayed them.

On the up-side, an impressive US victory over Iraq might strengthen Washington's hand in pressing both sides for a resolution to the Arab–Israeli conflict. As the prospect for peace in Israel was now tantalisingly close, it was feared that anti-Israeli terror groups would be pulling out all the stops to derail any peace settlement. Intel had shown that some terrorists were more than aware that a stable Iraq could lead to a settlement between the Palestinians and Israel. They had not been slow in organising their groups to flood into Iraq as soon as the invasion had started, but the longer offensive operations dragged on the greater the danger. The US would also have to insist on dealing with a Palestinian leadership that was truly interested in peace, which meant finding a successor to Yasser Arafat.

'So, who's going to take out Arafat and when?' Doug enquired. He had returned quietly some time ago, and until now had been listening attentively to what Dan had to say.

'We are, as soon as we've finished here,' Dan replied.

'Are you being serious?' I asked.

He laughed. 'No. Well, maybe . . . Hell, who knows?'

We'd been talking for a long time when Dan decided it was time to leave. 'You'll have to wait here until Kosrat turns up,' he said finally, then climbed aboard the lead Humvee and disappeared with his convoy into the night.

I had a better sense now of the burden of responsibility he was shouldering, Romero too, even if we didn't agree with some of his analysis, in particular the need to wipe out the Republican Guards units. But there was no doubt that the conflict was more complex and explosive than anything we had been involved in before.

I didn't expect Kosrat to turn up for at least another two days, and the idea of sitting around doing nothing wasn't appealing. But I knew why Dan wanted me to deal with him: for the past few days he'd been around Kirkuk, sussing it out and preparing for the Peshmerga to assault the city. If I was to stop the Kurds taking it, I needed Kosrat's influence to hold them back. On the radio, Massoud Barzani, Wajy's brother, and Zalmay Khalilzad, the US Special Envoy to free Iraqis, were giving a press conference in Salahuddin, in southern Kurdistan, detailing how more US troops would be deployed into Kurdish-controlled areas.

The following morning I was checking in with Tosh when I spotted a convoy of vehicles pulling up the track towards our LUP. It was Kosrat and his Peshmerga lads, with a SEAL team driving Humvees. Further along the road more US 173rd Airborne troops were tabbing into the area.

'Have we any tanks yet?' Kosrat called as he approached, his face creased into a smile.

'No. Some are on the way up from the south,' I replied, 'but they'll take several days to get here.'

Kosrat said he was eager to get into Kirkuk, but he wanted tanks in support and *didn't* want to wait several days. When Wajy joined us he, too, expressed his eagerness to move on Kirkuk. Kosrat looked at me long and hard. 'Why?' he asked, 'can't we do it without tanks? We have many, many people and all are ready to rise up as soon as they see us coming. We can take the city within a day.'

By now I was used to the Kurdish way: macho shows of strength were not uncommon – the more grenades and bandoliers you had strapped to you, the more of a man you were. But I also knew that, more often than not, they backed up these verbal shows of strength with action. In the back of my mind I could hear Dan's voice: no matter what, the Kurds had to stay out of Kirkuk.

'We need to look at the practicalities, and the aerial assets we can bring to bear,' I replied, as I struggled to find a convincing reason for them to delay.

'You look troubled, my friend,' said Wajy softly.

I glanced at him and said nothing. But there was no hiding the facts on this one: Wajy and Kosrat knew that something was up, and I knew that unless I levelled with them I'd lose their trust and they'd hare off to Kirkuk regardless. So, what did I have to lose, I asked myself, if I told them the truth? That the Americans would use 'any measures' to stop them taking Kirkuk. At least it might make them think twice before they did anything foolish. But if I did tell them the truth, I was taking one hell of a gamble. I had visions of being sent back to the UK in disgrace – Tosh would love that. Of all the decisions I'd made in my military career, this was the most difficult yet.

'Listen, both of you,' I began, still unsure of exactly how much I'd tell them, 'I'm sure you're more than aware of the Turkish position, and how they'd feel if you took Kirkuk. They'll not allow you to stay. Under no circumstances and not negotiable.'

Wajy nodded, and I knew that Dan's warnings of the previous evening were fresh in his mind.

'My advice, Kosrat, would be to use your people and network to locate Saddam. Make him your priority. Make yourself indispensable and well known internationally, then make your move to secure Kirkuk. You're going to have to plan long-term on this one, if you want the city back as yours,' I continued.

'Are you mad, my friend?' Kosrat was amazed. 'You know how much Kirkuk means to us. Besides, it is almost within our grasp. What do you think I have been doing for the past few days? I have many, many fighters poised to enter the city, from many sides, as does Massoud Barzani, Wajy's brother.'

It was time to bite the bullet.

'Wajy, Kosrat, I gave you my word and promised that I'd come with you all the way,' I said, 'and if that means you going into

Kirkuk, then that's where I shall follow.' I paused to battle with my fears as to whether I was doing the right thing.

'But you have orders to stop us . . . by any means,' Wajy said quietly, as if he was continuing my sentence for me.

I could see betrayal in their eyes, as they knew that what Wajy had said was true – they could read it in mine. Kosrat placed his AK47 on the table and held it there in front of us.

'No, Kosrat, we will not need that,' Wajy said calmly.

Just then Doug loomed into view at the tent opening, his GPMG half raised and ready.

'And we won't need *that*,' I said, waving his gun away. 'As Wajy may have overheard last night, those are indeed my orders,' I said, as calmly and sincerely as I could. 'But they are orders I'm not prepared to carry out. My word is my bond and I will honour it. When I promise something, I stick to it.

'Last night Wajy heard all about the bigger-picture scenario and why it's important that you do not take full control of Kirkuk at this moment,' I continued. 'The Americans feel the world is against them on this war. They feel they have to pacify Turkey, because Turkish troops moving into Iraq to do battle with you guys at Kirkuk would be a disaster for them. Plus, the Saudis and other states don't want you guys taking over Kirkuk's oilfields – well, not without any safeguards, anyway.'

'Then let the Saudis and the Turks come,' Kosrat replied defiantly. 'It is our city and we will fight and defeat them.'

'Kosrat, my orders are that if you take Kirkuk we have to stop you doing so by whatever means. As I've said, I will not carry out those orders. But I am going to appeal to you to trust me. Delay your assault on Kirkuk – at least hold back and remain outside the city's boundaries until we can sort out something to pacify the Turks, and all the other countries that have a take on this one,' I pleaded.

Doug came in now and sat down. 'Look, me old mates,' he said, as he plonked his GPMG down on the table next to Wajy's AK47, 'problem is, even if this one here refuses to carry out those Nazi orders, I'm afraid we know of some others who won't hesitate to do so. They ain't all as honourable as this one. And once that happens, there's going to be a lot of your people get hurt.'

'So, I am going to have to think about it,' Kosrat said.

'I swear on my family's lives, I will be with you all the way, whatever you choose,' I told Kosrat, as he stood up.

'I will speak with my brothers on this matter,' Kosrat replied, somewhat formally. 'Then we will let you know our decision. As for Saddam, he's mine already.'

'Whatever happens, know that my word is everything to me and I give it again now. I am with you. We'll cross whatever bridges as they come,' I told him.

'I trust you, my friend, I do, but this changes much,' Kosrat responded.

Wajy walked up to me, gave me a bear-hug, then stood back. 'Goodbye, my friend. May Allah always smile upon you and your family,' he said.

Wajy was clearly upset, and those bloody instincts of mine kicked in, telling me that this was the last time we would see him alive. 'Take very good care of yourself until we meet again,' I replied, trying to sound positive.

It was only then that I noticed that Twin One had been standing just outside the opening. He asked if he could stay with us, and Wajy said yes. To me that was an encouraging sign. Within moments, Wajy and Kosrat were good to go, leaving just a handful of Peshmerga with us. It was the parting of the ways all right.

'Remember – if you get hold of Saddam, make sure you have at least one US lad with you to confirm it was you who got him,' I shouted to Kosrat, as he made for his vehicle. 'If you don't, Mr Bush won't believe you.'

He smiled broadly. 'My friend, you worry far too much,' he shouted. 'You should be a Kurd, not an Englishman, and learn not to worry. I will find the lowliest American man I can to witness me capture Saddam, so as to rub salt in his wounds of humiliation. That will take away the glory that your Mr Dan longs for.'

As Wajy's driver put his Toyota in gear and moved the vehicle away, Wajy passed me with an arm outstretched. I brushed his hand in farewell. Within minutes the convoy had wound down the track below us and vanished.

'He's dead,' Doug stated as I turned back to our shelter. 'You know it and I know it.'

'Wajy?' I asked.

'Wajy.' He nodded.

'You got that feeling too?'

'We ain't going to see him again, not alive, anyway.'

I sat down at the table and tried to forget my premonition. After all, I had bigger things to worry about. I'd just told the Peshmerga leaders that we had orders to stop them 'by any means' if they went ahead and took Kirkuk. At this very moment, Kosrat was probably rushing off to tell his lot and all hell would be let loose. We could even end up in a direct confrontation with our Peshmerga friends, as Dan had warned all along. Not to mention all the SEAL lads presently stationed alongside the Peshmerga units across the region.

How many lives had I put at risk? I asked myself. How many might die as a result of what I'd just done? But there had been no alternative, as far as I could see. I sat down to compose a message to Dan and Quigly. 'Be advised have informed Kosrat *et al* of true nature of my orders re stopping them entering Kirkuk,' I began. No doubt about it, I was going to be in some serious shit this time. I had more than overstepped the mark. But I felt I had judged Wajy and Kosrat correctly – although I doubted that Dan and Quigly would see things that way.

'Reckon you might be losing me back to the UK for a court martial. At least it'll please Tosh,' I told Doug, as I scribbled out my message.

'You're not going anywhere, boss,' he replied. 'You're too good at this game and I think you called it right. If Wajy, Kosrat and their lot all tear-arse into Kirkuk, it's on their heads, ain't it? And if fucking Tosh thinks he's coming out to run the show in your place, I'll be leaving with you.'

Doug had no idea how much his remark lifted me. I think he had more faith in my ability than I did. I said a silent thank you that Destiny had put him at my side.

As I made myself some coffee Malcolm came up with a message from Tosh. I knew immediately that something was wrong.

'What is it, Malc?'

'Bad news, boss. You know your mate Steve, from UKLF– CSG (United Kingdom Landing Force – Command Support Group)?' Malcolm passed me a slip of paper.

My good friend Major Steve Baldwin had collapsed and died suddenly while deployed in theatre with the Royal Marines 3 Commando Brigade. It was sad news but I had been fearing worse – a message from Quigly, maybe, that the Peshmerga were turning on the SEALs as a direct result of my conversation that morning with Wajy and Kosrat. It was an hour or more since I'd sent my message to Quigly and Dan, and I had not received a response.

Half an hour later there were more messages from Tosh. One warned us to be on the lookout for Iranians now entering the area: they were believed to be on their way to spread further anarchy and mayhem. If they could destabilise Iraq, they hoped to install a puppet government that would ultimately be run by the mullahs. Bring it on, I thought. What next? Tosh's second message told me that again my full wages hadn't been paid into my account, which meant a cheque I'd given Victoria had bounced. Apparently she was pissed off with me big-time. There was nothing I could do about it but I'd try to call her, if I could get a signal on Doug's mobile.

When Quigly finally responded, it was an encrypted teletype message, and I was surprised by how measured it was. He recommended we sit tight and wait to see what the Peshmerga would do. Under no circumstances were we to relay to Head Shed, Cent Com or General Franks that I had revealed my orders to the Peshmerga, and especially not that I'd said I wouldn't carry them out. He ended that I shouldn't worry too much 'as we look after our own'.

Well, that was strange. I'd been expecting them to publicise my maverick behaviour as widely as possible among the high command. Instead, they seemed desperate to keep it under wraps. Did that mean the order to waste the Kurds moving on Kirkuk hadn't been sanctioned? It was possible – in my mind, it was an illegal act and tantamount to murder. Were Dan and Quigly keeping the whole thing quiet because they'd been acting on their own and didn't want it to get out? If that was so and we'd carried out the orders, doubtless we'd have been the fall guys, whatever the truth of the matter.

I spent the rest of the day listening to the short-wave radio and writing Victoria a long letter, forwarding it to Tosh in sections so that he could send it on to her. I spent an hour on stag (sentry duty) drinking far too much coffee, looking out towards Mosul and trying to evaluate what would happen if the Peshmerga tried to take Kirkuk. I felt certain that Dan would not hesitate to call in airstrikes on them – and us, if we stayed with the Peshmerga. In this war, most aircraft were delivering PGMs and could do so in the dark and in all weathers. The US military had also been using unmanned aerial vehicles (UAVs – pilotless aircraft, or drones) to track and attack enemy targets. All Dan had to do was retask a drone to seek out and destroy our position, and that would be the end of us. They'd put it down to just another sad incident of friendly fire.

I couldn't work out whether Dan and Quigly's dirty tricks had been sanctioned from on high. And what would it matter, if no one ever found out about them? I knew of one Iraqi colonel who had tried to surrender to coalition forces, and look what had happened to him. Neither Dan nor Quigly was ever going to be held to account for it.

That evening, Tosh confirmed that SAS, SBS and Delta teams were now being deployed into the western deserts to track down and destroy MAZ-543 Scud missile-launchers, just as they had during the first Gulf War. I knew he wished he could be with those SAS lads now – he hadn't wanted to leave the Regiment: he'd been forced out, after getting too familiar with one of the female officers. When their affair had been discovered, one had had to leave, and political correctness had dictated that it wouldn't be the woman. Granted, Tosh had also pissed off most of his troop with his bad attitude, but he was a bright, intelligent officer, which was why my little outfit had found itself a new member.

As we sat over dinner, Malcolm caught up with part of what Dan had been talking about the night before. 'So what's all this stuff about "crossover", boss?' he asked. 'And why's it causing us so much hassle?'

'It's when they finally cop they're in the shit,' Doug said before I could speak, 'and start baling out, like rats from a sinking ship.'

'Yeah. Crossover only happens when the war's well under way,' I put in. 'That's why covert operations like ours are so important, plus the use of deception and misinformation. Once Saddam's commanders believe the regime's doomed, they'll calculate the risk of remaining with him and facing an unsympathetic Allied coalition against the risk of attempting to overthrow him or refusing to execute his orders. That's when we hope they'll cross to our side.'

Once I'd finished explaining, Malcolm sat in quiet contemplation for a few seconds.

'It's all bollocks to me, boss,' he finally said, getting to his feet. 'Think I need another wank, as the boredom's getting to me.'

'Don't fucking use my water bottle,' Baby Steve remarked from where he was sitting monitoring the radio.

'Don't worry, mate, I've been using Guss's,' Malcolm replied, as he turned to leave. 'It's far more satisfying.'

As the night drew in and it got colder, I was stiff and aching. I was wheezing and I could taste blood, which wasn't a good sign. In fact, I was falling apart after so long roughing it and with so little down-time. I hate to think what was crawling around in my hair and my lips were chapped. I needed baby lotion fast.

It was during SAS selection that I'd discovered the wonders of baby lotion. I was being wound up about RTI (resistance to interrogation) and the nasty things that would happen to me – verbal and physical abuse, possible sexual molestation: if I couldn't accept it, I could leave. Of course, it was all psychological nonsense but I had my doubts, especially when they told me I needed to bring in a small bottle of baby lotion, a wooden spoon, a Durex, a latex or Marigold rubber glove, curry powder, women's tights and an onion. All kinds of images sprang to mind of being slapped with the spoon, made to sniff curry powder, and having an onion smeared with baby lotion forced up my backside, so I was pleased to learn that these items were considered essential for any SAS soldier's survival out in the field.

Tights were used as leg warmers and even head-overs. The wooden spoon was to eat with – it wouldn't clank against your metal mess tin and give away your position. The Durex had three uses: to keep grit and rain out of your rifle; to use as an emergency water container; and to protect your private parts, when wading through swamps or jungle rivers, by stopping any nasty surprises crawling up the urethra. And, of course, it was for protected sex, should the rare opportunity arise. The curry powder was to add to meals as it kills most bacteria when heated – and adds flavour to otherwise crap food. The onion was to keep sore throats and colds at bay; also, when you're exhausted a bite of a juicy, raw onion can give you miles more. The rubber glove was an emergency airbag to plug chest wounds, or a water-holder; I also learnt how to fill it with simple household chemicals to turn it into a device that could blow off a door or turn a car on to its side. The baby lotion was to keep exposed skin moist – as it dries out, cracks and bleeds all too quickly. Then the cracks become infected, and fairly soon you're unable to operate a radio or even your weapon.

I'd spent nearly twenty-four hours waiting for news of Wajy and Kosrat when Tosh came on the net, frantic. News of my open and honest talk with them had reached General Franks and Head Shed – in fact, everyone seemed to know. This time the fan had fallen into the shit. The real risk that the Peshmerga could turn on us was viewed as serious. I felt sick: I'd screwed up big-time. I was ordered to stand down and do nothing until further notice. The knock-on consequence was that all US troops in the north were ordered to pause for the next four to six days. The official reason given publicly was supply shortages and stiff Iraqi resistance, so I spent many tense hours kicking my heels.

Dan blew a fuse when his SEAL team were ordered to rest, having given close support to Peshmerga forces attacking Ansar al-Islam groups. I spent some time talking to Twin One, who missed his lifelong friend deeply, but was very proud of him. We took it in turns to catch up on sleep, but the longer the delay in hearing back from Wajy and Kosrat extended, the more con-cerned we became, especially Dan.

The Peshmerga lads continued with their tasks as Dan and Quigly tried to liaise with Massoud Barzani and Jalal Talabani to keep the momentum going. Dan deliberated on whether to let the other SEALs know the score so that they were on their guard if the Peshmerga turned on them. Then, contrary to my earlier orders, we received warning that we were to help direct airstrikes against Iraqi tanks, which were harassing a Peshmerga unit.

Doug, Athansa, Romero, Malcolm and I had started to prepare for the job, surprised but pleased after having been stood down, when Quigly came on the net with an urgent message: Wajy had made contact. He and Kosrat had reacted well to my honesty, and accepted that it was not in their best interests to take Kirkuk and stay there at this juncture in the conflict. I could tell that Quigly was hugely relieved – and I could have cried for joy.

The SEAL team working with Kosrat had sent his message direct to Quigly, but it was clearly meant to be read by us as well: 'You only had to ask us and we would have come to some arrangement,' Kosrat stated. 'You only had to trust us to be sensible and fair, as we are trusting you.' I was amazed at the grace, manners and respect his words displayed – especially when it was compared with the way we had behaved. Kosrat stated he had never truly trusted the US policy-makers and commanders – a clear dig at Dan – so he had not been surprised to learn of my orders to stop them taking Kirkuk 'by any means'. His final sentence said that he would deal with me because he trusted me. Suddenly, in Dan and Quigly's view, I had become an asset and the sun shone out of my backside.

I was good to go when Tosh sent an urgent encrypted message he'd received from Northwood, instructing me under no circumstances to go on the airstrike co-ordination job but to await orders and a new RV to meet up with Wajy and Kosrat. I said that Guss should go in my place but Romero shook his head. 'No way,' he said. 'We'll go as we are. Smaller the better.'

'Well, I'm staying with the boss,' Doug chipped in, and dropped his GPMG on the table. 'Take Ian in my place.'

'I'll go if I can have the Gimpy,' Ian said, and nodded at Doug's GPMG. It made sense: they'd have some serious firepower with them.

'What?' said Doug incredulously. 'You want my baby? Well, all right.' He handed it over. 'But if you don't look after her, I'll slot you my fucking self.'

I confirmed to Tosh that I'd received the message and would stand down. Malcolm squeezed himself into the passenger seat of the Humvee beside Athansa as Romero, checking the Pilkington laser target designators, and Ian climbed into the back.

A few minutes after they had left, Baby Steve came over, looking puzzled. 'Boss, there's something weird about that last message from Tosh,' he said. 'I can't find any call-sign confirmation for it.'

Each time we received a message with an order or some other item that required action, it always had an authentication code attached, which told us who had sent it and from where. So, if we received a message to withdraw, surrender, blow up the Peshmerga commanders or worse, we could confirm that the orders were genuine and not from a rogue source. But the message for me to stay put had no authentication code. As it had come through Tosh, we had not even thought to check until Baby Steve had pointed it out.

Doug suspected that Tosh might have sent the order himself just to stop me getting 'trigger time'. He got straight on to Tosh to get him to reconfirm who had sent the message. Tosh replied that he had obviously misplaced the authentication code, and blamed it on tiredness. Ten minutes later he came back to us: there was no authentication code, but the message had come from Head Shed in Northwood. The fuck-up was theirs, he maintained. My alarm bells were ringing and so were Doug's. I got on the radio to Malcolm, explained the situation and told them to watch their backs. Then I got both Guss and Tosh to confirm that the job was legit, and that air cover had been tasked to the mission. It took them half an hour to confirm that two F16s were dedicated to the mission and that it was indeed genuine.

I wondered if I was getting a bit paranoid and jumpy. I knew we were stressed and tired. But Doug was uneasy too. He went outside to set more claymores, and put extra Peshmerga lads on guard in a higher OP. I knew that the NSA boys in Maryland, USA, would have been monitoring all transmissions from Iraq, as well as the British intel people from 1001 Signals, at Rudloe Manor, an RAF base in Wiltshire, so maybe they had picked up my message to Quigly about coming clean to the Kurds. If they had, Head Shed might know about it, despite Quigly's efforts to keep them in the dark. Either way, there wasn't much we could do about it but wait.

Romero had his team in position just before sunrise and spent an uncomfortable day holed up in a LUP directing as FAC. We sat and listened to sitreps from Malcolm until the early hours. It was the beginning of April and my son's birthday at the end of the month and I'd promised him I'd be home for it. Now, that was looking unlikely. A signal from Head Shed warned us to put on chemical suits as US Infantry were about to enter Baghdad's Red Zone. We didn't bother. A message also informed us that Major General Stanley McChrystal had confirmed that two top Iraqi Republican Guards units, the Medina and Baghdad divisions, were no longer credible forces as they had been bombed senseless.

We kicked our heels for another twenty-four hours, and frustration mounted. At lunchtime Quigly came through that Romero's FAC work had been spot on: satellite imaging confirmed that the Iraqi arms sites they had targeted were completely destroyed. Guss relayed this to Romero, with instructions for them to return immediately to our position. An hour later they were due to check in with a sitrep, but nothing came through when Guss tried to raise them on the radio. Tosh had heard nothing either. We spent the entire afternoon and early evening trying to contact them, but with no luck. Something had happened to them.

Eventually Tosh informed the CSAR chopper and gave them the co-ordinates of the ERV Romero had identified prior to his departure. Doug wanted to go out and trace their route, in case we could find them, but I decided against it: we had to stay put so that we could move at a moment's notice if they called for help, but also in case Wajy and Kosrat decided to turn up. As awful as it was, we had to sit and wait. We told ourselves that Malcolm, Romero, Athansa and Ian were big enough and ugly enough to look after themselves.

'Do your spook bit, boss,' Doug said, as he passed me some dinner. Curry again. He wanted me to try my sixth sense to work out what had happened to them. Usually if I sat down, relaxed and concentrated on something, I got a feel for what was going on. It worked well when I was tired. I did my best, and I had the impression that the lads were in trouble, but would come out of it all right. Using the main roads to hare round the war zone had always been a gamble, but the length and breadth of our operational area was too large not to.

We waited for the CSAR chopper to head into the ERV at the predetermined pick-up time, 01.00 hours that night. We listened in on the comms as it went in, and I prayed that Romero and the boys would be there. The chopper put down and waited, but no one turned up. Tosh was our liaison with the aircrew and I asked him to encourage the pilot to stay on the ground as long as he dared. Five minutes maximum is all you are normally allowed: a large bird on the deck makes an inviting target. The CSAR crew stayed there for a full ten minutes. When they pulled out empty-handed, the mood in our tarpaulin tent city was sombre.

Three hours later, one of the Peshmerga lads on sentry came rushing into our position, whispering excitedly. He and Twin One had seen figures moving towards us, but they couldn't make out who it was. As I grabbed my weapon, Doug was already in the aim, following the outline of a shadow cast against the tarpaulin by the light of the moon. Whoever was out there must have known exactly where our security perimeter was to have been able to sneak through it.

'Fucking shit security,' we heard Malcolm announce.

Then Romero eased aside the tarpaulin and his head popped into view. 'Your guards are shit,' he said, with a grin.

'Yeah, well, you almost got your arses shot to fuck,' Doug replied, barely able to suppress his delight at seeing them.

After a major back-slapping session, we radioed Tosh and confirmed that all four had returned safe and well, then sat down to hear their story. They'd taken the main road back to our LUP – they knew that every Iraqi in the region had more sense than to use it with all the Allied aircraft on the prowl. They'd been burning down an open section when Malcolm had noticed a bright glow, like a flare, shining off to the right. Athansa had taken one look at it, screeched to a halt and was out of the door and running as he yelled, '*Incoming!*'

The others bailed out in separate directions and, moments later, a Maverick missile slammed into the Humvee, turning it into a ball of flame. As it burned, an Apache AH68 chopper appeared over the horizon and pounded the wrecked vehicle with 20mm cannon fire. As the Humvee was a blazing wreck, the pilot had decided not to use thermal imaging, or so Romero believed. If he had, he might have spotted the four bodies lying in the immediate area.

Once the chopper had withdrawn, they started to make their way back to the LUP, as they were nearer to it than they were to the ERV. It had been sheer good luck that Malcolm had seen the tail-end rocket flame from the Maverick as it headed towards them, and even more so that Athansa recognised it.

At sun-up we received a message from Wajy. He wanted us to meet him and also Kosrat's forces on 6 April at a major junction on the approach to Kirkuk just south of Arbil. We had twenty-four hours to kill so took it in turns to heat some water for a mess-tin wash. After weeks of living in filth, it felt like luxury to have some boiling water for a hands, underarm and crotch wash. We hadn't shaved for weeks and looked wilder than the Pesh lads. I glanced into a mirror and was horrified at the state of me: I had spots all over my face, red eyes and dirty beard.

Late that evening I sat in one of the Humvees and managed to get a call through to Victoria. It was a bad line, but at least we could talk. I leant against the door, feet up, and tried to relax as we chatted. Victoria panicked when she heard me swear, then a clang and a loud thump. We were cut off and she thought the worst, until I got back to her. I'd been leaning on the Humvee door, opened it by accident and tumbled out. She laughed, but in the next breath she was singing Tosh's praises. When she paused, I told her that, once I was back, I was out of this game for good. She didn't say much, and by the end of the conversation I'd decided I wouldn't call her again. From the start, Doug had decided not to call Sara: he believed it wouldn't improve his concentration and focus. A good text session about sex was a different matter, he joked. Now I had to agree with him.

The following morning we packed up our kit and headed in a convoy of four vehicles for the RV with Wajy, Kosrat's lot, Dan and many of his SEALs at a crossroads thirty miles south-east of Mosul. As we drove along the main road, we could see coalition aircraft carrying out airstrikes on distant Iraqi positions. Guss liaised frantically with the aircrews – we didn't want a repeat of the Apache blue-on-blue incident. We arrived at the RV, to find several trucks and other Peshmerga already there. I laughed when I saw pictures of Bush and Blair taped across their munitions pouches. The landscape was sweeping, rolling hills.

The crossroads was a major junction, with Iraqi positions clearly visible less than a kilometre away across the valley. B52s were pounding the Iraqis while F15s and F18s were giving CAS. One strike sent up huge plumes of debris and many Iraqis ran out of their fortified positions across a bridge that spanned the river, only to be cut down in a hail of fire from a group of Peshmerga who had set up a position at the other end of the bridge. The sun was climbing higher as well as the temperature when Dan's convoy rolled into view, an assortment of pick-ups and desert-coloured Humvees that stuck out in the green surroundings.

Wajy was still some twenty minutes' drive away and I was glad to know that I would see him again, after all. Dan didn't say much, but directed his SEALs to fan out into defensive positions as two began to direct F15s on to Iraqi targets. We were in open country so we couldn't hide the wagons. Malcolm spotted an Iraqi T55 tank moving towards the bridge below us, where the Peshmerga were positioned. Romero and Athansa linked up with Dan's SEALs, and moved down towards the bridge area to deal with it. When I looked north, I saw Wajy's convoy heading towards us. I got on the net and informed Tosh that we were only waiting for Kosrat now.

Dan walked to the main crossroads with several of his SEALs to Wajy. As the convoy stopped, people greeted each other. I saw a camera crew filming; when they swung in our direction I turned my back. There was going to be trouble with the T55 tank, I realised, because it had been joined by another, with more following. I took a message from Tosh that Kosrat had been delayed by some thirty minutes, which, I reckoned, should give us time enough to deal with the tanks. Doug and I jumped into our wagon and headed for the bridge. We had several LAW 80s with us, which could easily deal with a T55. By the time we got there, the SEALs were on the air to a pair of F15 pilots.

Suddenly Dan arrived behind us in a Humvee, having decided he would help deal with the tanks. Doug and I took a LAW 80 each and armed them. We ran alongside the slightly raised riverbank out of sight of the tanks to try to hit them as they turned to manoeuvre. As the first tank edged on to the far end of the bridge we'd found a suitable position. Dan and his SEAL FAC lad had better get their fingers out, I thought. We could hit the tank opposite us and the one just behind it but not the one now almost on the bridge. Rounds started biting into the dirt just above our heads – the tank commander had seen us.

We scurried along a little further, then popped up. The rounds switched to our new position. I levelled the LAW 80, flipped up the green perspex sight screen and tried for a site picture but dirt was kicking up in front of me from impacting bullets as others cracked overhead. Then there was a whoosh as Doug fired his weapon and ducked out of harm's way. His aim was spot on: he'd hit the tank just beneath the main gun mantle at the front. The commander tried to leap out but an explosion tore through the vehicle, immediately followed by another, which sent the turret up and to the right on to the commander. Flames roared upwards as if they were being bellowed in a furnace. The commander and gunner from the T55 behind it jumped out and fled while the driver started backing it up.

All the while I could hear the pitch and whine of the two F15s circling overhead. I rolled over, set the LAW 80 back to safe and scanned the sky to see where the F15s were, expecting them to be almost overhead. They were further back. I watched the first plane dive and release its bombload. I followed the trajectory of the brightly painted white bombs with red stripes falling fast.

Idiots! They'd released them far too early – no way would they hit the tank on the bridge. They must be aiming at another coming in from behind us, I thought.

'Fuck! It's gonna be a blue-on-blue!' Doug shouted, and jumped to his feet.

11

CONVOY OF DEATH

From our position we couldn't see the airstrike, only hear the explosions. We ran back to our wagon as Dan stood up, his face ashen, as the SEAL next to him frantically called the F15 pilots to abort a second run and attempt new co-ordinates. The T55 on the bridge clanked to a halt and its crew abandoned it. I realised our lads might have been hit. We jumped aboard our wagon, and as we crossed the brow of the field we could see several vehicles well ablaze at the main crossroads, their occupants as well as engine blocks and chassis.

As we bounced towards the road, I saw Malcolm and Ian rushing towards the strike zone. My fears grew for Romero, Athansa and Wajy. We pulled up two hundred metres short, dived out and ran forwards. I could see a cameraman filming, panning the scene of carnage as a journalist talked. Several vehicles were burning fiercely and small-arms ammunition fired off in the flames. I was carrying my medikit, Malcolm had a full field trauma pack and Ian saline solution bags.

It soon became apparent that many were beyond help. Smouldering body parts lay among the burning debris. Those who had survived were marked with shrapnel wounds, some serious. SEAL lads were already ministering to the wounded who were lying around, some in agony. And still I could hear the journalist talking as he was filmed.

'Fucking diabolical,' Doug said, nodding at them.

Three vehicles, including what looked like Wajy's Toyota, were relatively intact but with flames pouring out of the sides. As we rushed from vehicle to vehicle, it was obvious we could do nothing for those still inside, but where were Wajy, Romero and Athansa? Several SEALs had been injured but it was difficult to tell who was whom, as the dead were badly mutilated. Further along, another vehicle was beginning to burn. Several Peshmerga and SEALs were trying to pull out the driver, who was pinned into his seat by the steering column.

As two Peshmerga tried to douse the engine fire, which was growing in intensity, flames licked down on to the road, ignited the spilt fuel that ran under the vehicle, then leapt to the rear and the fuel tank.

'It's going to blow!' yelled a SEAL.

All dived away except one Peshmerga who was still trying to pull out the still conscious driver when the vehicle exploded into flames, throwing him backwards, his upper torso and head alight.

The trapped driver screamed, '*Kill me! Kill me!*' in agony. Two SEALs were knocking out the flames on the lad who had been blown backwards, but through the smoke to my left, I saw a figure emerge, aiming his C7 straight at the vehicle. Bang! Bang! The driver stopped screaming. It was Romero. He was safe, thank God, and had ended the driver's agony. Athansa was busy administering first aid. The few who had life-threatening injuries were being treated where they had fallen. I went from person to person asking after Wajy.

As the flames died away, leaving burnt and smouldering shells, we could see the remains of those inside. We checked each vehicle, looking for Wajy, but to no avail. Twelve vehicles had been destroyed; seventeen fighters and a civilian translator were now dead. It was fifteen minutes before Kakameen Mustafa, the KDP regional commander who had been travelling with Wajy, informed us that Wajy had been seriously injured in the head and was being rushed to a hospital in nearby Arbil. He kept telling us it wasn't our fault: 'We don't blame you. This is war, and everything happens in war.'

But that didn't take away the gut-wrenching feeling that it was our fault. It was only as I turned back to the reporter, who was still talking about the scene from hell he was witnessing, that I recognised him as John Simpson, the BBC world affairs correspondent. We still had Iraqis less than a thousand metres away to contend with as well as co-ordinating the airstrikes, so I grabbed Romero and Doug. It was then that a truly horrible thought struck me.

Dan was with the FAC lad who had co-ordinated the air-strike, and his words about Wajy and Kosrat echoed in my mind: that whatever force necessary should be used to stop them taking Kirkuk. Perhaps this 'friendly fire' incident had been intended to resolve the situation. Thankfully, Kosrat's lot had been delayed or they too would have been among the casualties. *No, surely not.* I felt incredibly angry in case it was true. Wajy had better survive, I thought, and stay calm and get the facts before you go off on one.

'Boss, let's see what help we can give here. Phil can check the situation down there,' Doug suggested. Many injured and shocked individuals were still milling about.

'Boss, you need to calm down,' he added.

Even Romero nodded in agreement, but I was hyped up as I set off to confront Dan. Doug grabbed my arm and stopped me. His face said it all. And he was right: we had casualties who needed help, as well as the remainder of the Peshmerga to refocus.

Malcolm rushed over to tell me that Kosrat had heard the bad news. He wouldn't now link up with us at this location but would head for the remainder of his forces and Jalal Talabani's massing around Kirkuk. He had also requested that I join him as soon as possible. Massoud Barzani's brother had been on the net via one of the SEALs' radios, extremely angry and upset, wanting details of his brother's condition.

Then Quigly came on demanding a full update: they were getting images live from BBC News 24. Tosh was sending request after request for a sitrep, but we left him until last, then confirmed we were OK. He was receiving demands from General Franks, at CentCom, and Northwood for a full sitrep. As I headed to our wagon for the field surgery packs I nearly stood on someone's head. It had landed in the grass and looked perfectly normal and undamaged, as if the owner was asleep, but from the neck down there was only a section of spine, covered with blood and strips of muscle. It didn't look real. I grabbed the medical supplies and headed back.

John Simpson had been accompanying the convoy of US Special Forces and Kurdish fighters, with Wajy's group, and even now was still broadcasting. 'Well, it's a bit of a disaster . . . I was in a convoy of eight or ten cars in northern Iraq, coming up to a place that has recently been captured. American Special Forces in a truck – two trucks, I think, beside them, plus a very senior figure,' he blurted out as one of the specially trained SEAL medics approached him. 'Shut up, I'm broadcasting live!' he said loudly. The SEAL said something to him. 'Oh, yes, I'm fine – am I bleeding?' he asked.

'You've got a cut,' he answered.

'I thought you were going to stop me filming,' Simpson replied, and continued to broadcast, stating that he had shrapnel in his leg and that the man was an American Special Forces medic. Simpson had counted ten or twelve bodies around him. He went on to explain in detail that there were Americans dead, that an American plane had dropped the bomb.

'This is just a scene from hell here. All the vehicles on fire. There are bodies burning around me, there are bodies lying around, there are bits of bodies on the ground. This is a really bad own goal by the Americans,' he said loudly – mainly because his eardrums had burst during the explosion.

Apparently the presenter Maxine Mawhinney, at BBC News 24, asked him to recap. Simpson apologised for being so excitable and repeated that a US Special Forces convoy had been hit and, yes, many were dead. I was half pissed off that he was still broadcasting but also half impressed.

'I saw this American convoy, and they bombed it. They hit their own people – they may have hit this Kurdish figure, very senior, and they've killed a lot of ordinary characters, and I am just looking at the bodies now and it is not a pretty sight,' he stated.

As Simpson signed off I knew it was time I got moving. Later he filed a report stating that the officer in charge of the American Special Forces had seen an Iraqi tank on the plain about a mile from us; it was firing in our direction and he had called in an airstrike to deal with it. Simpson had seen two American F15 planes circling quite low overhead and he had a bad feeling about it because they seemed closer to the convoy than they were to the tank. He said he had seen the bomb coming out of one of the planes and watched it come down. It was painted white and red and crashed into the ground ten or twelve metres from where he was standing. It took the lower legs off Kamaran, his translator, and he got shrapnel in parts of his body. He would have got a chunk in his spine, had he not been wearing a flak jacket – it was buried deep in the Kevlar. A piece of shrapnel an inch long was taken out of the producer's boot.

Simpson told the world that, as far as he could work out, there was a burned-out Iraqi tank at the crossroads and he suspected that either the pilot had got the navigational details wrong or that he had seen the burned-out tank, assumed it was to be hit and dropped the bomb. Simpson concluded that mistakes happen when you are fighting a war.

It was some fucking big mistake all right.

As I walked to the end of the convoy, I saw a woman checking the smashed windscreen on a sports utility vehicle. I asked if she was OK as she looked a little disoriented. She was telling me that she was a radio reporter from the Canadian Broadcasting Corporation and her name was Margaret Evans when a mortar round landed almost smack in the centre of the blast crater from the airstrike. The Iraqis were still trying it on.

It was another forty minutes before we'd done all we could to help and load the dead with over forty injured on to vehicles. Among them, Massoud Barzani's son, Mansour, was slightly hurt and, in Wajy's absence, now commanded the KDP Special Forces.

With the imminent arrival of US troops and back-up, there was nothing more to do except get the rest of the convoy moving again. I went to the FAC location to find Dan, but he was nowhere to be seen. Only the young SEAL FAC lad was carrying on as if nothing had happened. I felt like kicking him as he sat on a Humvee, calmly calling in the next IP and co-ordinates as the fighting continued less than two hundred metres away. Soon Romero heard that Dan had moved out to catch up with Kosrat's lot and to meet Massoud Barzani: he wanted to explain what had happened and placate them.

Senior KDP commanders Saeed Abdullah, Abdul Rahman and Mamasta Hehman had also been injured in the attack. We found out that there had been three other FAC operators in our area and any of them could have been responsible for the error – or maybe

239

the pilot hadn't checked his way points and absolutes, perhaps a little over-confident.

The battle lines were changing over a huge distance between Pir Dawad and Dibagah 25 miles south-west of Arbil, but like everyone else I wanted answers and, most importantly, I needed to know that Dan hadn't orchestrated the attack; I had no idea what I'd do if he had. Shoot him myself?

Many of the Peshmerga still with us reorganised themselves ready to reinforce attacks in Dibagah, where we should have been going once linked up with Wajy. Driving Iraqi forces from Dibagah would cut the main road connecting Mosul and Kirkuk.

As we collected ourselves, though, our thoughts were with Wajy.

Doug did his usual impression of a rally driver when we took off after Dan. Soon we heard, from Hoshyar Zebari, another senior KDP leader, that Wajy's condition was so serious that the US were about to airlift him to a better hospital in Germany. He assured us that this incident would have no negative impact on our relationship with the Kurds. 'It doesn't undermine our resolve to work together,' he said.

Doug and I glanced at each other. We had a feeling that Wajy was already dead but hoped we would be proved wrong. By now the war was hotting up fast all across the country. Baghdad International Airport was secured and US armoured combat troops had entered the heart of Baghdad, defeating Iraqi forces as they went. As yet, no chemicals had been used as they crossed into the Red Zone, and one of the last bridges leading to Mosul had been captured by the Peshmerga.

Tosh was going mad demanding a sitrep so I got Malcolm to tell him we'd link up with Kosrat and Dan just outside Kirkuk. Then, and I don't know how, Malcolm pulled out another full flask of coffee and poured us all a cup as we sped off.

We passed streams of US 173rd Airborne on foot and in Humvees. Kurds and Peshmerga were all over the place, in an assortment of vehicles ranging from military trucks to tractors, and it was almost dark when we crossed the Little Zab river. Tosh came on-line to inform us that eighteen people were confirmed dead from the airstrike. Investigators from JAG (Judicial Adjutant General) were already interviewing the pilot on board his carrier out in the Mediterranean.

Later Tosh told us that, sadly, Wajy had died from severe head trauma at the USAF military hospital in Germany. We had many of his KDP Special Forces with us and we weren't looking forward to telling them. When Dan turned up, he could tell them, I thought, and then explain to me the facts behind the blue-on-blue.

Phil had received orders requiring him to assist in the push south and head towards Iraq's capital. A large number of Kosrat's lot were with him or en route towards Tikrit, although they had been advised to wait until US forces could move into position near and around the city as it was accepted that some of the fiercest fighting would take place there. Most of the inhabitants were pro Saddam Hussein because it was his birth-place and hometown. Kosrat was convinced that he would be there. I had to agree.

Eventually we arrived at an RV in an old car park on the outskirts of Kirkuk at a former beauty spot, where we met Romero's SEAL friend Ryan, but no Dan. He'd been redir-ected to the furthest side of Kirkuk to meet Jalal Talabani, if he was there. Intel was coming in that the Iranians were now trying to kick off on the borders, and it was feared that they might try to settle some old scores or grab some land. We needed a large number of Peshmerga to move and engage any cross-border insurgents discreetly. Doug thought that the next forty-eight hours might prove to be the defining moments that would dictate how the war unfolded – whether it would be contained or spill over into a larger conflict with Iran, Israel, maybe Syria and Turkey.

By the early hours of 9 April, I found myself surrounded by vehicles and Peshmerga, many of whom were now smartly dressed in modern new combats, all ready and eager to storm into Kirkuk. They were excited. One of Dan's SEAL teams, with KDP Special Forces, had seized a strategic and heavily defended hilltop, called Maqloub, overlooking Mosul. It had been used as a munitions dump and a hub for air defences. Not wanting to be outdone, the three hundred Peshmerga with us, all heavily armed, were eager and good to go. Many more had moved into positions surrounding the key oil centre at Kirkuk. We had a further fourteen SEALs with us while in Mosul and Kirkuk crowds went on to the streets waving white flags as others looted.

I tried to steal some sleep while we waited. I woke after an hour in the back of the wagon and Malcolm passed me a signal that had just come in from Dan: 'Remember, do not allow Peshmerga to advance on the city proper. If they do you are to stop them at all costs. Use of extreme force authorised.'

'Fuck off, Dan.' I snorted, and passed the paper round the rest of the lads. Then I moved over to Guss and shook him out of his sleeping-bag. 'Quick, I need you to get on to Quigly, as well as your NSA and CIA lot, and get confirmation of this order,' I said, as I passed him the paper. 'I want absolute confirmation – one hundred per cent. You got that?'

'Roger, boss,' Guss replied, and tried to look alert. 'I'll get right on to it.'

'Good lad,' I told him.

I called a Chinese parliament (a meeting of all parties at which all ideas are put on the table), and we agreed there was no way we could carry out such an order, even if we wanted to. As we were talking, Malcolm received news that the Turkish government had viewed the images of the friendly-fire incident and had been surprised to see so many well-armed and organised Kurdish troops being supported by US Special Forces. Ankara was shaking the diplomatic big stick and making clear how nervous it felt about Kurdish autonomy – more so if the Kurds seized Kirkuk and its oil. But Massoud Barzani would soon be with us and he would know the Peshmerga commanders' plans.

I was about to send a sitrep saying that we couldn't stop the Peshmerga rolling into the city, when Quigly came back with confirmation of Dan's order. I was so shocked that I laughed. I asked him to reconfirm. While we waited to hear from him I called the Peshmerga together to tell them about Wajy's death. I stood on the back of one of the Land Rovers where they could see me, with a Peshmerga lad who spoke good English as my translator. 'Right, I've got some bad news for you all,' I began. 'As you know, Wajy Barzani was injured in the US airstrike that hit your convoy. He suffered extensive head wounds and died during the night.'

As the translator finished speaking, there was total silence, apart from the distant rumble of bombing runs. The excited chatter about taking Kirkuk had stopped and all eyes were on me. I felt apprehensive: the Peshmerga were volatile and emotional – if they were going to kick off, now would be the time. Doug was behind me and I heard him switch off his safety catch. A man pushed out of the crowd and walked towards me, Peshmerga patting him on the back as he went. It was Baban, one of Wajy's most trusted senior deputies and a cousin of Twin One. He stopped in front of me. 'Wajy trusted you and followed you,' he exclaimed. Then he faced the crowd. 'That is good enough for me, also.'

I had a lump in my throat – I could see the pain in his eyes at the loss of his friend – and also felt humbled by his words. 'Thank you,' was all I could say in reply.

Baban addressed the crowd, raised his AK47 in a form of salute and was picked up on the shoulders of two Peshmerga, as everyone cheered.

'Out with the old and in with the new,' Doug whispered, as we watched.

We had lunch in a makeshift tarpaulin shelter, and I chatted with Baban and some of the other Peshmerga commanders about Kirkuk, and Turkey's threats should the Kurds take it. Half-way through, in walked Mam, the highly respected Kurdish veteran whom I'd befriended at the cave complex. Clearly he had the respect of the other commanders, who fell silent as he took a seat. They waited for him to speak. Mam greeted me and we exchanged courtesies. He had come from the front lines around Chamchamal. Outside Kirkuk, he outlined how many Peshmerga and other Kurdish fighters were poised to enter the city. Despite what the Turks were threatening, he said, they would start their assault on it in the early hours. Indeed, Kurds living in Kirkuk had already started to liberate the city from within.

Doug, Romero and I were all thinking the same thing: now the shit really was going to hit the fan.

As news of the coming assault filtered to the Peshmerga outside, they were ecstatic to be finally going into action: nothing I could say or do would stop them. Still, I took Mam and Baban to one side and tried to warn them of the 'serious consequences' they risked if they took Kirkuk against the express wishes of coalition commanders. As Wajy and Kosrat had before them, they looked at me as if I was mad when I tried to convince them to hold off their assault on the city.

I went and had a quiet chat with Romero about whether I should level with them, as I had with Wajy and Kosrat, about the specific nature of our orders. We didn't have much choice: either we shot them, then drove on to the other Kurdish leaders and finished them off too – although clearly we'd be dead before we'd left our tent if we tried it – or we came clean. I thought this should be a decision for the whole team, so I called them together for a quick heads-up. When I'd explained our predicament, Guss declared that we should follow orders. He was in favour of taking out the Peshmerga leaders, and even offered to slot them himself.

'Twat, then what do we do about the other three hundred?' Doug asked.

'Take out the leaders and the rest will do as they're told,' he said.

The rest of us could hardly believe he could be so stupid. In a way Guss was cut from the same cloth as Dan, but with just half of the grey matter Dan had.

'Put your brain in a bird and it'd fly backwards, buddy,' Romero remarked.

'Look, we can slot 'em quietly and say they were taken out by the Iraqis,' Guss continued. 'Once we do that, we tell the rest of 'em they'll have to follow us.'

'Are you really that fucking stupid?' Doug asked incredulously.

'Guss, do that and the leadership falls to the next in line.' I tried to defuse what was threatening to turn into a major Guss–Doug showdown. 'It won't work, and besides, I'm not one for cold-blooded murder, especially of people I know, admire and respect.'

'Oh, well, there goes my career and pension,' Romero joked.

With Guss the only exception, we all agreed that we had no choice but to level with the Peshmerga leaders. Mam approached us, concerned to know what we were planning. He was a good man. Thirty years of fighting and now some smart-arse with a 'bigger picture' had ordered that he and the rest of the Peshmerga commanders should be stopped. Just like that. It was too easy to tell others to do the dirty work. Of course, war has always been dirty, and covert wars especially so, but it was me who was standing in my shoes right now, and it was me who'd have to pull the trigger.

So, I sat down with Mam and Baban and told them we had been ordered to stop them at all costs, with use of extreme force authorised. As I did so I had visions of us all ending up as hostages of the Peshmerga, or of me joining their side and going in with them to liberate Kirkuk, or of ending up an outcast from my own side, court-martialled later for disobeying orders. But there was little time to dwell on any of that, as the Peshmerga lads were preparing for the assault, and carloads were already heading for their positions around the city.

'Those are our orders,' I repeated to Mam and Baban, 'but we will not be carrying them out. In fact, we'll be entering the city alongside you. I promised Wajy that I would be with you all the way and I intend to keep that promise.'

'Are you mad?' Mam was amazed. 'This is our land, our city, our most sacred city – and of course we know what your orders are if we enter it. But if we get bombed by the Americans that is our business. It is our blood for our city, and we do not expect you to waste yours. You have kept your promise to Wajy and all of us. You have honoured us this far and that is enough. No, you must stay here when we enter.'

Clearly Wajy had explained the situation to him.

'Mam, we have come this far and we will go the rest of the way,' I said firmly.

Mam put a hand on my shoulder and looked me in the eye. 'Wajy was right, my friend. You should be a Kurd. Now, I will give you my word. We will take Kirkuk but we will not stay. We will leave again within forty-eight hours. We just want to make a show of strength. After all, the city is rightfully ours. But we do not want war with our American "friends".'

With that, he smiled and walked away. I didn't know what to

make of his last words, but putting a time limit on their stay in Kirkuk wouldn't stop the US airstrikes. There had to be a better way than letting these people, our allies in this war, be bombed by coalition air power. I racked my brains. Let the diplomats earn their salaries on this one, I concluded, and told Malcolm to get on the net to Tosh. We'd go for the nuclear option: we would send a message to Quigly and Dan, then get Guss to forward it to General Franks, the NSA, the CIA and anyone else we could think of, saying we could not stop the Peshmerga taking Kirkuk as many were already in the city and liberation was well under way. Therefore we would enter the city alongside them. The politicians would just have to get the Turks to wind in their necks for once.

'You know you may have just signed our death warrants, don't you, boss?' Doug remarked, once the message had gone. 'If they decide to bomb the fuck out of the Pesh as they move into the city and we're with them, we're all fucking dead.'

'I know,' I replied quietly. 'That's why you lot are going to stay put while I go in with them. It was my call and my promise, not yours.'

'Fuck off, boss, you melodramatic arsehole,' Doug replied. 'No one said you had to be the only fucking dead hero around here. You go, we all go – ain't that right, Guss?'

There was silence as Guss bent over his radio set, busy sending out our message. Malcolm was pouring yet more coffee from his flask but he gave me the thumbs-up. Baby Steve smiled and nodded. Romero and Athansa both gave a thumbs-up. Ian was asleep in one of the wagons, so I would put the same to him when he woke.

'OK, guys, it's your funeral.' I grinned.

It was an amazing vote of confidence in me that they were all volunteering to come on the death run into Kirkuk.

'Not sure it's a good idea,' Guss said, as he turned away from the radio.

'Well, you can fuck off, then, mate,' Doug snarled.

Just then Dan's SEAL deputy, Ryan Zinke, rushed over to me, looking concerned. 'Listen, bud, I just got a whole bunch of orders tellin' me to stay firm and not to enter Kirkuk,' he explained. 'Like, under no circumstance enter Kirkuk. Is that where you're figuring on going, buddy? 'Cause if you are, I've been ordered to stop you. So whadda I do?'

Clearly, the shit had hit the fan again, this time as a result of our radio message.

'Send a message back that we've already left with the Pesh so there's nothing you can do,' I told him.

'OK, bud, I'll give it a go.' He headed back to his vehicle.

'Malc, get on the net to Tosh,' I said. 'Tell him we're already on the move into Kirkuk. Ask if he can contact Heather and Ben, or even John Simpson, and get them here as soon as possible. Tell them there's a big story brewing.' If we could get enough news crews into the city, it might just cause Dan and Quigly some problems in taking out the Kurds.

Then I asked Guss to get on to Quigly and get him to reconfirm who above him had sanctioned the orders: I wanted 100 per cent confirmation that they were genuine. Tosh came back to say that Heather and Ben were already in the area, with a host of other news crews, and heading for the city as I'd requested. He advised me to stay put. I responded with a negative, and he told me he would make sure my car was returned to Victoria and that he would look after her.

Quigly came back on the net informing us that all aerial assets available to us were being withdrawn until further notice. He had decided to play hardball. Groups of Peshmerga started calling in, asking why the SEAL FAC teams with them were refusing to co-ordinate airstrikes along their front lines. By this time, Kurdish forces had surrounded Kirkuk as US air power pounded Iraqi defences in the city. As I had gone for the nuclear option, so now had Quigly: it had become a game of brinkmanship to see who would back down first. I was taking a gamble on the US forces not hitting the Kurds. I told myself to stand firm and trust my instincts.

12

TAKING KIRKUK

At 03.30 hours Mam informed me that the remainder of his group would be heading into the city at 04.00. We could already hear plenty of gunfire and explosions from RPGs so we knew the assault was being prosecuted. As Mam was readying his men, several women Peshmerga arrived. I wondered if Layla was with them, but SEAL Ian soon established that she wasn't. Kirkuk is hugely oil-rich, which had been the source of conflict over this city for decades: I could not see how murdering the Peshmerga leaders now could make the slightest difference to the region's long-term peace. I put those thoughts down and sent them to Quigly, Dan and Tosh. If I was going to get shit further down the line for my actions, I wanted it all noted and on the record. I had concrete reasons for disobeying my orders, and I believed they were the right ones.

Ryan Zinke approached me with his radio man in tow. He offered me the set. When I took it, Quigly came on the secure sat link in person. He was far from stupid and he knew that we weren't already on our way into the city, as I had signalled earlier.

'It's me,' Quigly announced. 'Listen, buddy, I'm gonna level with you. I need you to stay where you are, with all your team, and not enter that city.'

'No can do.'

'Hear me out,' Quigly said. 'I got a task I need you and your boys for as a priority. I ain't shittin' you on this one and I know what you're thinkin', but this is for real. We got a site on the outskirts of Kirkuk, real big WMD facility, and we need you to go secure it, 'cause if your Kurd friends get there first, we ain't fucking around no more, we are taking them out. Period. And you can understand why.'

'I'm listening,' I told him.

'All right. Now, if you do this one for me I'll do my damnedest, I'll pull all the strings, I'll shout at anyone who'll listen, to get the Turks to back off if the Kurds take Kirkuk. You hear me?'

'They're already taking it,' I told him. 'It's happening.'

'I know. So, will you take the job to secure that facility? It comes right from the top, this one, bud, from the very top.'

'You think I give a shit?' I told him. 'Listen, I'll do it only if you promise no airstrikes on the Pesh troops. They're already in the city and there's no way I can stop them. You promise me that and I'll take all of my team and the SEALs to carry out your request. It'll be problem solved all round.'

'Deal,' Quigly confirmed. 'Shit – you think I want sixty thousand Peshmerga turning on us now, at this stage of the game? Buddy, you think I want that?' He paused. 'All right, this is the intel on this WMD facility. It's over at the Kirkuk airbase, on the eastern side of town.'

Quigly explained that there was a series of giant S-shaped bunkers at the airbase known to be used as storage for 122mm artillery shells and rockets fitted with chemical warheads. Intel about it had been used to help make the case for a pre-emptive war in the first place. Satellite images were now showing scores of military vehicles moving around the base, raising the fear that Iraqis were preparing to use the weapons against the Peshmerga and US forces, or even against the city of Kirkuk. Quigly wanted us there as fast as possible to stop whatever was happening. If by chance they were Peshmerga forces, they, too, would have to be stopped.

I gathered the SEAL lads and my lot together, then quickly outlined the situation, explaining that we had to be discreet but leave fast. Then I called Mam and Baban over. 'We're just moving to a better location to co-ordinate things, as you lot are moving in all over the place and far faster than we anticipated.'

Mam looked at me suspiciously. 'I am meeting Massoud and Jalal Talabani in fifteen minutes' time,' he announced. 'Do I tell them that you have run out on us or that you have hidden because your planes are indeed about to stop us as you warned?'

'Mam, I give you my word, if it still means anything to you, that once I have settled this lot into a new location, I will find you and stand with you,' I told him. 'If the bombs fall, we will both be beneath them, my friend, and if they hit us we will be walking together through the gates of heaven.'

'Or the gates of hell,' Mam said, breaking into a smile. 'If you do not come, I will come to find you,' he added ominously.

As we pulled away from the car park, we joined a main road heading towards the city. It had raw excrement running down either side of it as the sewerage system had been neglected for twenty-five years or more. The closer we got to the city, the worse the smell became.

'If it all stinks like this, they can keep their fucking city,' Doug remarked.

'By the smell of things, chemical warfare's already started,' Malcolm added.

As we headed around the outskirts, we broke out our NBC suits and checked the respirators in case chemical weapons were being used at the base.

'Well, guys, if there is chem shit at that base and we get a hold of it, you know our president's gonna love us all for ever,' Romero remarked from the rear of the wagon.

'Fuck your president.' Doug snorted. 'He's a fucking cretin and a wanker, wouldn't you agree, Guss?' Guss was in the rear of the vehicle, trying to monitor signals traffic, and ignored Doug's little dig.

We arrived at the airbase as the sun came up, and broke into two convoys, moving into positions that effectively surrounded the bunkers. For several minutes we kept watch, but there was little sign of life. We spent the next four hours moving through them, securing each in turn and using classic room-clearance techniques. It was incredibly hot and intense work, trussed up in the NBC suits and masks, and eventually we could confirm that the base was deserted. Evidently the Iraqis had feared it was a prime target, and the movement the satellites had picked up must have been them legging it. As the SEAL lads took up defensive positions, I called in a sitrep to Tosh and Quigly: the base was deserted and no WMD had been found. Quigly came back, asking us to check again for any signs of chemical weapons or delivery systems.

'Looks like your president's going to be disappointed,' Doug remarked to Romero, as a team went to recheck the bunkers.

'No medals for us, then, eh?'

By 10.00 hours the sun was well up and we were sweltering in the growing heat. The second search had revealed no WMDs. I sent a message to Quigly that, no matter how many times we searched it, there were no WMDs on the airbase. On the radio we could hear Luke Harding reporting amid a cacophony of hooting, whistling and cheering, with many people shouting in the background, 'We love Bush. We love Blair.' The report continued that Iraqi northern front lines were crumbling and the US was preparing for a big offensive. We laughed: we knew it was disinformation and propaganda to scare any remaining Iraqis into fleeing, all part of General Franks's April Fool plan.

I got on the net to ask who was at the oil sites, and received an answer that Dan and some SEAL teams were monitoring them. They couldn't move on to the oil wells: the media were there and might claim that the war was all about oil after all. How bloody fickle, I thought. On the one hand our bosses didn't care a damn about ordering us to murder the Peshmerga leaders to stop them liberating their own city, while on the other they were hanging back from the oilfields in case they got a bit of bad press.

I told Guss to contact Mam and work out his location so that we could head in and link up with him. I'd stuck to my side of the bargain with Quigly, and now I had to deliver on my promise to Mam. When Guss finally got a fix on where Mam was setting up his forward command post, I took Doug, Guss, Baby Steve and Athansa in one of the Toyotas, leaving Romero and Malcolm in charge at the airbase. As we headed into the city, the streets looked more like a carnival scene than a war zone and no one paid us much attention. We arrived at Mam's location, to discover that he'd set up base in a large, gated courtyard surrounded by palm trees.

As I climbed out Mam pulled me into a bear-hug. He was ecstatic, but sewerage lay everywhere and the stench was horrific. He explained that he had just left a meeting with Massoud Barzani and Jalal Talabani. He confessed that he had told them about my orders to use all force to stop them taking Kirkuk. When we had moved off to check the airbase, and they had seen no US forces in the city, they had taken it as confirmation that they were being deserted and that the US was going to bomb them. Jalal Talabani had ordered his Peshmerga fighters to pull out of Kirkuk by the end of the day, which he hoped would ease Turkish concerns about the city's future. Then forward elements from the US 173rd Airborne Brigade would start to enter and do high-visibility patrols, particularly where news teams were positioned, so that the images would soothe Ankara, especially as Mosul had now fallen to the Peshmerga and SEAL teams with the surrender of the entire Iraqi 5th Corps. My arrival was a relief to him. I could see that his men were reinforcing their positions, and it didn't look as though they were preparing to leave Kirkuk any time soon.

We set up position with our vehicle near the compound's central fountain and settled in for the evening. In spite of the stench there was a party atmosphere, as celebrations continued into the night. Sporadic gunfire could be heard and many dogs were barking. I called in a sitrep to Tosh that there were no signs of the Peshmerga leaving the city, certainly not that night. Malcolm sent a signal asking if he and Romero could join us: the SEAL lads were driving them mad and he had heard there was a big party going down.

In the morning Baby Steve woke me early with a signal from Dan: he would be with us shortly.

He turned up just after breakfast, climbing down from his fully armed-up Humvee and dressed in full combats with no Arab apparel. As he strode across to me, I took a deep breath. I still wanted answers for the blue-on-blue in which Wajy had been killed. But Peshmerga lads were wandering about, cleaning their weapons and grabbing food, and I knew that everything we said would be overheard. Somehow I had to bite my tongue. Dan held out a hand to me, but his smile disappeared when he registered the anger I was unable to hide. I led him to our tarpaulin awning and sat him down opposite me.

'No good old British hospitality today, then,' he said.

'Fuck off, Dan,' I retorted. I wasn't going to beat about the bush. 'I know you too bloody well by now and I want the truth about that strike the other day on Wajy.'

He said nothing, so I placed my M16 on the table in front of us with the barrel towards him. 'You said if he couldn't be stopped you might just have to arrange it, maybe by a friendly-fire accident. So, did you?'

I felt Doug move in behind me as Baby Steve sat down and passed round four cups of coffee.

'Cheers for the coffee,' Dan remarked, then glanced at the M16 muzzle. 'You should know I don't intimidate easy.'

'Not trying to intimidate you,' I responded. 'I know you too well, and just what a cold, heartless fuck you are.'

Dan slammed his fist on the table and stared hard at me. For once, though, he was lost for words.

'It's simple, Dan, explain yourself,' I added. 'Wajy being taken out of the equation was bad enough. But killing your own men? Come on, surely even you feel guilty about that.'

'You stupid fucking English asshole!' Dan exploded. 'Don't you dare pull the moral fucking high-ground trick with me, you jumped-up fuck.'

I felt Doug move towards him and raised my arm to hold him back. 'Not bad, Dan, four expletives in two sentences,' I said. 'Just explain yourself, that's all. You're a big boy. Surely you can do that.'

'You still have no idea, do you?' he sneered. 'Well, let me spell it out so even you can understand it, with your delusional high morals and your saintly ethics. The blue–on–blue was a fucking accident. Jeez, I was doing this shit when you couldn't wipe your own arse.' He sat back, picked up his coffee and sipped.

'Go on, Dan,' I said.

'All right, get a fucking load of this,' he snapped. 'Wajy's death was fuck-all to do with me. There were three FACs on the go. Go speak with the F15 pilot and see how fucking gutted he is. Now you want to go off on some fucking crusade of yours, then let me tell you something. You give these fucking Kurds autonomy right now, with all this oil for them to pump out and sell as they fucking see fit, then oil prices go AWOL. The Saudis won't stand for it and on top of that the entire world economy is governed by the price of oil. These fucking Kurds are a law unto themselves. Let them pump the stuff out cheap and you have world-wide economic meltdown on the fucking horizon. So don't you dare presume to judge me. And if it had been necessary, and it still fucking may be, if I was ordered to take him out – Wajy, Massoud, Mam, Talabani – I'd have taken out the whole fucking lot of them, including you, buddy, to stop that happening. So, d'you read me? That's what I'd do, and that's what makes me a good soldier.'

'When are you going to give these people a bit more credit for being able to run their own affairs properly?' I asked.

Dan guffawed. 'Still, after all these years, you don't get it, do you?' he said, through gritted teeth. 'You still have those naïve fluffy-bunny illusions. I expected more of you. You may consider yourself intelligent, a thinker, a moralist and philosopher, but you're just a fucking dreamer and that makes you dangerous. A liability, out here. We give these fuckers autonomy, regardless of fucking oil, they get their new, recognised state, and it's game on in Palestine with the rag-heads there demanding autonomy too. We can't give it to this lot but not the Palestinians. Then you got Israel and a whole pile of shit landing on your doorstep. We've been planning and strategising this for years, but you wouldn't understand that kind of long-term planning, now, would you?'

Before I could respond, Mam appeared at the edge of our gathering. He cleared his throat. 'My friends, great news for you. All our commanders, Massoud and Talabani included, have given their word that they will indeed leave Kirkuk within twenty-four hours. You gave your word and kept it. We will do likewise. We Kurds believe in keeping our word,' he added, then turned and walked away.

Dan sat back, surprised. Then he said, 'Fucking lies and

bullshit! They're playing you for a fool. They're simply stalling for time. If they don't leave, you'd better be prepared to slot them or face the consequences.' With that, he got up and headed for his Humvee.

As Dan left, my mind was spinning. I didn't know if anything he'd told me was true. And I didn't know whom I could trust any more. There seemed to be no signs of the Kurds preparing to leave Kirkuk, so maybe Mam was indeed playing me for a fool, as Dan had suggested. Right then, the only thing I was certain of was that I wanted out of this game once and for all. I wanted to go home, settle down and maybe realise my dreams. In the interim I would do whatever it took to ensure that I could – and that meant surviving the rest of this dirty war.

On 11 April Turkey announced that it had the option of deploying more troops to northern Iraq if Kurdish fighters failed to relinquish control of Kirkuk and Mosul. By late evening I was getting seriously concerned that maybe Mam had hoodwinked me. Perhaps Dan had been right all along that I'd trusted them too much. I sat up with Mam and had quite a lengthy discussion on Sharafnama and Kurdish history, then went over the latest intel on the progress of the war. At around about 03.00 hours on the 12th, Mam stood up and said that he was leaving, as per his orders. What orders? I asked.

'Just follow me, my friend,' he replied. 'We have organised everything.' He got into his Toyota pick-up and asked if I would be following. I asked where he was going.

'We are off to Tikrit. Our American friends are sending the 1st Marine Expeditionary Force and we cannot have them steal the prize if Saddam is there,' he stated, and signalled for his driver to leave. As he pulled away, he turned back. 'As I told you, we Kurds keep our word.' His driver accelerated out of the compound.

When the dust had settled and we were alone in the courtyard,

I got on the net to Tosh to let him know that the Peshmerga forces were pulling out of Kirkuk, as they had promised, and were now on their way to Tikrit. We were preparing to follow them.

Within ten minutes I received a message ordering us to move to a new RV point outside the city where a CH47 Chinook would pick us up.

At the RV, we met up with Malcolm, Romero and the rest of the team from the airbase and received another message: we were to head back to our main FOB, at Cizre in Turkey. Tosh, Dianne and Big Matt had already been collected from the caves. Tosh told me I had some serious explaining to do and forwarded me the end of the message: 'Clarification required. Full debrief – why risk taken to tell Kurds.' So, this was the end of our war. At first I was glad. Any 'explaining' I had to do was of minor importance compared with the fact that we were getting out of Iraq alive.

'If some bastard wants you out the way, boss, then the chopper ride's the time to do it,' Doug remarked, as we waited for the CH47 Chinook to show.

'I'll walk, then, if it's all the same to you,' said Baby Steve.

When the helicopter landed I saw Tosh waving from the back. Within minutes Pilot Steve was welcoming us aboard and the loadie was passing round coffee. We sat in silence on the long flight, exhausted and lost in thought about the weeks we had just endured. Suddenly I had a lump in my throat and thought I was going to cry.

We arrived back in Cizre, and made for the ops tent for a full debrief. We were quiet as we wrote up our notes. When I'd finished I went outside and sat alone for some time – I could see the river Tigris in the distance. Eventually, Baby Steve brought me a cup of coffee. He also had some mail and a parcel from Victoria, which contained razor blades and sweets. As I walked back to the mess tent with him I opened my letters.

'Yeah! Here's the main man himself,' Tosh announced, as I entered.

Everyone in the mess tent raised their mugs of tea or coffee towards me in a silent salute. Whatever I had done in the field to piss off my superiors, my team was still well and truly behind me. I joined them at the tables, and thought what a gaunt and desperate lot we looked. The weeks in theatre had taken their toll, and we all needed time to recover. Dianne was buzzing, though: she had done all that was asked of her and more, despite her initial fears of inadequacy.

'What are we all going to do with our big fat wage cheques when we get home?' Tosh asked.

'Big wage cheques?' Guss queried. 'I'm on standard CIA rates.'

'You mean you weren't offered a fortune?' Malcolm asked. 'We all were — ain't that right, D?'

'Didn't put my arse in the sling for nothing. And I need the extra spons to pay for my boat,' Doug replied.

'Yeah, and I'm hiring four hookers to wait on me hand and foot,' Malcolm said.

'Dianne there would do it for free,' Doug retorted, 'and you could save yourself a packet.'

'In your dreams,' said Dianne, and everyone burst into laughter. Matt was gazing at her, smiling.

Tosh kept on at me about what I would do with my pay, so in the end I told him to mind his own business.

We all laughed and the conversation ended as we headed off for some food.

Over dinner Tosh wanted to know how Doug and I had been so certain that Wajy would be killed, days before his convoy was hit in the errant airstrike.

'It's the Force, mate, which you ain't got,' Doug joked.

'Just a gut instinct, Tosh,' I added. 'Soldiers in the field develop a sixth sense.'

'I'm curious,' Tosh said. 'About this Force, as you call it.'

'Niall's having you on, mate,' Doug told him.

'So, if you've got the Force, Niall, why don't you tell me what you think your long-term prospects are with Victoria?' he persisted.

I glanced up at him – and saw Doug's hands twitching at the other side of the table. 'Why don't you tell me, Tosh? You seemed to be communicating rather frequently with her while I was in theatre.'

Everyone laughed except Doug, who was scowling at Tosh. I suspected he knew something I didn't, and made a mental note to ask him about it later.

'You joke about the Force, guys,' Romero said, 'but I tell you, every day we were in Iraq an inner voice was telling me that this was the war that was gonna get me. Now, I ain't never had that before, so someone tell me what that's all about.'

'It's bollocks, mate,' Malcolm replied. 'Proof is your war's over and it didn't get you, did it?'

'Voice is still with me, and maybe it ain't over yet. I just been praying it'll be quick and my wife and daughter will be fine.'

'I'll look after them for you,' Tosh volunteered, 'From what I saw of your wife's photo she's a damn pretty lady.'

'She's too damn pretty for a ponce like you,' Romero shot back, which shut Tosh up.

'Way I see it,' I continued, 'life's like a hangar. You enter through the front door and the object is to get out the other side. You can walk the straight path through the middle, or take one of the less direct routes. Death gets you when you reach the exit and there's no way to avoid it.'

'Well, I know where I'm going,' Doug observed. 'Straight to hell – and when I get there I'm going to put out all the fires.'

We all laughed. In our work we had all been forced to come to terms with death. We were all aware of our own mortality, and often wondered about God and life after death. Some of the conversations we had had wouldn't have been out of place in a philosophy club.

'I don't agree,' Tosh said. 'The future's not set in stone and I can prove it. Your instincts are telling you your relationship with Victoria will work, aren't they, Niall?'

'Well, my instincts about you being a fucking twat proved 100 per cent correct,' Doug interjected, coldly. 'The Force sure worked there, didn't it, Tosh?'

'Very funny,' Tosh replied as everyone laughed.

'I think we stand a good chance,' I replied guardedly. Why did he keep going back to my Victoria? And why did Doug look like he was about to slot him every time?

Something was eating Doug about Tosh, but the operation was over, so perhaps it didn't matter. I was curious to find out what it was, though. As soon as I had the chance I'd ask him.

Later, after a lot more banter, I headed for the signals tent. I couldn't relax – I had a suspicion that we had more to do, although as we were close to the end of the ground offensive I couldn't imagine what. I sat down at the radio and was checking for messages when I received a signal from Head Shed that we were to stand down. Our war was indeed over. I sighed with real relief. I went to tell the others and Doug told me to get off to bed. In the morning, he said, he and Dianne would force me to return to Konya for a full check on my chest – I was still coughing up blood.

As I lay in bed, I read through the other intel and sigint (signals intelligence) messages. One from Dan had been meant for Quigly only, but had come back to me via Head Shed. It related to the deployment and use of the MOABs. I read the last paragraph with amusement: 'Warning! Not for close-support operations. Too destructive and lethal.' Someone in Northwood was trying to tell me something: this was not the first set of messages that had been sent my way and was not for my eyes. But it didn't matter now. We were on our way out of there.

Dianne had given me some powerful pills to help with the pain in my chest and I fell into a ragged, drugged-up sleep. I dreamt that the Iraqi desert was awash with fire: burning tanks, vehicles, bunkers. War is a dirty business of pain and death and I had always known that. It was not so much death itself that shocked but the horrific nature of it. And fire is the worst, the smell of burning flesh. Even a simple gunshot wound burns. I recalled a friend who had been blown up in front of me as he drove a Land Rover in Northern Ireland. We had to place sandbags in his coffin to add some weight after his remains had been shovelled into a body-bag.

I awoke late with a muzzy head and those horrific images running through my mind. I turned back to my letters from home to try to get them out of my head. One was postmarked 'Lincolnshire', which was where John lived. His wife said that he was OK and seeing a psychotherapist. At first he had been too proud and stubborn to confide in her, but eventually he had broken down and, for the first time, cried in her arms.

There was a picture in the envelope that John's two daughters had drawn, showing them all sitting in their garden. They thanked me for sending their daddy home. Christ, if I hadn't felt emotional already, I did then.

PART THREE

DESERT OF NO RETURN

13

GENERAL PARACHUTE

Head Shed had received a request from Barzan Abd al-Ghafur Sulayman Majid al-Tikriti, the senior Iraqi general of one of the feared Special Republican Guards units based around Tikrit. With Kosrat Rassul's Peshmerga coming from the north and the entire US 1st Marine Expeditionary Force, as part of Task Force Tripoli, about to crash down on him, he wanted to negotiate. No large combat operations had occurred so far that day, Cent Com reported. The 26th US Marine Expeditionary Unit had arrived to augment the 173rd Airborne Brigade in the north, securing all strategic sites in the region. It appeared the war was almost over, but our services were required.

We'd been given his details previously and had thought somehow that he would want to cross over with his unit. Sure enough, intel via the CIA and Kosrat Rassul's network had confirmed the general was now saying he could convince his unit not to fight coalition forces as they approached Tikrit. The planned assault on the town was days away and, according to all intelligence reports, at least 2500 regular and paramilitary fighters, including professional remnants of the Adnan Special Republican

Guards Division, despite heavy air and ground attacks, were fortifying their positions.

Tikrit was Saddam's hometown and most of the inhabitants were his staunch supporters, so it was viewed as the place that would see the war's bloodiest fighting. The chance of a local general offering such an opportunity couldn't be ignored. Of course, it might be a trick but the potential gains were worth the calculated risk of trying to liaise with him. Besides, PsyOps (Psychological Operations) had been beaming and broadcasting messages into Tikrit since the countdown to war had begun, encouraging Iraqi soldiers not to fight. Quigly had sent a signal requesting that I deal with it. I'd told him that, if such an opportunity arose, I wanted it and so our very brief stand-down was cancelled, as was any trip to Konya for a full check-up.

Doug came into the tent, grunted at Tosh and sat down next to me. He picked up a cup of coffee someone had just made and drank it. Might have been Tosh's for all he knew, but he didn't care. Guss came in, waving several orders sheets covered with intel notes he had scribbled. None of us had had much sleep so this little nugget of an opportunity was not welcome. On top of that the painkillers I had taken were making me drowsy. The four of us sat round the small wooden table and Guss told us the game plan.

We would be flown by Chinook, refuelling en route, to Buhayrat ath Thartha, a lake west of Tikrit. From there we would meet up with a junior officer of the Republican Guards who also wanted to defect. He would lead us to a location near the railway that runs just north of Tikrit. We would stay the night in a train siding with lots of rolling stock parked in it. The following evening, we would move on to meet the general at a pumping station on the outskirts of the city. If we ran into any major problems we would only need to hide out until the Peshmerga arrived from the north. Pilot Steve was still with us so hopefully we could get him to fly us in.

As Guss finished speaking Tosh went into speak-and-be-heard mode, and emphasised how crucially important this mission was: Tikrit was causing serious concerns up the chain of command. As if we didn't know that already! As I sat at the table, my instincts were screaming at me to stand this one down. But how could I? I had specifically asked Quigly to let me do this type of job. As I tried to make a decision, an image from my dream flashed into my mind – the Iraqi desert, burning tanks, vehicles, bunkers, people. I knew that if there was the chance to avert such serious bloodshed, I had to give it a go.

I ran through all my ancillary concerns: what was the chance of being bombed by coalition forces as we lay up in the railway siding?

'No worries there,' Tosh assured me. 'The area's been designated as of no military value. Besides, there could be mobile chemical laboratories within the rolling stock, and we wouldn't want to destroy evidence of that, would we?'

What about the junior Iraqi officer? I asked. How trustworthy was he?

'He's genuine. He gave details of his family which were independently confirmed on the ground,' Guss explained.

'What about the general?'

Guss threw some photos on to the table of a middle-aged Iraqi officer, sporting the biggest moustache I had ever seen. 'General Barzan Majid al-Tikriti,' Guss announced. 'Or General Parachute, as he's known to his friends.' He jabbed at the moustache with a forefinger.

I looked round the faces in the ops tent. Romero and Athansa had joined us by now, as well as Baby Steve and Malcolm. 'Who wants to go and meet General Parachute?' I asked. 'I want to keep the group as small as possible. We go in quietly, but heavily armed in case of trouble.'

'I'm fucking going if you are, boss,' Doug said.

'My people say I gotta be there,' Guss volunteered. 'Can't say I'm keen, but orders is orders.'

I knew Doug wanted to leave Guss behind, but there was no time to argue this one with his people in Langley. Malcolm, Baby Steve, Ian, Romero and Athansa all said they wanted to go, but I wanted just six, which meant leaving two behind. I decided to leave Malcolm and Ian at base: I wanted two serious operators in reserve in case a rescue force had to come in and bust us out of there. They were seriously pissed off, but slightly mollified when I told them they were the QRF (quick reaction force) and should be ready to go at a moment's notice.

'We'll wear Arab dress on top of our combats, as before,' I told the team. 'That way, we can blend in with the locals, unless they get up very close and personal. Last thing we want is to be captured in Arab clothes and no uniform – they'll try us as spies.'

'Fucking nice one, boss. Why not keep it cheerful?' Doug said, with irony.

By the time the planning, briefing and team selection were done, we had barely two hours before dusk. Pilot Steve would fly us in under cover of darkness, so we had to get ready to go. I looked over my kit, got a full supply of ammo and rations, then checked we had the correct broadcast frequencies for the tacbes. I drew an extra pistol from the armoury, a Universal Service model. Within hours of having received the warning order, I found myself lifting off from the FOB with Doug, Romero, Athansa, Baby Steve and Guss. I sat near the rear of the Chinook as I always do, given the choice. I wanted out in a hurry if we went down. It was somewhat oversized for just the six of us so we could all stretch out a bit.

Guss was tooled up like Rambo, with knives, pistols and an M4 assault rifle with a 40mm grenade-launcher attached. Romero, next to him, was cool and collected as always. Athansa sat beside him, with Doug opposite, winking at me and sucking boiled sweets. Baby Steve had fallen asleep within seconds of takeoff. Three Brits and three Americans: we all felt as if we had had our baptism of fire in Iraq. Nothing could have prepared us for what was to come.

An hour into the flight Pilot Steve pointed out Mosul, to the left of us on the horizon. We could see the glow of the city lights. We all had memories of it and reflected on them briefly – apart from Baby Steve, who was still dead to the world. I thought of Wajy, Layla, Mam and the rest of the Peshmerga, who had become our friends. I laughed as I remembered Kosrat and what a wild character he was. I hadn't imagined, though, that we would be going back so soon into the area on another operation. Thanks, Quigly.

It was noisy as we thwoop-thwoop-thwooped our way across the desert, just feet above the featureless terrain. Between the thirty-sixth and thirty-fifth parallels central Iraq is flat and featureless so it was an easy job for Pilot Steve. Far easier than those trips into the Kurdish mountains. I got up, went to the cockpit and linked up to the intercom. Pilot Steve informed me we were nearly at our LZ. Ahead, I could see a shimmer on the horizon: the early-evening sky was reflecting off the surface of the Buhayrat ath Thartha lake.

We banked sharply to our left and took a bearing south-east. Co-pilot Mark was confirming our identity to all other military air traffic around. By this stage of the war we no longer had to worry about ground radar or scanners detecting us as Iraqi air-defence and electronic-warfare capability was zero. Pilot Steve pointed ahead and to starboard. He was wearing PNGs as well as a FLIR (forward-looking infrared) thermal-imaging system and could clearly see a strobing flash about eight miles away.

We slowed to a hover as the loadie, Richard, swung the fixed minigun aside and lowered the tailgate. It was only then that I realised how close to the deck we'd been flying – I'd felt no discernable descent as we touched down or, more correctly, hovered just off the ground. Doug was out first, on his belly, weapon up, sights, observing, followed by Baby Steve, Athansa and Romero, with Guss almost up his arse. I checked we'd left nothing essential then jumped off and gave a thumbs-up to Richard. The Chinook lurched forward and was gone.

That left the six of us lying on our bellies in all-round defence, feet touching each other. There was no cover. We waited until the chop-chop sound of the Chinook's rotors had faded, leaving an eerie silence. I lay there, mouth wide open – it acts as a sound-wave collector, enabling you to hear better. I hoped that I'd memorised the emergency tacbe frequencies in case we'd landed in the proverbial brown stuff again.

We lay still, covered with fine desert sand kicked up by the Chinook's downdraught. Romero, facing east, kicked my boot and I pointed towards the glow on the horizon that was Tikrit. We were just ten miles from its northern airfield, still under Iraqi control. A lone figure was walking gingerly towards us. Suddenly a voice boomed out: 'Hey! Americanos!' It carried across the flat desert landscape like a foghorn.

When the man was almost upon us, Doug jumped up in front of him, and pulled him swiftly and efficiently to the ground, hand across his mouth.

We soon established that this was Magdi, the young Iraqi officer we were to meet. I wasn't impressed with his loud arrival, but he had been afraid of missing us. Also, he knew the area well and was confident that no one was within a ten-mile radius of us. He was wearing local Arab dress, not uniform: he'd deserted at the beginning of the air campaign and had been hiding out here ever since. He'd made contact with US forces on a mobile phone, and had convinced Head Shed, Northwood and CentCom that he was genuine with the information he'd supplied about troop strengths and deployment around Tikrit, which had proved accurate, and with location details of his family. We had operated with much less credible informants and defectors in the past but I couldn't shake off a sense of foreboding. Now, though, I had to go with the flow.

We headed out across the desert towards a wadi where a small vehicle awaited us. Ever cautious, Doug kept his weapon on the Iraqi. I felt exposed – we stuck out like sore thumbs. We were moving fast, which was non-tactical but time wasn't on our side if we wanted to make the railway sidings before sunrise. As we ran in single file, with Romero at the rear, constantly turning to check behind us, I thought of the last time I'd felt so vulnerable. I'd been in Afghanistan stranded on a billiard table-flat plateau with no cover for miles.

Suddenly I heard a thump. I whirled round to see that Romero had fallen – he'd tripped while running backwards. We all waited for him to compose himself, then set off again. We found the vehicle, an old Russian Gaz military jeep, checked it for booby-traps, then squeezed ourselves in and on to it. Magdi switched on the engine, which roared into life – the exhaust had had it. Magdi apologised with a grimace.

He drove the Gaz like a rally driver with no lights on – and Doug found out, at last, what it was like to be driven by a madman. On the horizon in front, we could see flashes and feel the percussion of bombs falling around Tikrit. To the right we could see even bigger flashes from the direction of Baghdad. Soon the sun was climbing into the sky, and we could see many coalition aircraft, which was alarming: we were all worried that some trigger-happy pilot would see us and decide to upset our day. Images of Wajy's bombed convoy flashed through my mind.

The ground ahead was greener and more fertile now as the land sloped towards the railway line, which ran from Al Qamishii in northern Turkey, through Mosul, Tikrit and on to Baghdad.

Beyond it we could see the shimmer of water from the Tigris River. Magdi drove us into the railway yard and towards some rolling stock in sidings. The place appeared deserted and, sure enough, it was. The Iraqis had assumed that such a prime target would soon be obliterated as part of the coalition war effort. Little did they know the yard wasn't being targeted as it was viewed as essential for after the war, and besides, it might contain mobile chemical weapons laboratories.

We swung round a siding and, in complete darkness, drove up two ramps into the back of a cargo container. We clambered out into stifling heat. Immediately Athansa and Romero set out to do a recce of the area. Doug got on the net and checked in with Tosh: 'India Alpha One One, message. Over,' he whispered.

Tosh must have been busy as he didn't respond on voice comms but sent a teletype on-screen message in acknowledgement. All he had to do was press a preset code and it would reply to us.

I checked out our location on the map. So far, everything was going to plan. Our RV point with the general, a pumphouse on the banks of the Tigris, was just over an hour's walk away.

For the rest of the day we lay up in the container, taking it in turns to keep watch, eat and sleep. I quizzed Magdi on the plan for our meeting with General Parachute that night, and he seemed to have everything sorted. I soon established a good rapport with him. He told me he had known nothing in his life except Iraq under Saddam Hussein. He loved his country and hated Saddam for what he had done to it. Magdi was an engineer but had been drafted into the Iraqi Army engineers. He said he was a builder, not a destroyer. I decided he was genuine, and Doug made it clear to him that if there was any funny business or even the hint of a stitch-up he would slot him on the spot.

Using our maps and Magdi's local knowledge, we planned our route to the RV point. Magdi explained that the pumphouse was a small block containing two pumps that irrigated the surrounding area. It had a stone wall round it topped with barbed wire. There was only one gate into the compound with enough space inside to park two or three cars. The surrounding terrain was flat and open. Our Iraqi general was supposedly visiting the site to find out if it had been targeted by coalition bombing. It seemed a low-priority job for a general, but it was the only semi-plausible excuse he had for travelling out there. Of course, a man in his position could do more or less as he pleased, but he needed a cover story if he was not to arouse undue suspicion. He would be accompanied by his own personal bodyguards and one truckload of Iraqi Republican Guards.

I outlined the plan from our side to the lads. A single-lane dirt track led off a main road from Tikrit directly to the pumphouse. Athansa and Romero would hole up about a mile away on that road, maintain comms with Tosh at the FOB in Cizre, and act as a cut-off group in case any other Iraqi forces tried to come along the track. They would also warn us when the general and his entourage were on their way. On arrival, Doug would keep his GPMG fixed on the Iraqi Republican Guards in the truck. The rest of us would cover the general and his bodyguards.

14

FLESH AND BLOOD

The thump of explosions from Tikrit and Baghdad flashed across the ever-darkening skyline. The container was rank and airless, but at least we could have a decent meal: it afforded us cover and the chance to brew up and cook. We all knew what we were going to do and were fully tooled up. Half of me prayed that Kosrat's Peshmerga and the US 1st Marine Division would seize Tikrit before we'd got going, but if they did, many would be killed on both sides. This job had to go ahead and succeed, I told myself.

We checked the radios, both personal and comms with Tosh. A signal came through that Watban Ibrahim Hasan al-Tikriti, Saddam's half-brother, had been captured south of the city but warplanes and artillery continued to bomb it in the hope of wearing down any attempt at a last stand. The feared Special Republican Guards, however, as far as intel was concerned, had vanished. I hoped Tosh would keep the AWACs and CAS bang up to date with our position and progress so that we didn't join Wajy.

After dark, we cleaned up all trace of our presence in the container, set off on foot from the sidings and headed towards the

Tigris, with Magdi guiding us. Doug was behind him, wearing a fixed grin to make it clear that if he messed up or led us into a trap, he wouldn't see the sun come up again.

We maintained complete silence for the sake of opsec (operational security). In this billiard-table terrain, even the slightest sound carried for miles on the still desert air. Magdi led us quickly to the main tarmacked road, which led to Tikrit and the dirt track. We crouched low and kept to a shallow ditch. It provided next to no cover, and I was praying that any Iraqi Army units within range of us had no NVG (night-vision goggles) or we'd be well and truly stuffed.

Within fifteen minutes, we located the dirt track. There was no ditch, so we had to hoof it along the centre as fast as we could. It was another fifteen minutes or so before we reached the designated ERV point, about a kilometre short of the pumphouse. Here, we left Romero and Athansa as the blocking group; it was also our meeting point if we were compromised or became separated.

As we provided cover, Romero and Athansa located a little culvert running beneath the road in which they could hide. As they crawled in, I hoped they wouldn't meet any scorpions, snakes or the dreaded desert camel spiders. With barely a whispered goodbye we left them and headed on down the road.

Minutes later, a squat black building appeared ahead, silhouetted on the dark horizon. It was the pumphouse. We stopped some two hundred metres short, and took cover, lying down at the edge of the road. I motioned for Magdi to go forward alone to check out the lie of the land. He had assured us the place would be deserted as it was an unmanned, automatic pumping station. He had told us that the locals were convinced it would soon be pulverised by some trigger-happy coalition pilot.

I glanced at Doug and we grinned at each other nervously. Baby Steve was watching our rear, while Guss seemed to be checking his GPS repeatedly. I wondered why. We were clearly in the right place – as there wasn't another building on that flat, featureless landscape. I looked back at Doug, and he was staring over at Guss in obvious disgust. He started gesturing that the silly sod should use his eyes if he wanted to check where we were. So what the fuck was he fiddling around with his GPS for?

I pushed the throat mic against my neck, pressed my personal radio switch and spoke to Romero as quietly as I could. 'India Two, this is India Sunray Zero. Sitrep. Over.'

My earpiece crackled with Romero's reply: 'India Two. All OK. No spiders of ridiculous size, out.'

I laughed inwardly. And at least everything was all right back up at the ERV – our mad dash hadn't attracted any unwanted attention.

Magdi was scurrying back towards us in a crouching run. Had our situation not been so horribly exposed, it would have been seriously funny. No matter how low he was, he still stood out sharply on the crest of the track. Still, I was amazed at how well his soldiering skills had progressed since our first meeting less than twenty-four hours earlier. He was learning fast, and was proving himself to be a smart and resourceful individual.

Once he was close enough, Magdi gestured for us to follow him towards the pumphouse. Without a word, we got up and scurried after him, except Baby Steve who was covering us in case anything unpleasant developed. As we approached the main gate to the compound, Magdi pulled out a huge set of bolt-cutters. I was impressed: how the hell had he hidden them on himself? He cut through the chain securing the gate and within seconds we were against the pumphouse wall, adjacent to the door. Even though the desert night was cold, sweat was pouring down my face, causing my throat mic to slip ever lower down my neck.

Doug signalled to Baby Steve to come in from his position on the road – he placed a hand on his head, meaning 'on me'. As

Steve ran across to us, Magdi was already cutting the chain securing the pumphouse door. I was worried about the noise if the chain fell – normally, we would have wrapped it in hessian to deaden any sound. But there was no stopping Magdi. As it was, the chain dropped away quietly, yet the door still refused to open. Magdi glanced at me, as if for guidance. I tapped Doug's shoulder and pointed at the lock. Doug passed me his GPMG and dropped to his knees to take a closer look.

Guss was edging up on me from behind. 'Shoot it off,' he whispered hoarsely – and a little too loudly for my liking.

I turned, half fearing that he would already be levelling his weapon at it. At the same time Doug looked back at him with a killer stare. I could barely make out the words he muttered under his breath, but it was something like 'Shut the fuck up, you dumb Yank'. But Guss didn't need to hear him: the expression on Doug's face had said it all. Any plan Guss might have had of shooting off the door lock and alerting the whole Iraqi army to our presence was rapidly abandoned.

Doug pulled out a matchstick-thin length of C4 plastic-explosive charge from his webbing. Gently, he rolled it even thinner between his palms, until he was able to feed it into the keyhole. When he attached the fuse to the small protrusion still hanging from the lock, it was bigger than the charge. After a second or so's hesitation – he was clearly doing a last-minute mental check that he'd got everything right – he fired the fuse with an electric detonator. A split second later there was a barely audible thud – far quieter than firing any silenced weapon would have been – and slowly the door swung open. Bingo! We were in.

We checked the building for booby-traps, then took up our prescribed fire positions. I checked my watch: 23.45 hours. Five minutes ahead of schedule. It had taken us just under the hour I'd allocated to get there. I glanced around the darkened interior of the building. With only one door, no windows and no emergency exit, it was not the best of positions to be caught in if we were compromised. On the other hand, any enemy would have a hard job getting at us as there was only the one way in: through the door.

For a moment, I toyed with the idea of taking up defensive positions outside, but it was all open, exposed ground. Yet we needed a set of eyes out there. After some deliberation, I motioned to Baby Steve that he should take up a position outside the pumphouse to one side of the doorway. He managed to squeeze his considerable frame under one of the two large irrigation pipes that ran from the pumphouse, through the perimeter wall and into the fields. From that position he could give us early warning of any Iraqis trying to sneak up on us. Now it had become a waiting game.

While the rest of the team seemed icy calm, I could tell that Magdi was jumpy. He kept pacing up and down, then glancing out of the doorway in the direction of the road. This worried me: it was the first sign of nerves I'd seen in him. Even when Doug had threatened to slot him earlier, he had remained remarkably calm.

'What's up, Magdi?' I whispered, as I pulled him over into the shadows by the side of the doorway.

'The general. I am worrying he will not show up . . .' Magdi mumbled. 'I am worrying he is not coming.'

'You think that's likely?'

'I hope not. I hope the general comes . . .' He glanced nervously at Doug. 'But the general, if he fail to come, maybe it's me who get the blame.'

'Don't worry, Magdi,' I whispered, trying to reassure him. 'No general, we call the mission off. Simple. You've done your part – getting us here. Calm down. Let's wait and see what happens.'

We settled down in the darkness to wait. Show-time for the general was midnight. As the minutes dragged by, the only interruption was a short sitrep from Romero at the ERV, telling me that they were dropping back to the ditch at the junction of the main road: their position in the culvert was too exposed. I wondered if in fact a swarm of giant screaming desert spiders had pounced on them. When we got back to Cizre I'd rib Romero about it big-time: Delta Force running scared of a few arachnids.

I glanced at the others. Doug was sitting on the opposite side of the doorway, Magdi directly behind me. Guss had taken cover behind one of the giant pumphouse turn wheels, giving him a clear line of sight out of the door towards the entrance gate. He kept searching the darkness outside through the night-vision scope on his M4 assault rifle. No one spoke.

Midnight came and went, and there was no sign of the general. Instinctively I knew something was wrong, as did Doug. A cut-off point had to be laid down, beyond which we would wait no longer for the general to show. Finally I broke the silence. 'Go fetch Baby Steve, will you, mate?' I whispered across to Doug.

He nodded, disappeared into the darkness, and returned a few seconds later with him in tow.

'Show-time for the general was some fifteen minutes ago,' I whispered, as the lads gathered round. 'There's no sign of him. It's quiet as death out there and nothing's moving on the road. It doesn't feel right to me. We'll give him until 01.00 hours. If it's still a no-show we head for the ERV and get the hell out of here. All right?'

'Sure thing, boss,' Baby Steve whispered. Doug nodded.

'You, Guss?'

'Whatever you say.'

'Magdi?' I queried.

'Yes.' Magdi hung his head.

'OK, 01.00 hours and we're out of here, whatever happens.'

As we settled back into our positions I knew that the general wasn't coming. Whether he had bottled it at the last minute or had never intended to defect, I didn't know. But I was certain he wasn't going to show. As we crouched there in the darkness, my sixth sense was screaming at me to get the hell out. I could feel the hairs on the back of my neck standing on end and was tempted to ask Doug if he was feeling the same, but I wanted to appear calm and relaxed in front of Guss, Baby Steve and, particularly, Magdi.

I checked the ground outside the pumphouse through my night-vision monocular for any movement. I saw and heard nothing, but as the minutes ticked by towards 01.00 hours, I felt a burning, suffocating sensation inside my chest from where I had been hit by the .50-cal round. Sweat ran down my back in rivulets and my body armour felt like a straitjacket – like I was in a trap.

Eventually I could bear it no longer. I shuffled across to Doug. 'What d'you reckon, mate?' I whispered. 'You feeling what I'm feeling?'

'Fucked if I know,' Doug grunted. 'But I don't like it here one fucking bit. Most likely the general's bottled it. Time to fuck off out of here, that's what I say.'

I nodded and moved back across to the opposite door jamb. Every ten minutes I had been sending the same two-word message to Romero: 'Wait out.' He would then forward it to Tosh, who would send it to Quigly, Head Shed and Guss's lot. Those two words must have been driving them mad with frustration: all anyone would have deduced from them was that no one had a clue what was going on.

01.00 hours came and went. Still nothing.

'Time to go,' I said abruptly, getting to my feet and stretching. My limbs had seized up with inactivity and the desert chill.

Doug was up in an instant. He gave Magdi a look that would have scared anyone. Magdi raised his hands in silent protest. I moved out of the building covered by Doug and Guss, then to Baby Steve, whose knife was on the ground in front of him with a skewered scorpion on the tip. It had wanted to get a little too friendly with him. He and I covered Doug and Guss as they headed for the main gate to exit the complex. I got the thumbs-up from Doug to approach. Baby Steve and I stood up and started to run towards the gate.

All hell broke loose. The night was suddenly filled with gunfire. Green tracer rounds were zipping through the gates and hitting the walls of the pumphouse, the enclosure and the ground all the way up to the entrance door where I saw Magdi jumping out of the line of fire just in time. Baby Steve and I were out in the open, between the pumphouse and the gate, with tracer all round us. A small wall separated the car-parking area from the pumphouse and I dived behind it, closely followed by Baby Steve.

The crack of rounds over our heads was tremendous. I knew I had to look up to assess the situation, but the amount of fire power zipping overhead and thumping into the wall was just stupid. My earpiece had fallen from my ear as I'd dived. As soon as I put it back I could hear Romero asking for a sitrep. Before I could send a reply there was a lull in the fire so I looked over the wall in time to see Doug lean out from the gateway and fire his GPMG. It was almost reassuring to hear the 7.62mm burst into life.

As he fired I saw sand and dust kick up close to him as rounds bit into the ground, but still he kept firing. Then Guss leaned out on the opposite side and fired his M203 40mm grenade-launcher towards the incoming fire. There was an explosion two hundred yards down the track but it had no effect on the fire being directed towards us. Guss started to run back to the pumphouse. As he approached, tracers arcing towards him, he sprinted for the door, which was stupid given that the enemy fire was concentrated on that area. Doug was still hammering away with controlled bursts.

'*On me!*' I yelled at Guss, as he careered past.

At first I thought he hadn't heard but then he swung round in a large arc. He was about ten feet away when he dived, landing heavily between Baby Steve and me just as more rounds thumped into the wall. He was out of breath, his eyes bulging with adrenaline. I gave him the thumbs-up and he gave one back, then smiled, excited. Baby Steve looked across him to me and winked, as cool as a cucumber. Despite his youth, I was glad to have him with us.

I was about to look up to see how Doug was getting on when he crashed over the wall and hit the ground like a ton of muck, GPMG still in hand. 'Could've given me some fucking cover, you wankers,' he rasped, trying to be heard above the noise.

Romero was trying frantically to get some sense from me on the radio while at the same time sending out a contact report to Tosh. It was obvious we were seriously compromised. I radioed Romero and told him to request immediate ex-fill (ex-filtration) and for some CAS angels on our shoulders. He couldn't hear me properly, but I ordered him to stay put anyway until we could gauge how many we were up against. Going by the accuracy of the incoming fire I figured the area had been purposely sited as a killing zone with fixed machine-guns. We hadn't seen them on our way in, which showed serious pre-planning by the sods outside. Romero wanted to come in from behind the Iraqi positions and take them on in order to get us out but I declined. We had no idea what we were facing.

It was becoming obvious that either we had been stitched up or something had gone wrong. No point risking Romero and Athansa needlessly. I also needed Romero to stay put to control the air cover and ex-fill bird when, hopefully, it arrived. But first we had to get out of there before we had any chance of being lifted out.

Rounds were now concentrating on the wall we were behind and slowly chipping away at it. With the amount of fire coming our way, it would be just moments before the bullets penetrated it. We had to move. At that moment Magdi came running out of the pumphouse door, an AK47 in his hands. Doug and Guss raised their weapons, naturally thinking he had stitched us up, but as he came out he was firing from the hip towards the Iraqi positions outside the complex.

As he ran towards us, Doug and Guss kept their aim on him but held their fire. Just as he neared us, he was hit in the stomach. He was wearing no body armour, and even with the noise of gunfire and bullets zipping overhead, we all heard the sick squelch. He spun sideways but managed to stay upright and run, finally dropping in front of us. As rounds bit into the soil around him, Baby Steve lurched out on his belly, grabbed Magdi's collar and pulled him to us. Blood was pouring from his mouth and the effort of trying to speak above the din of the battle was half killing him. I leant closer to him. 'Not my fault this, not my fault. Something very bad wrong. You must move back into building, not safe out here.' He coughed. He was clutching his belly but blood was pouring through his fingers, clearly visible as it shimmered with each tracer round that flew overhead. Doug pushed Magdi's hands tightly into the wound, then rolled him sideways to check his back. Sure enough, blood was oozing from a large exit wound. Doug glanced at me. We both knew he'd had it.

'Fucking idiot, we know it ain't fucking safe out here,' Doug shouted at him.

Time was running out fast. If we got up one by one and ran for the relative safety of the pumphouse, we could be picked off one at a time. Usual procedure was to get up and run as a cluster, thus confusing the enemy. All they would see was a mass of arms and legs and be unable to count how many of us there were. The only advantage about the pumphouse was that the walls were thicker but the doorway was obviously zeroed as a killing ground. If we stayed put, we were going to die for sure. If we could get inside, we could try to hold out until either Kosrat's Peshmerga lads arrived or the US Marines from the south a few miles away.

I yelled into Doug's ear: 'Get your GPMG on top of the wall, mate. With the barrel rested up there, you should be able to put down some covering fire, right?'

'Fucking right.'

I motioned to Guss to follow Doug's lead, so that he could put down extra covering fire with his grenade-launcher. Guss nodded. As Doug raised the GPMG over the lip of the wall, a green tracer round zinged off the barrel and bounced straight up into the air.

I turned to Steve. 'Right, on the count of "three" I lob a white phos grenade at the gate and you throw two smoke grenades. We grab Magdi and run like hell for the pumphouse while Doug and Guss keep the fucking Iraqis' heads down. Got it?'

Steve raised an eyebrow, then nodded coolly. It wasn't the best of plans and I knew it – standing up in full view of the enemy with just a little smoke for cover so that we could make a mad dash towards a death trap. But I was damned if I could think of a better one. I grasped the pin of the white phosphorous grenade. Once I pulled, it was game on. I breathed deeply and glanced at Guss. He was gritting his teeth: I could see them gleaming green-white every time tracer zipped overhead. His hands were flexing round his grenade-launcher, and he was taking short, sharp breaths to keep himself calm. He glanced back at me, expressionless, and I nodded that I was ready. I saw Doug and Steve shrug at each other, as if to ask what all the fuss was about.

I slung my weapon round my neck and pulled the pin on the phosphorus grenade. For a moment I held the retaining clip tight. I could be dead within the next few seconds, I thought. I had felt that sensation several times before, but this time the chances of survival were close to zero. This time my life truly was in the lap of the gods. More tracer snapped past, lighting up the scene. Several rounds embedded themselves in the wall above me, fizzed and flickered then choked out. The most frightening thing was the knowledge that between each of those rounds there were another five normal bullets.

I released the grenade retainer arm by straightening my fingers. The brass clip flew into the air, and I watched it rise in slow motion, glinting in the eerie light. I was committed. I reached for Magdi with my left arm, then hurled the grenade up and back-wards over the wall, aiming it blind towards the pumphouse gateway. Simultaneously, Doug opened up with a deafening barrage from the GPMG. It bounced madly up and down on the wall, forcing him to grasp it tightly round the trigger mechanism with both hands. Then Baby Steve threw his smoke grenades.

My white phos grenade exploded, spewing out a brilliant gout of white flame and throwing off thousands of tiny glowing phosphorous balls all over the entranceway. As Baby Steve's grenades spewed out a thick cloud of smoke, Guss turned on to his knees and fired an aimed shot with his grenade-launcher towards the entrance. Doug followed suit, spinning round on to his knees and taking aim with his GPMG, firing controlled bursts at the enemy. The area was ablaze with green tracers coming our way, and red going in their direction. My ears were ringing to the point that I could no longer hear the rounds whizzing past me.

I leant down to grab Magdi, but Baby Steve was ahead of me. He jumped to his feet, grabbed Magdi's collar as tracer spat round him, whipped the injured Iraqi on to his shoulders in a fireman's lift and pounded towards the pumphouse doorway. Not quite as I'd planned it but, then, what plan ever survives contact with the enemy?

Magdi was bouncing about like a rag doll on Steve's shoulders, as if he weighed nothing. I could see rounds biting into the dirt all around them. The tracer seemed to grope in the darkness for a kill. As Baby Steve lunged towards the doorway, several tracer rounds smashed into the masonry on either side. He dived forward, throwing Magdi ahead, and suddenly they were inside.

Lungs burning, I raced after them expecting to be hit. I could just make out that in the darkness someone had got a bead on me because rounds were kicking up the dirt just behind me and closing rapidly. I dived for the doorway, felt a kick to my left foot which caused me to spin in the air, and landed hard on my left side, just inside the pumphouse. For an instant I saw Baby Steve pulling Magdi out of the line of fire, and then I was rolling to the opposite side, as rounds poured in after me, walking up the centre of the floor towards the main pumps. As they hit the pipes, bullets zipped and pinged off the thick metal casings, ricocheting all over the inside of the building.

I readied my weapon – an M16–A2 with a 40mm grenade-launcher attached – as Baby Steve did the same. Over the noise of the incoming fire, I could still make out the throaty roar of Doug's GPMG firing in bursts, and the hollow *bloop!* of Guss's M203 – they were still alive and fighting. I lay down as close to the base of the doorway as possible, aiming my weapon towards the main gate, which was still blanketed in smoke. I could hear the screams of an injured enemy soldier, but my ears were ringing so loudly that I couldn't tell exactly how far away.

At my signal, Baby Steve and I opened up on the Iraqi positions. As we did so, Doug and Guss glanced back our way, and then they were up and running. They covered the open ground at breakneck speed, but three RPGs whooshed in their direction. One exploded just in front of them and I was convinced they were going down – but a fraction of a second later they reappeared through the swirling dust and tracers, running even faster now. Just as they neared the building, there was a sudden lull – almost as if someone had ordered a momentary ceasefire to enable them to make it to the pumphouse alive. Then they were diving inside and rolling clear of the doorway.

A huge explosion occurred near the main gate. What caused it I'll never know. Perhaps we'd hit a crate of RPGs or similar but the screams that followed will stay with me for the rest of my life. I'd heard screams before but at that moment we could all hear very clearly a scream that was of absolute terror and pain. I can't put the sound, or how it seemed to come from the deepest part of someone's soul, into words – they don't begin to convey the reality of it.

For some reason I thought of my eldest brother. When we were children I'd led my gang on to the Colchester MCTC (Military Corrective Training Centre) assault course at night and Craig had come with us. When a Land Rover turned up we all ran and Craig got separated from us. From the safety of the woods, all I could hear was Craig screaming because he was lost.

Doug lay down on the floor to the left of the doorframe with just his GPMG barrel sticking out round it. As Baby Steve checked Magdi, Guss decided for some reason that he would sit up on the metal walkway that spanned between the two pumps, putting himself in the direct line of incoming fire. He started to bum-shuffle backwards to the rear of the pumps where they went through the walls and propped himself up. As Doug calmly took out a belt of fifty 7.62mm rounds and clipped them to the few rounds left on the belt in his weapon, Baby Steve caught my eye. He was holding Magdi up against the wall and shook his head, indicating that the Iraqi was dead. He jumped up, dashed across and moved next to me.

We checked our weapons and got out all the grenades we had, ready to throw. Then I heard Romero going mad on my earpiece, still dangling from my neck. I put it back into my ear. Baby Steve yelled at Guss to get down and find better cover.

'Fuck that,' Guss yelled. 'If them motherfuckers are coming for me, I want to see them coming, and I want them to see who's sending them to Allah!'

I was about to intervene, when I stopped myself. So far, Guss had been a big surprise to us all. The American 'loaf' had emerged from the contact as a man with robotic killer calm. Doug smiled, winked and took aim. The shooting stopped and all we could hear were the moans of those we had injured. Whoever had screamed in such pain and terror was silent now.

I radioed Romero. 'Hello, India Two, this is India Sunray Zero, message. Over.'

'India Two, send. Over?' Romero replied calmly.

'India Sunray Zero, sustained contact with enemy. Holed up in target building. Size of enemy force unknown. Over.'

'India Two, requesting go-ahead to do a CTR. Over.' Romero wanted to sneak up on the Iraqi positions from the rear to ascertain what numbers we were up against.

'India Sunray Zero, negative. Stay put, call in an extraction chopper and chase that CAS. We need angels on our shoulders now. Over.'

'India Two, well copied. Out.'

It was dark, smoky, and the air stank of cordite and burning flesh. My phosphorus grenade had made its mark. It was then that I noticed the heel of my left boot had been shot clean through the middle. That was what had hit me as I dived through the doorway.

Doug lay perfectly still behind the GPMG, his eyes fixed firmly on the aim. The pumphouse complex only had one entrance and the surrounding walls were high, thick and solid. All we had to do was keep the entrance covered. It was only some twelve feet wide, which gave us a serious advantage against any attacking forces that wanted to come in. Thank God for Doug's GPMG: without it we stood no chance. Romero confirmed back to me that he had requested immediate recovery. The nearest unit already in the air was a US Special Forces team en route back to Turkey. They had declined to help even though they were just ten minutes' flight time away.

Tosh sent back a message that he would confirm who they were and have them sent back for us as it would take two hours minimum for one of the dedicated CSAR choppers to reach us. Kosrat's convoy was delayed, perhaps another eight hours away, and the US Marines were bogged down dealing with insurgents and Iraqi regulars in the village of Abuja, right on Tikrit's doorstep. I knew I couldn't call the CSAR helicopter directly into this immediate area as it was far too hot: as soon as a helicopter appeared, one well-placed RPG or concentrated ground fire would bring it down on top of us. And how ironic that would be, I thought.

Romero came back that Tosh believed the SF helicopter nearby was one of Dan's lot, but they had refused again to come to our aid. As soon as he had said this, I felt it like a blow to the stomach, punching the life force out of me. It was one thing to have been betrayed and ambushed by the Iraqis, but quite another to be abandoned by your own side, when they were just a short flight time away. The betrayal seemed personal – especially if Dan Meany was involved, which now looked likely.

Three RPGs exploded to our front. How they missed the building I don't know. They were immediately followed by a hail of tracer rounds, plus an added .50-cal heavy machine-gun. The darkness and smoke meant we couldn't see anyone, just the tracer rounds zipping towards us. We had to conserve our ammunition so we didn't fire back blindly, and the gunfire stopped as quickly as it had started. Suddenly we saw Iraqi troops running towards us firing from the hip. I did a double-take: there appeared to be at least a hundred racing towards us in that cramped parking area.

They'd reached the midway section where the small wall was when I heard a *bloop* and a whoosh as Guss fired a 40mm grenade straight past me out of the door. It exploded among the Iraqis, throwing several sideways as well as body parts in all directions, but still the main group kept coming. Doug opened up in full auto mode without stopping for controlled bursts as they were practically upon us. As Doug fired from left to right, Iraqis were falling, spinning as they were hit, while others were kicked backwards by the force of the rounds hitting them. As men in the front sections fell, most mortally wounded, the others kept charging over them, still firing.

I opened up as Guss fired another 40mm and Baby Steve rolled into view to take aim. Rounds were snapping past my head and dust was being kicked up all over the place. Doug did the fastest reload of a belt of ammo I have ever seen and blasted away, first to his left, then the middle and then right. Grit was in my eyes, which streamed. Now Guss was firing on full auto as the Iraqis came even closer.

I aimed my rifle at the lunging mass ahead, squeezed off a round and saw it hit the centre of one man's face. His eyes bulged out and his nose imploded into his head. He fell and I fired again, hitting the man standing directly behind him in the chest. He fell forwards too – not backwards, as you see in movies. I fired again, hit another man. Fuck, I thought, I'm firing in a straight line and men behind are being funnelled through that entrance directly into our fire path. How the hell are we going to stop this onslaught? I fired again and another went down. I went on until the magazine ran out.

As I was changing it, the noise was unbelievable. All I could see was Doug shifting from one aim point to the next and firing, Guss firing off round after round of 40mm grenades as quickly as he could reload and Baby Steve lying practically in the doorway on the floor firing at everything, only stopping to throw a couple of hand grenades. Normally you would throw a grenade and duck but we didn't have that luxury. Fortunately for us, and unfortunately for the Iraqis, their bodies were taking the main force of the explosions or we would have been peppered with shrapnel.

The fire coming from the Iraqis was not accurate now, but they were within ten feet – which is nothing, believe me – when those still standing turned and ran back towards the main entrance gate. In films you always see soldiers being noble and letting them retreat. Stuff that, I thought, as they would come back, so we kept firing, taking aimed shots this time as they ran into the cover of the smoke and dust. It was bloody and awful having to kill men like that, but I focused on the promise I'd made to myself that I would get home. Now I had to do whatever was necessary to keep it.

No sooner had they disappeared than the heavy machine-guns opened up again. I dived for cover behind the doorway as Doug rolled out of harm's way. His GPMG barrel was steaming hot. As rounds hit the pumphouse, Guss made himself into a very small target up against the back wall. Baby Steve and I checked ourselves and our ammo. Doug did a rapid barrel change. If it gets too hot it can cook off rounds prematurely or blow up in your face, so you carry a spare that you can change in seconds. I noticed then that the doorway was covered with blood, as were we. Bits of flesh and bone were strewn everywhere.

I peered round the corner and saw carnage. The entire car park area – in fact, all of the area – was covered with dead and seriously injured Iraqis. I could see bodies slumped against the inner wall and across it. Some had fallen on top of others. I ducked behind the wall again as more rounds kicked into the ground and doorway.

A pool of blood was slowly edging its way in from the dead outside. It shimmered like an oil slick in the dark. Baby Steve beckoned me nearer to him. 'Fucking waste of time carrying Magdi back, wasn't it?' he yelled, above the noise.

I gave a thumbs-up.

'At least he protected my back.' He grinned.

Doug took up his fire position again. The rounds coming our way had died down to just the odd one here and there but I was convinced Guss would take a hit at any moment, and he refused to move. Did he want it over and done with quickly or what? I wondered, as he sat up high, almost mesmerised. Doug winked at me again. Part of me thought that maybe he was enjoying this – he looked so calm. I wiped away sweat from my forehead, then saw my arm. It wasn't sweat but blood. Not mine – from the dead and dying outside.

Romero came over the net: Tosh had got us transport out. Only problem was the helicopter wouldn't reach us for another hour and a half and we would have to rendezvous with it several miles away. No problem, I thought, if we ever got out of this hole. After all we'd been through I didn't want to die here. I was sure the Iraqis would soon bring up a tank or heavy armour, or just place a large bomb at the back of the building and detonate it with us inside.

'This is karma pay-back big-time, boss, for us fucking off them rag-heads earlier,' Doug called from his side of the doorway.

'Looks that way,' I replied, with a wry smile. I assumed Doug was referring to the Iraqi colonel who had given us his co-ordinates and offered to surrender in the Kurdish hills, only for his men to be bombed into oblivion by US air power.

I had felt wretched when that happened, but somehow I didn't feel that we were the guilty party. We had passed on his co-ordinates in good faith, believing that the US commanders would honour their pledge not to target them. I'd done as I had to save lives. And somehow, deep inside me, my instinct was telling me that, bad as things were now, we would get out of this one alive.

'The karma's bad, but it ain't that bad,' I called back to Doug.

15

THE KILLING FIELDS

After the suicidal assault they'd just made, it would be insane to do it again, I thought. But then I recalled intel reports that on 4 April, US Marines in Kut had had over eighty AK47-wielding Iraqi soldiers attack them in a deliberate suicide assault against a single tank, so I knew they were more than capable of it. As we all sat with our thoughts, the odd round bouncing through the door, I thought of Victoria. If she could see me now, I thought, covered with blood and gore, trapped in a hell-hole . . . She hated fights and I was in the middle of one. I thought of my parents, too, and especially my children: they would all be upset if I didn't get out of this alive.

I took out my PNGs to get a better look outside, but as I switched them on I realised they had been damaged. Back to good old-fashioned standard army-issue mark one eyeball. A sudden burst of heavy machine-gun fire forced us to shield our eyes as dust and brick debris flew everywhere. It was followed by the screams and shouts of another full-frontal assault towards us. I decided we would wait until the heavy machine-guns stopped firing and the Iraqis were almost on top of us before I would lean out to shoot. The heavy-calibres kept firing.

Doug made himself as small as possible and, despite the heavy incoming thumping all around him, started firing – he knew that if he didn't we were as good as dead. Guss fired another 40mm as Baby Steve and I decided we had to fire too. Baby Steve rolled past me straight into the pool of blood in the open doorway and fired off his M203, followed by bursts of fire.

I leant out and only just had time to level my weapon as an Iraqi was right in front of me. I fired off on auto and he shot backwards, his helmet smacking into the face of the soldier behind him, who stumbled forward on to his knees. I squeezed off another burst that tore straight through the top of that soldier's helmet. Blood and brains spurted out from the rim in a shower of red. I raised my aim – bang! Another one went down. Bang! Another.

I shifted to aim to my left as an Iraqi was nearly on top of Doug and aiming straight at his head. I fired a burst that tore into the man's side, shoulder, face, and took off the top of his head. He fell on to Doug. As Doug pushed him away, countless more converged on the doorway. I got away from it as Baby Steve sat up and fired another 40mm straight into the middle of the group, as did Guss in perfect harmony.

Baby Steve's round went straight through the first man, which was providential for us – if it had exploded I'm sure it would have done us damage too – and detonated in the man behind him. The concussion from the explosion threw me on to my backside against the first main pump pipe. I found myself sitting with my back to it, Baby Steve next to me and Guss up above and to our rear. Doug, meanwhile, was firing off bursts as he kicked his way backwards to us. All we could see through the smoke, dust and cordite fumes was the odd anguished, aggressive, terrified face of an Iraqi soldier. We could see now that they were conscripts, as they tried to push into the room. I thought my heart was going to burst it was pumping so hard.

I glanced left and saw Baby Steve grimace as he fought to maintain aim, firing on full auto, empty cases flying up in the air. Doug was firing with the butt of his GPMG held into his thigh as his left hand fed in the ammo belt, which was getting very short very quickly.

As I looked up again I fired off the last round in the magazine as an Iraqi was pushed in front of me by his colleagues shoving from behind. I kicked his legs hard and he fell down next to me. I smashed the butt of my rifle as hard as I could into the back of his now exposed head without looking – I was too busy staring up the barrel of another AK47. I thrust my rifle up, knocking it away as the Iraqi fired. Problem was, I knocked it towards Baby Steve. The rounds cut across the top of his shoulder webbing, missing his head by a fraction.

The Iraqi fell towards me – his comrades were behind, pushing frantically. All I could do was lunge the barrel of my weapon hard into his face. It caught his top lip and split it. As he continued to fall, the muzzle of my rifle caught his upper lip and nose, tearing it up and off to reveal brilliant white bone. A round hit him from behind, vaporising the right side of his face. It struck me then that the poor sods were not so much aggressive, brave and dedicated but were being shot at from behind and trying to get into cover.

Romero, I thought, had disobeyed me and come behind them. Then I realised I could still hear the heavy thump of the .50-cal outside. As the assault had gone in, the Iraqis outside had not stopped firing as their own men came into the killing zone. They had continued to stop us firing back. It was a heartless tactic that the Russians had used on their troops in Stalingrad during the Second World War. I could see the terror in the face of another young Iraqi conscript as he was pushed towards me by the mass of his comrades. He dropped his AK47, fell to his knees and looked straight at me, hands clasped as if he was begging me not to shoot him.

The soldier behind him took a direct hit from the .50-cal, which threw him forward against the young man kneeling. Their heads cracked together with a sick crunch I could hear above the battle. Both fell forward on to my outstretched legs at which point Doug, now surrounded by Iraqis trying to stab him with bayonets or get a clear shot, pulled out a phosphorus grenade, lunged on to his back, pulled the pin, let the retainer fly and lay there.

We'd been overrun. This was it. Doug was going to take out as many with us as he could.

Baby Steve clocked what he'd done. 'Scotland for ever,' he yelled.

Steve has nothing to do with Scotland, but his favourite film is *Braveheart*. I started to laugh. So this was where I was going to die. I'd often wondered how I would feel when the time came, but as I sat there I still couldn't believe this was it. There were things I wanted and needed to do. I'd told Tosh I had a future with Victoria that included children. I'd been wrong. I just hoped I wasn't wrong about there being life after death.

The Iraqis in the room froze, even though .50-cal rounds were still incoming and now a hole had been breached in the wall to the right of the door. We were all transfixed by the phosphorus grenade Doug was holding up, pin and retainer gone. Any second now it would go off and kill every living thing in that room. The Iraqis outside saw Doug's last-stand gesture, turned and ran. It seemed like an age as we all stared at each other, friend and foe alike, waiting for the bang. Then, suddenly, an Iraqi stumbled over his dead comrades out of the room, quickly followed by the others.

As they fell and crawled over the dead to get out, Doug jumped up and was about to throw the grenade when another Iraqi stood up, in full view despite the smoke in the doorway.

'Out of the fucking way, rag-head,' Doug yelled.

The Iraqi raised his hands and gestured as if to apologise, then ducked accordingly. Instantly Doug threw the grenade and dived out of the blast zone. Thanks, Doug, I thought. Baby Steve and I were on our backsides stuck against the pipes, several dead Iraqis at our feet and in full exposed view. Fortunately the grenade exploded as it hit the ground. It threw up some pieces of bodies, thus taking away a lot of the force from the initial detonation. The blinding flash meant we had to close our eyes for a second.

I opened them in time to see the whole doorway awash with white balls of burning phosphorus that came flying into the room and through the breach in the wall. Guss got down from his exposed position and started to kick bits of it towards the open floor just as Doug pulled me out of the line of direct fire. Phosphorus balls sizzled in the pool of blood, giving off a smell like burnt steak, sweet and sickly. I gagged.

The shooting stopped, I think in part so that the Iraqi commander, whoever he was, could ascertain who was now in control of the building. The question of whether he was genuinely looking to cross over with his unit was now academic. Doug dragged me across the floor and against the wall. I was covered from head to toe with blood, as were we all, but he thought I'd been hit.

'You fucking all right?' he yelled, which resulted in another burst of .50-cal coming our way.

'Looked at yourself lately, you mad fuck?' I yelled back.

Baby Steve scrambled across to us. 'Don't fucking mind me, will you?' he joked.

Guss was still kicking out bits of burning phosphorus. We glanced at the bodies in the doorway and back to the small wall. This was madness, I thought. What kind of commander would send his troops into such a full-frontal suicidal attack? But the buggers would have got us that time, had it not been for Doug's mad gesture with the phosphorus grenade, the results of which the Iraqis had seen earlier. As we all looked at the bloody mess I started to laugh, as I often do when I'm stressed. 'We ever get out of this, I'll buy you a *Braveheart* sword,' I said to Baby Steve.

'I could fucking do with one now, boss,' he replied, 'the way this gang-fuck's going.'

Guss was clambering back up on to the framework joining the two pipes. We all looked at him.

'Hey, I was safe up there so I'm going back, OK? Any problems with that?' he asked.

Doug took out another belt of 7.62mm. He linked four together making a belt of two hundred. 'That's all I have left and the fuckers can have it with interest,' he murmured.

Thank God he was with us, I thought, and on our side. Without his GPMG we wouldn't have stood a hope in hell of beating back the assaults. Baby Steve was checking his mags and how many 40mm grenades he had left. We could hear groans and moans from outside, and someone shouting orders in the distance. Romero was asking me for sitreps every minute, until I assured him we were still intact.

I reloaded and cocked my weapon. My M203 grenade-launcher was seriously dented from a bullet strike and I couldn't fire any 40mm rounds from it so I passed the ammo to Baby Steve, who gently pulled my muzzle towards him. A chunk of flesh was wedged in the muzzle flash eliminator. He prised it out with his fingers and held it up. A lump of that size could have caused the barrel to explode if I'd fired it. As he held it up we realised together that it was part of a nose. He flicked it to the ground and we took up our positions again.

This time we used the dead bodies as best we could to make a shield. I was certain the commander would send troops to the back now to breach the wall but they never came. I was trying to formulate some kind of plan for us to get out. We could blast a hole in the wall and leg it out the rear, but I reckoned that that was what the Iraqis wanted us to do and that they'd be waiting. We were running low on ammo – although we had plenty of Iraqi ammo and weapons now. Our grenades were rapidly running out too. I knew we couldn't hold out for much longer: this was their country and they could bring in shitloads of reinforcements. Also I'd no idea just how many were outside already.

As I pondered our dilemma, I knew I had to action a plan pretty quickly if we were to meet our helicopter ride home. Baby Steve wondered about the likelihood of a couple of Apaches coming to our aid. Then Romero came through with the one positive piece of news I was hoping for: we had dedicated CAS angels on our shoulders for the next four hours.

All was quiet for about fifteen minutes as we listened intently. I considered requesting SPIE (special procedures insertion/extraction): would the CSAR be prepared to hover over the site long enough for us to get in if we could put down adequate suppressive fire coupled with an airstrike from our angels? SPIE was similar to STRABO (Specialist Tactical Recovery Airborne Operations), a cable suspended beneath a helicopter to which you attached yourself by your own D-ring and were hoisted away rapidly. With STRABO, you swing all over the place, but with SPIE, you don't, so you can still fire your weapon. I relayed this request to Tosh via Romero.

The groans had stopped – the injured had obviously bled to death. No one was risking a visit out to rescue their friends. Any moment now, we knew, another assault would come. As we sat there I took out my last sweet and sucked it. Blackcurrant, the best I've ever tasted. Then I got out my water bottle, which was covered with blood. I wiped it clean but I could still taste iron. Doug asked if he could have some of my sweet as he only had lemon ones. I took what was left of mine out of my mouth and passed it to him. 'You got any diseases, boss, that I catch, you're fucking dead.'

Romero came back that Tosh had received a negative to our

request as the CSAR didn't have the SPIE harness set up. Doug and I glanced at each other: they most certainly would have – or should, being CSAR.

'Maybe wank-features Tosh didn't bother to forward the request,' Doug exclaimed.

'No, he would have,' I replied, and tried not to think too hard about it.

I stared out of the door for a few seconds as I racked my brains for another escape plan and drew a complete blank. Well, if I couldn't come up with a plan, I'd use the opportunity of being stuck to clear up a few things with Doug. Like why he hated journalists. And what was his problem with Tosh?

'Come on, Doug, tell me – what's the big score with journalists?' I asked matter-of-factly.

Doug glanced at me. 'You really want to know, boss?' he asked, then re-aimed on the space to our front.

'Sure he fucking does and so do I,' Baby Steve interjected.

'All right, then, as we're never going to fucking get out of here alive, I'll fucking tell you.' He kept his aim on the GPMG. 'After nine years in the Reg I started dating this gorgeous bird. Only trouble was, she worked as a fucking reporter on the local rag in Hereford. I made her promise she'd never divulge anything about my work and told her about a few of the ops I'd been on. I'd fallen hook, line and fucking sinker for her. She was all I could think about when I was away. We've all been there. Instead of concentrating on me work, I was always looking forward to getting home to her. I knew I couldn't continue with the job, 'cause I wanted to settle down with her.'

He paused for a second to listen, in case the enemy were trying to creep up on us undetected. 'After the Iranian embassy siege, the SAS were hot news,' he continued. 'By now this bird had moved in with me. The CO warned me at the time I was on thin ice, with her being a reporter and all, but she just kept telling me I could trust her and not to worry. Well, I came back from the Falklands and told her I was leaving the Regiment so I could be with her always. She got very angry, and said she only wanted a man who was in the Regiment. I couldn't believe she was so shallow, but she was serious. She said if I left the Regiment the relationship was over. Well, no one was going to fucking blackmail me, so I called her bluff. I told her I was resigning and leaving the Army. At the time I meant it, too.'

'So, what happened?' I asked – he'd gone silent on us.

'What happened?' said Doug. 'In the Falklands I'd been sent into Argentina to do this CTR on the main airbase. We were going there to give early warning about the Argies' fighter bombers. They were using their French Exocet missiles against our ships, remember? Well, we were about to hit the LZ when the officer in charge decided to abort the mission. We flew on to Chile, then set about destroying the Sea King by sinking it in a lake. Problem was, it didn't sink. Well, me and all the lads got a lot of stick afterwards that we'd bottled it. So, with all that on me fucking shoulders I confided in me bird.' He almost sighed.

'So, she went to the fucking papers?' Baby Steve prompted.

'Too right she fucking did. That night she packed her bags, wrote an exposé on the whole mission and several prior operations and sent it to the *Sunday Times*. A bidding war started between them and another paper, and the love of my life stood to make a small fortune. I confronted the bitch, begged her to withdraw the story and come home, but she wouldn't. She was hard and cold towards me, like only a fucking journalist could be. Just saw me as a story. Tell you the truth, it broke my fucking heart. I vowed I'd never let a woman put me through that again.'

'Fucking bitch! So what the fuck did you do, mate?' Baby Steve asked.

'I didn't do fuck all. It was decided for me,' Doug continued. 'The newspaper that got the story was stamped on by the MoD, so it never came out. But the damage was already done, wasn't it? It was all known to the Regiment, and I was asked to leave. I had to go voluntarily or be RTU'd. I was fucking devastated. Lost the first love of me life, the Regiment, and now the other love of me life, that journalist bitch. You want to know the rest of it, do you? Well, I went to a very bad place and did a lot of drinking. Would've killed myself, most likely, if it hadn't been for getting myself recruited as a retread. I volunteered for any and all ops to try to make up for it. Got back on terms with the Regiment. But when you've been down as low as I was, you don't fear much. Not even fucking death. That's why I count every day as a blessing, 'cause I was that close to topping myself. It's what led me to Buddhism too, but that's another story.' There was silence.

'So that's why you didn't take to Heather. Pretty female journalists like her can't be that high on your likeability scale,' I commented.

'Nope. They aren't,' Doug confirmed. 'I've tried dealing with it, but I can't get it out of my system. Journalists? They're scavengers. Parasites. Especially the fucking women.'

After his revelations I was itching to ask him why he disliked Tosh so much, but before I could Romero called in: Tosh could confirm that one of Dan's teams was still in the area, less than ten minutes away, and he was trying to raise them but we had to get out and away from the concentration of Iraqi troops outside.

The plan I came up with was brutally simple. We would wait until another assault came in, which couldn't be long now. Then, whichever direction it came from, we would rush out to meet them head on. We would discharge all of our grenades while staying in a diamond shape of four – me at the front, Doug at the rear, Baby Steve and Guss on either side. We would charge out of the main gates and make for open desert. It was daring, maybe, insane, perhaps, but we had no other option, as far as I could see. We could sit and wait, knowing that, sooner or later, we would be overwhelmed. Or we could go on the offensive. We had been trained to fight that way – to go on the attack when the enemy least expects it.

If we waited until they attacked we would be out and among them before they knew it, which would make it difficult for them to fight us without shooting their own. While this might not worry the Iraqi commander, it would certainly cause the troops up close to hesitate. Once out of the pumphouse complex, we would let rip with as many smoke grenades as we had and run hell for leather to the ERV. Most importantly, just before we charged I would give the signal for our CAS to drop all the munitions they had on the area. During the resulting chaos, noise and confusion, we would make good our escape, link up with Romero and Athansa and leg it to the helicopter PUP (pick-up point). It seemed simple enough, and as I explained it to the others it even sounded vaguely doable.

Tosh came back, via Romero, that Pilot Steve was attempting to get refuelled and was more than willing and able to come in for us. A Chinook can take a lot of damage but not RPG rounds. The CSAR CH53 Pave low was a lot sturdier and capable of looking after itself.

It was only minutes but it seemed an age as we sat viewing the scene that lay before us. Guss was muttering something to himself. 'He's praying,' Doug whispered.

Suddenly the .50-cals opened up again. This time they'd been moved and resighted: the fire was coming straight through the door very accurately. The rounds smashed into the dead Iraqi bodies we'd stacked up, knocking them down like tissue and throwing body parts all over the place. Also small-arms fire and green tracer streamed in through the doorway and the breach hole. Doug leant out and tried to fire off a burst but the heavy incoming forced him to dive out of the line of fire on to his back.

Green tracer and large .50-cal rounds zipped past us like a

fantastic light show. Bullets were ricocheting all over the place, causing us to duck and shield our faces. Guss just sat up top, like a Buddha, still not moving. I thought he'd lost the plot. My great plan of rushing out to greet the Iraqis head on suddenly went pear-shaped with their new tactics. Even to stand up would be inviting instant death.

The heavy machine-gun fire died down a little as up to thirty Iraqi conscripts rushed towards us yelling and firing. Some were stopping to take aimed shots this time. As soon as they stopped, Doug fired well-aimed bursts at them. A 7.62mm at close range literally tears a human body to pieces. Through the dust and smoke I caught glimpses of Iraqis. As soon as I spotted one I fired and they would drop. I became oblivious to the rounds thumping around me. Didn't have time to think or worry about it.

'Do we go?' Baby Steve was shouting.

Too many Iraqis were funnelling through the narrow entrance and rushing our way, and still the .50-cal was firing at the doorway. I saw at least five go down having been hit from behind. Some bright spark had got a bead on my position and was firing accurately towards me, the bullets ripping into the bodies I had dragged in front of me. In the haze of smoke, dust and vaporised clouds of blood, I rolled across the entrance and next to Doug. Several Iraqis appeared, running at speed towards us, jumping over the dead and wounded. Doug took out four with a burst as I raised my aim to take out the man nearest to us. I was about to fire when he was hit in the knee from behind. He crumpled to the ground, stunned. He was rolling backwards when he was hit again in the shoulder from behind. As he fell backwards his gaze fell on me and our eyes locked.

Suddenly another figure appeared right in front of me. He'd obviously come round the side. I shot him in the groin as he'd stepped straight in front of my muzzle. Baby Steve yelled as an arm appeared from the top of the doorway and a grenade was lobbed in. 'They're on the roof,' he shouted, as he jumped up, caught the grenade and threw it back out.

The Iraqis in the line of the grenade parted. It exploded, throwing several into the air and dropping others where they stood. The roof of the pumphouse was solid concrete so we couldn't shoot up through the ceiling. Baby Steve dived off to the right and took up firing again. The number of bodies was now a major obstacle to the attacking Iraqis in the confined space left.

I sent a signal to Romero for our CAS angels to drop danger close. We had to get out of this place. I signalled to Doug, Guss and Baby Steve that we were going for it. Doug was running out of ammo and Guss gestured he was down to just one 40mm grenade for his launcher.

'Fire in the hole in sixty,' Romero came back.

This meant sixty seconds. We couldn't do fire for effect as we would have on a normal fire mission. This was rapid improvisation on the go. We heard the screech of the F18 Hornets above almost instantly. My only concern now was whether they would drop directly on the pumphouse or forward of it, as requested. Some of the Iraqis paused, looking upwards. That was all it took for us to sight and drop them. I was now down to one magazine of rounds. The F18s pulled up fast and I waited for the explosions.

As Iraqi soldiers jumped for cover, I buried my face and covered my ears. A thunderous, almighty roar went up. Not a bang, a truly awesome roar that seemed to get louder as the ground shook violently. I felt the air pressure outside drop, then blast back with a furious howl. Before the noise had begun to die down I was up, followed by Baby Steve to my right, Doug to my left and Guss somewhere behind. I rushed forwards, leaping over bodies.

In the dark, smoke and chaos I prayed I was heading in the right direction. I could smell avgas from the F18s' after-burners as lots of little fires illuminated the ground. The smell of burnt flesh from the grenades was strong, as was the choking smell of cordite. We could hear screaming and shouting ahead but at least the heavy .50-cals had stopped firing. Half of the outer pumphouse enclosure wall had been flattened as we ran towards it. Anything beyond that should hopefully have been obliterated by the airstrike.

I was wrong.

As we charged through the shattered gates, the curtain of smoke blew aside, and we could see dozens of Iraqi soldiers rushing towards us from every direction. Worse, they opened up again with the heavy .50-cals. A carpet of green tracer raced towards us from all directions. A great number of dead Iraqis, whom the airstrike had taken out, lay on the ground, but I had no idea where the hell the others were coming from. If we ran towards them to attack, as was my plan, we were dead for certain. They were everywhere and there was nowhere for us to take cover.

Doug grabbed my shoulder. '*Plan fucking Z,*' he yelled as he pulled me back.

'Plan Z' was the phrase we used when all other plans had gone to rat shit. In an instant we were running back the way we had come, towards the pumphouse. Just as we reached the doorway we careered into Guss, knocking him to the floor.

'Hey, guys, you came back for me!' he shouted.

We hadn't even realised we'd left him behind, and as we dived back into the cover of the pumphouse, the pursuing Iraqi soldiers opened up on us again. As a barrage of rounds hammered through the doorway, Doug, Baby Steve and Guss returned fire, and I got on the net to Romero. From the glimpse I'd had of the enemy concentrations outside, I reckoned that we were up against at least a battalion-sized unit – up to a thousand men. And the Iraqi soldiers advancing on us now weren't conscripts: they were dressed as Republican Guards, unlike the cannon fodder that

had been used on us up to now. But for the fact that the assaults
had been funnelled through the entranceway, and were being met
by a wall of fire from us, we would have been overrun.

I sent an urgent message as priority that we needed a MOAB,
and we needed it dropped danger close to our position, as the last
airstrike had not done the job properly. I knew that the MOAB
had been designed to take out large troop concentrations, wiping
them out in thousands. It was such a massively destructive
weapon that the concept of 'danger close' wasn't relevant where
it was concerned. I used the phrase more to demonstrate the
desperate nature of our situation – that we were totally surrounded and about to be overrun. I also suspected that by the
time they had loaded a MOAB aboard a C130 Talon and had got
it into position, it would be all over for us. But if we were to die,
better to take the Iraqis with us.

A minute passed, then Romero came back, saying that the
MOAB was almost in position and to stand by. All they wanted
from me was the signal of when to drop it. I was stunned. How
come they just happened to have a C130 Talon with a MOAB on
board in the area exactly now? It could only mean that it had been
called for hours ago when the fire-fight had first kicked off. The
implications did not bear thinking about. I forced the dark
thoughts of betrayal from my mind – and the certainty I was
now feeling that we had been used as bait by our own side – and
tried to concentrate on the job in hand. Survival. We had to
survive. Somehow we had to get out of this thing alive – and then
I could hunt down Dan, Quigly and the rest of the duplicitous
bastards in my own way and in my own time.

Romero begged me to allow him and Athansa to cause a
diversion, but with the MOAB on its way there was little need. I
radioed him to stay put and wait for us at the ERV, then
instructed him to get the US fly boys to drop their MOAB as
soon as possible, two kilometres south of us. Then I double-

checked with Romero that he had the exact co-ordinates of the pumphouse to pass up to the US pilots – 'Ask them not to fry us,' I added as an afterthought.

There was no time for fear, or even thoughts of 'death by MOAB': the Iraqis were pushing ahead with another assault. Doug was firing off short bursts, trying to make every bullet count, and Baby Steve had gone on to single-shot mode. Doug fired the last of the belt on his GPMG and sat up to grab his pistol. An Iraqi soldier collapsed on top of him – Baby Steve had shot him through the head. I heard the *bloop* of Guss firing his last 40mm round, which passed between the shoulders of two Iraqis at the doorway and exploded among the group behind them. I knelt up, aimed at the nearest man to Doug, still grappling to get his pistol out of his leg holster, clicked my safety to full auto and opened up with my last magazine. I sprayed from the left and worked my way across to the right, and suddenly Doug had two dead men on his back. I could see that his arm was trapped and he couldn't undo his pistol holster, so he grabbed for his knife.

The Iraqis were stumbling all over the place, firing wildly into the room, as more of their number pushed from behind. Click! I was out of ammo. I threw the gun backwards so it hung on its sling and drew my pistol. Doug lunged his knife upwards into the solar plexus of the nearest Iraqi and kept on ramming it home, heaving him backwards out of the doorway, only to be forced back again by the press of bodies outside. Baby Steve and Guss were firing in bursts as they moved towards the rear of the pumphouse. Doug tried to lever himself to his feet, but lost his grip and fell. I lunged over to grab him with my left arm. As I did so, an Iraqi soldier – clearly Republican Guard – took aim with his AK47 at where my head had just been and opened fire.

As he tried to correct his aim, I stuck the muzzle of my pistol into his face. He looked like a nasty shit, and no way was he going to be the one to kill me. I squeezed off a round, and the bullet passed straight through his head. With my left arm I grabbed Doug by his webbing strap and pulled him up, hard. As I backed away half dragging him, he finally managed to get out his pistol. Both of us were firing now, going for headshots, as more and more Iraqis surged through the doorway, forcing us to the back of the room. One grenade would have wiped us all out, and I felt certain they had been ordered to capture at least some of us alive. Well, there was no way the bastards were going to, I told myself – and found I was praying for the MOAB to arrive.

We had our backs against the wall in the corner of the pumphouse now. My Glock ran out of ammo, so I dropped it and grabbed my back-up pistol from my inside holster. Doug grabbed an AK47 from the floor, as Baby Steve and Guss took aim with their pistols. As more Iraqis approached through the swirling smoke, we kept firing aimed shots at them. Guss hopped backwards, climbed up on to his perch and fired down on them. An Iraqi soldier's head exploded in front of me, which had to mean that the .50-cal had started firing from behind again. It was already difficult to breath, and as I gasped for air a lump of the man's flesh went up my nose to lodge in the back of my throat. I gagged, snorted and swallowed. For a second, my throat swelled as if I was about to vomit, but there was no time for that: more Iraqis were upon us.

I stood up and aimed my pistol, but a huge soldier lunged out from beside me with a knife aimed at my throat. I only saw him at the last second, and just managed to block the thrust. He closed on me, grabbed me in a bear-hug, the knife coming round for a second go at my throat. He was incredibly strong and I couldn't pull away from him. I tried to kick my boot down his shin and headbutt backwards, but he didn't flinch. As his knife drew ever closer to my throat my energy was fading. I could see Doug trying to get a clear shot at him, but the man was using me as a shield. I couldn't elbow him, as I dared not lose my grip on his arm.

Out of the corner of my eye I saw Baby Steve stand up, covered with blood, his knife at the ready. A wounded Iraqi lurched in front of him. Baby Steve kicked the man to his knees, twisted him round and knifed him in the throat. The Iraqi holding me dragged me backwards until we were hard up against the main pipes. Still holding the man he'd just stabbed, Baby Steve lifted his right arm, snapped it backwards and brought his knife down towards the face of the Iraqi who was trying to kill me. My grip was slipping on the man's hairy arm, as blood and gore flooded over us.

'Have this,' Baby Steve announced, as he stared at the Iraqi.

We all froze for a second, then Baby Steve thrust the knife into the Iraqi's left eye socket. He let out a horrible scream as the blade bit deep, and I twisted away from him. He staggered backwards, tripped over a dead body and crashed to the floor. With blood streaming from his ruptured eye socket, I could see him searching for a weapon. Suddenly he grabbed a discarded AK47. As he tried to push himself backwards and raise the muzzle of the weapon, Doug fired his pistol, emptying two rounds into the Iraqi's chest before his gun ran out of ammo. By rights the Iraqi should have been dead, but he was still raising the gun muzzle towards us. But as he tried to level his aim, the barrel jerked to a stop. The sling was caught round the leg of a corpse. Frantically he tugged at it as he tried to shuffle backwards and away from us, but the bodies stopped him.

I knew that unless I did something he'd yank the gun free and cut us down. I dived forward, landed on his bloodied chest and slammed my fist into his ruptured eye socket as hard as I could. He let go of the AK47, grabbed me with both hands and threw me backwards. I rolled over and up on to my knees. As I did so he grabbed the AK47 again. As he swung it towards me and struggled to free the strap, I flailed for a weapon with which to hit back at him. My right hand made contact with something hard. Without thinking I grabbed it and swung it at him. As my improvised weapon made an arc through the air I realised what it was: the lower half of someone's severed leg.

Two feet of muscle topped with six inches of jagged white shinbone slammed into the Iraqi's forearm, knocking the AK47 out of line as he squeezed off several rounds. By now I was in an animal state. I felt strong enough to tear anything apart, limb from limb. I kicked away the AK47 and thrust the shattered bone into the man's chest as hard as I could, putting my full bodyweight behind it, forcing the sharp bone into him. I clenched my teeth as I stared into his one good eye, and saw the life force drain out of him. The pupil in his eye blew, and I knew he was dead. I breathed a sigh of relief, and pulled away from his corpse.

As I did so I felt like I was coming out of a trance. I glanced round to see Doug, Baby Steve and Guss staring at me. The room was littered with dead bodies. Some near the doorway lay four or five deep. The entire pumphouse was covered with blood, and so were we. It was a scene from hell. The giant Iraqi who had refused to die lay slumped against a wall of dead bodies. His one eye was still open, and the leg was still stuck into him. As I stared at his corpse, the weight of the boot twisted the leg so that the foot faced downwards. It was the most gruesome sight I had ever seen.

'Is that what you call putting the boot in?' Doug enquired.

I didn't know how to answer. I just grabbed myself an AK47 off the floor, and crawled towards the doorway. Somehow, Doug had found a belt of fifty GPMG rounds hidden in his webbing, and he fed this into his weapon. Where the fuck was the MOAB? Something was still stuck at the back of my throat and, no matter what I did, I couldn't shift it. I lay down in the doorway with Doug next to me as Baby Steve policed up some extra AK rounds. As we lay there I was struck by the horrific smell. Men lay where they had fallen, body fluids, blood, half-digested food and ex-crement everywhere.

I radioed to Romero that I needed that MOAB within minutes. No way could we sustain another onslaught. I gulped down some water but my thirst was unquenchable. Romero came back with the news that it was now all down to my mark. We could hear the C130 Talon some distance off, circling, as well as the F18s. They'd obviously got a pilot who had agreed to fly the mission or somehow rushed the air certification through.

It was now 04.50 hours and it would soon be full daylight. 'Plan Z again,' I said. A wounded Iraqi who had been lying still tried to sit up, raising his AK47. Baby Steve fired a shot at him and he slumped back to the floor.

An early-morning breeze blew gently into the pumphouse enclosure, swirling the clouds of smoke into little plumes, starting to clear the area. It was then in the twilight that I could see just how many dead were lying around. I knew we were not responsible for all of them as many had been hit from behind. The last wave had been made up of mainly Republican Guards and Fedayeen militia troops. One was lying near to me in his smart uniform. I couldn't tell for certain but they looked like the élite of the élite, the Special Republican Guard, not just your average Republican Guard. He was either a glory-hunter or had pissed off his superiors. The silver wire and braid badges on his arms glinted in the firelight. They were fixed on by popper studs, not sewn, so I took them off his jacket and put them inside my body-armour vest pocket.

'You'll be wanting their ears next,' Doug joked.

If I ever got out of this I wanted something to remind me that it had been about humans – not just a job, a kill-or-be-killed scenario. Corny, perhaps, but that was how I felt. Also I could use the badges to identify the unit the soldiers had come from.

It was then that another wave, conscripts this time, rushed our way. The .50-cals weren't firing this time, just small arms – but they can still take off your head at six hundred metres. Immediately Doug opened up. Baby Steve and Guss started firing AK47s, which was a bit unnerving – we had been attuned to the noise they made as that of the enemy's weapons. This time the onslaught was nowhere near as heavy or as committed. Doug aimed at one Iraqi. He fell dead. He moved left to the next. He fell dead. He moved to the left again, and dropped another man. Baby Steve kept his eyes at the top of the doorway, expecting more hand grenades to come in.

16

SAVING PRIVATE AHMED

At that point I looked left following Doug's GPMG barrel and noticed the young Iraqi conscript who had been shot in the knee and shoulder from behind. He was propped up against the small wall, clearly in pain, holding his hand across the wound in his chest where the round had exited. He had sat there all that time, watching the battle unfold before his eyes. What thoughts had gone through his mind?

His eyes locked on mine and, for a moment, we were transfixed by each other's gaze. I was covered with blood, so what a sight I must have been. His eyes were wide, hazel green, much like mine, not the characteristic dark brown. He tilted his head and raised his other hand. I sensed he'd resigned himself to death and was waiting for it to take him.

I saw the barrel of Doug's GPMG align on him. I grabbed it and pushed it away. It burnt my hand as the rounds went off just to the side of the Iraqi.

'What? He's still fucking alive. Slot him!' Doug yelled at me.

'There,' I yelled back, as more Iraqis came for us.

Immediately Doug swung the GPMG into the aim and started firing at them. I looked back at the wounded man and our eyes

316

met again in a strange understanding. He tried to smile, as if in thanks. He'd seen what I'd done. I cannot explain it, but I felt a strong affinity with him.

Whether it was simply because our eyes met or that he posed no threat, I don't know, but it told me that even among this carnage humanity was still present. For a moment I was oblivious to everything else around us. All seemed to become quiet and to slow down. I'd heard and read many accounts from veterans that they had experienced exactly this state of heightened awareness.

I felt myself rock as Doug shook me, trying to get my attention. With every bang, the Iraqi flinched and grimaced. Now the sun was breaking on the horizon. I could see Doug yelling at me, but couldn't hear a word he was saying. A tracer round flashed between his head and mine with a loud snap. That brought everything back into focus and my head was full of noise again.

'Time for Plan Z,' he yelled.

I gave a thumbs-up and sent the signal to Romero. As I went to squeeze my transmitter prestle switch, I saw it was broken. I lay down behind the bodies to take a closer look at it. Thankfully, the two halves were still attached by a piece of plastic. I put them together, held them and pressed the switch. I pushed the microphone tighter against my throat and spoke. With a throat mic you don't have to yell, no matter how loud the battle noise is: it reads the vibrations from your voice directly. 'This is my mark. Say again, this is my mark in ten starting now.'

I waited for a response as more rounds kicked up in front of the pumphouse. Baby Steve was aiming and shooting, aiming and shooting. Magazine ran out, quick change to another, and bang-bang off again. Guss was using his pistol to maximum effect as the sobering staccato thumps of Doug's GPMG sent a hail of murderous fire towards the still oncoming Iraqi soldiers. Romero didn't respond but I heard the C130 Talon high above. Had he called in the MOAB airstrike? I knew we couldn't wait much longer.

Suddenly the Iraqi soldiers broke off their assault. Many more now lay dead, with as many squirming in agony from horrific gunshot wounds. One stood up and staggered away, his left arm hanging from his body by a tendon. I gestured 'on me' and the four of us lay down beside the wall of bodies. I made it clear we were going to try for the break-out. We still had no idea of how many more Iraqis were outside but our position was now untenable. We didn't even know if Romero and Athansa were still OK or if they'd got the message to use the MOAB. I rolled on to my stomach and looked towards what was left of the main gate area in time to see the Iraqi whose arm was hanging off stagger out of view.

'Let's go,' I said, jumped up and grabbed the nearest AK47.

As I stood up I glanced at the wounded Iraqi soldier, still propped against the wall. I started to run but as I got near to passing him I glanced down. He forced a smile. Without thinking I turned, grabbed his uninjured left side and pulled him up. I indicated for Doug to take his other side, which he did. 'What you doing?' he yelled.

'Taking him back with us so he can testify that his own people shot him from behind,' I yelled back.

A feeble reason, I know, but for some reason I couldn't leave him to die. The Iraqi looked puzzled, then almost passed out as Doug and I grabbed him firmly under his arms. He faced backwards as we started to run towards the gateway, the odd round and the occasional tracer snapping past us. As we moved I glanced at the sky, just in time to see the MOAB deploy – a tiny flash of orange-red as it exited the C130 Talon. So, Romero had got the message out. Problem was, we were out and committed to our plan. We couldn't turn back this time.

As we raced forward, Baby Steve was firing off aimed shots as figures moved on the ground or walked across our path through the smoke. I hoped the wind wouldn't blow the MOAB in our direction – no matter how deep we dug ourselves into the ground, the massive vacuum and the fireball would kill us. At least if it went off where I hoped it would, it would create the most spectacular mini-nuclear-type diversion imaginable. Baby Steve ran in front, as Doug and I dragged the Iraqi soldier, Guss following. We went out through the gateway, and ran for all we were worth through the smoke and dust. As we put some distance between us and what was left of the pumphouse compound, the air began to clear.

Then, as if we had stepped through a curtain into open land and clear air, we saw Iraqi Republican Guards running in our direction as many more climbed out of slit trenches that had been dug into the ground as far as the eye could see. We'd walked straight through all of this, just hours earlier, and not seen a damn thing. It also proved that they had been waiting for us, and that our entire mission had either been a trap to capture us, or we had been deliberately sent in to set the cat among the pigeons and show where the feared Republican Guards actually were in Tikrit. To intelligence, they had simply disappeared. Well, now we knew where they were. At that instant I saw a flash in the sky from the MOAB about eighty metres up in the air and about two kilometres away. The primary charge had detonated.

'*Down!*' I screamed, and pushed the Iraqi to the ground with such force that Doug fell forwards ahead of us.

Before we hit the deck the secondary charge detonated, igniting the airburst of fuel. A tremendous wind blew us down hard from behind as the fuel ignited ahead with such force that it caused the desired vacuum, which sucked all the oxygen from the surrounding area into its centre. This was followed by a thunderous roar, which sent my ears off the scale with a high-pitched shrill whine. I buried my face and covered my mouth with my hands. I screamed as I'd been trained to do: it gets all the air out of your lungs and stops them collapsing – an explosion from heavy ordnance can cause that to happen as it sucks the very breath out of you at such speed. Screaming also stops your ear drums bursting.

Instantly the shockwave smashed into us, throwing debris, stones, rifles and bodies over us. Oh, for a steel helmet. The roar kept getting louder and louder, the vibrations from the blast and the ground seeming to shake the very core of my bones. My head was humming and I felt nauseous and dizzy as it vibrated. Any minute now, I thought, and the fireball would incinerate us.

The wounded Iraqi, between Doug and me, was on his back, and his good arm flailing. The dust and debris flying our way meant I dared not look up as it would have gone straight into my eyes. Then the heat blast hit us but, thankfully, no flame. It blew over us so hard I felt certain it would tear the clothes from my back. The temperature was still rising and I thought again that this was it. Then the stones and debris stopped smashing into us and the blast wave began to subside, as did the roar of the explosion. The wind started blowing backwards over us, towards the centre of the explosion again. The air was cooler now.

I looked up, thinking the worst was over, and saw a massive cloud of dark dust rolling towards us at speed and, towering above it, a rapidly rising plume of smoke, which rushed skyward looking remarkably like the mushroom cloud of a nuclear bomb. I lay face down and placed my arm over the Iraqi's face to shield him as the dustcloud rushed over us. I expected lumps of rock and body parts again, but this time it was just dust. We all coughed and spluttered, gasping for fresh air. A couple of minutes passed, and then there was silence, apart from the breeze now swirling the dust around us.

It was hard to see and I had to pull the shemagh over my mouth so that I could breathe properly. The Iraqi was coughing and spitting blood. I stood up and tried to lift him, but Doug gestured for me to leave him. I looked down at the man, whose eyes gazed into mine. I knew I couldn't leave him to die. I bent down to pick him up and my shouldered weapon lurched forward, hitting me on the head. 'Fuck!' I yelled, and Doug gave a hand again.

Baby Steve and Guss got to their feet. Guss was smiling. 'Fucking awesome,' he yelled, clearly half shell-shocked.

We moved off, heading, I hoped, for the main tarmac road to link up with Romero. I couldn't make contact with him now as my throat mic and the prestle switch had been blown off during the explosion. As we walked forwards, as fast as we dared, the Iraqi told me his name was Ahmed. 'Isme Ahmed, Isme Ahmed,' he kept saying, half unconscious and in agony.

'Fuck off, Raggy, you ain't no fucking brigadier,' Doug yelled at him.

'No, he's saying his name is Ahmed, not Ahmid,' I shouted back to Doug, 'ahmid' being Iraqi for 'brigadier'.

My ears were ringing loudly and it was difficult to hear properly. The four of us stayed close to each other as the dust was everywhere and we didn't want to get separated now. Through the dustcloud I found the tarmac road and as we turned on to it we found ourselves stepping over dead Iraqis who had been nearer to the MOAB's detonation point. The dust was clearing quite fast now as we picked up our pace. Every now and then an injured Iraqi soldier would loom into view. They just passed us by. The further we ran down the road the more bodies we saw and the more twisted and grotesque they became. One Iraqi rushed past us praying as he tore off his clothes. More and more pieces of clothing and weapons had been abandoned.

We carried on for about a mile towards Romero and Athansa's position, passing more and more Iraqi soldiers coming out of the desert area west of us and running towards Tikrit, throwing off their clothes. Many were burnt. Those who had been caught out in the open when the MOAB detonated lay in contorted positions, smouldering, blackened heaps of flesh.

The ground was covered with a fine ash. The Iraqis took no notice of us. Perhaps to the survivors we looked as bad as they did. You certainly couldn't tell what uniforms we were wearing as they were so badly torn, singed and covered with blood and sand. And we were dragging Ahmed with us. He was still calling out his name, which must have made them think we, too, were Iraqis. Or perhaps they were all so shell-shocked they didn't care. We stepped over more and more bodies and my mind raced. Had the MOAB taken out Romero and Athansa too? If they were OK how would they tell it was us approaching them? I started to shout in English: 'Coming through. English coming through!' Absurd, I know. Doug laughed.

After another fifteen minutes or so the dust cleared, as did our view. It was now dawn, and light. I looked down as we passed another burnt body. The face had completely gone. I stopped to catch my breath – my lungs felt as though they were about to burst. My throat was so dry that I went for my water bottle but it had been ripped off my belt. My body-armour vest and cops (Covert Operations) vest were just a mass of shreds. I pulled off my shemagh and took a deep breath. Ahmed fell unconscious. As I laid him down, I could hear the familiar chop-chop-thud of helicopter rotor blades in the distance.

I stood up straight as Baby Steve, Guss, Doug and I strained to hear where the noise was coming from. Devastation stretched out before us in all directions. The land was flat and burnt as far as the eye could see. Smoke was rising from the area of the pumphouse. Everything was covered with fine black dust and the ground was smouldering. Bodies lay everywhere and I couldn't begin to count how many there were. The breeze wafted the remaining smoke into little swirls. Iraqis kept streaming past us out of the desert on to the road. What looked like burnt clothing hanging off their arms and legs was flesh.

An Iraqi walked straight into me – he'd been walking head

down, just following the path. As he stood up straight, we stared at each other. His eyes were bloodshot and he was holding his right forearm. As he took away his left hand, the burnt flesh on his forearm stuck to it and peeled off, like a banana skin, from wrist to elbow. He gazed at the brilliant white bones. The Iraqi looked back at me, his arm and then just walked off.

The chop-chop of rotor blades was louder now but we still couldn't see the helicopter. We stood motionless, looking around for it, except Baby Steve, who was applying rags to Ahmed's wounds in an attempt to stem the bleeding. Ahmed came round and muttered something in Arabic, pointing. Doug, Guss and I turned. In the ditch that ran parallel to the road we saw three dead and badly burnt Iraqi soldiers. One had lost his head, which had rolled on to the road and was facing us. The teeth were white, fixed in a perverse grin. The eye sockets showed the burnt eyeballs – the lids had gone. This had obviously freaked Ahmed.

Guss went over to the head, glanced at Ahmed, picked it up and talked to it as if it were a hand puppet. I shook my head, no, as Guss looked at Ahmed and smiled.

'Put it down,' Doug told him, but Guss tossed it up and caught it as if it were a baseball. He wore a look on his face that was almost pleasure.

'Put the fucking thing down, you twat!' Doug roared.

Even for Doug there was a limit and Guss was crossing it.

Eventually Guss dropped the head and Doug went for him, pushing him hard in the shoulder, as the skull went in two directions. *'You fucking animal!'* he bellowed.

'Enough!' I yelled.

Doug gave Guss another shove, but Guss just stood there, grinning. I could see that he was in shock. People react in strange ways to cope. Doug turned at me, as if waiting for me to say he could smack him one. *'Well, boss?'*

'*No!*' I yelled back.

Ahmed was staring at Guss in horror, but then he pointed weakly at me. 'Boss,' he muttered.

Doug gave Guss a final shove, then came over to me, his eyes on Ahmed.

'Boss, please, Mr Boss,' Ahmed pleaded fearfully.

Doug knelt down with Baby Steve and began to help him with Ahmed.

'Yes, he is boss. Big boss. Very good man. Understand,' Doug said to him reassuringly. He looked up at me and winked. Doug never ceased to amaze me.

Ahmed nodded and tried to smile. 'Thank you, Mr Boss. I understand little. Thank you. You big boss. Thank you.'

Baby Steve injected morphine into Ahmed's thigh. I turned to look towards where we'd left Romero and Athansa. A dustcloud was swirling on the road about a mile away when suddenly it parted and a CSAR CH53 Pave low Super Sea Stallion hovered into view, then vanished into the dustcloud again.

'*Follow me,*' I shouted. I grabbed Ahmed and hoisted him up, Doug helping.

We began to run towards the dustcloud. My lungs stung with all the smoke I was inhaling. We were coughing and our ears were bleeding. The helicopter was chopping into the air, getting louder. It loomed out of the dust into full view when we were about three hundred metres from it. It was one of the most beautiful, most welcome sights of my life. It meant safety – life. It meant going home. It meant seeing Victoria and the children again. I began to feel overwhelmed. Don't lose it now, I told myself. I gritted my teeth and ran faster, practically dragging Ahmed and Doug with me.

Guss overtook us and sprinted for the helicopter, hovering just feet above the road. I was convinced that an Iraqi would appear and bring it down with an RPG. As I got to within a hundred metres I spotted Athansa and Romero in the front doorway, egging us on. Guss rushed ahead.

Baby Steve was racing along behind us with an AK47, ready to drop anyone who got in our way. The door-gunner was training his minigun to cover us. At fifty metres Doug and I were struggling to run and carry Ahmed, but Romero jumped from the rear of the helicopter and came towards us. At that point several Iraqi soldiers ran past the helicopter out of the dustcloud. As they passed it, they glanced at it but didn't stop.

We were about to pass each other, them looking at us, and us looking at them, when the helicopter gunner opened up with his minigun. The four Iraqis blew to pieces before our eyes. Romero reached us and took over from me with Ahmed. The door gunner gave a thumbs-up and a big grin as Guss dashed up the rear ramp.

What could I say? The gunner had been doing his job. Maybe he thought the Iraqi soldiers were going to hit us. I was grateful the he was a good shot and hadn't taken us out too.

We clambered on to the huge chopper. The same crew had picked me up previously, but they didn't recognise me because of the state I was in. Guss reached out to grab Doug, the last man on, whose legs were still dangling out as he lay on his stomach trying to wriggle in while the helicopter moved forwards and up. Guss pulled Doug in by his trousers – a little too hard. Doug rolled over in pain. 'Twat!'

Baby Steve and one of the aircrew were sorting out Ahmed's wounds. He'd lost a lot of blood and more was seeping on to the floor. He passed out as he was given more morphine. One of the PJ loadies grabbed a saline solution bag from a medical kit and got a line into him.

As we lifted higher into the air we looked down at the devastated area below. Those Iraqis who were still alive were heading towards Tikrit. The road was littered with clothes, weapons, helmets and bodies. Little fires were blazing every-where. Each one was the smouldering body of an Iraqi Repub-lican Guardsman still in his foxhole.

'Phew, boss,' Doug shouted. 'Now was that fucking Zulu Dawn?'

I smiled but inside I was like jelly. I sat back and closed my eyes. How on earth would I ever explain all that had happened to people? Would I want to? I must have dozed off with the rhythmic chop-chop of the rotors, and woke up feeling as if I was choking because my throat was so dry. Guss was taunting the now-conscious Ahmed, saying he was going to throw him out. Ahmed's English wasn't good but I could see he'd got the idea. Doug was asleep, exhausted. I nudged him awake. He looked at me, then Guss.

'Full permission granted!' I shouted to him.

Doug winked at me, then at Ahmed. Then he gestured for Guss to lean closer. Guss did so, expecting him to say something, and Doug's fist came up very fast and hard in a classic French uppercut punch. Guss went backwards like a sack of shit. His eyes rolled and he was out. Doug grinned, then rubbed his hand as he'd hurt it. Baby Steve was laughing, which set us all off – even Ahmed. Romero gave me a thumbs-up.

A few minutes later Guss came round. He sat up and rubbed his chin. He must have known he'd been hit but couldn't figure out by whom or why. 'Don't worry about it, mate,' Baby Steve told him. 'It's an initiation thing. After a first big op, everyone gets a smack on the chin. It's to show you've been blooded.'

17

JUDGEMENT DAY

As we touched down at our base in Cizre, the full reception party was there to meet us, including Tosh, Dianne, Malcolm and the SEAL lads. As I fell out of the chopper doorway Dianne rushed towards me. I was stiff and aching and I knew we looked like the walking dead. As I approached Tosh, he looked about to burst into tears. When Dianne saw all the dried blood she thought I must be injured, but I finally got the message through to her that I was all right – and it was our Iraqi wounded, Ahmed, who needed her attention.

'He should be dead,' she shouted, and immediately went to work on him.

I stood away from the chopper door as Dianne threw out all of the soaked padding we'd stuffed into Ahmed's wounds to stem the bleeding. He just lay there, high on the morphine. As Dianne got a fresh saline drip into him, I felt a massive wave of emotion welling inside me but I knew that if I started to cry then I'd never stop. I had a lump in my throat and fought to maintain my composure as I muttered over and over again, 'After all of this, please, God, let this man live . . .'

Tosh kept asking questions, but I was oblivious to them,

willing Ahmed to survive. I kept pushing Tosh away, until Doug placed a hand on my shoulder. 'Boss, come on, it's OK,' he said gently.

I let him turn me away from the chopper and push me towards the medical tent, his arm across my back. I heard a helicopter power up behind me and turned to see Pilot Steve waving from the Chinook cockpit. I watched Dianne and Matt place Ahmed on a stretcher and rush him over to it. They were going to fly him to a British military field hospital and then onto Basra, where his wounds could be properly treated. As he was lifted into the chopper's hold, I just saw him give us a thumbs-up. Dianne mouthed, 'Don't worry, I'll look after him.'

Tosh brought me a coffee as I watched the Chinook take off. I had got hardly half a mug down me when I had to rush to the back of the mess tent and throw up. Tosh found me there and looked at me with what amounted to disgust, although whether at the puking or at the sight of me scorched all over and covered with dried blood I don't know. I handed in my weapon without bothering to clean it, stripped off the ragged remains of my dish-dash and combats, then got into a shower. I sat under the stream of warm water for nearly two hours.

Afterwards I went into the signals tent. I found Guss still in his tattered uniform, covered with blood, sending a full coded sitrep to his people. He tried to hide it from me but I didn't read much into that. We used to joke among ourselves that Guss was so secretive with his sitreps because he was unsure of what he was doing and didn't want to be shown up. As I took a seat Romero passed me a signals sheet for my attention. I nearly threw up again at the thought of yet another operation. No doubt about it, my nerve was almost exhausted. I looked at the signal and almost cried with relief: 'Return to UK immediately.' I asked Tosh to get it confirmed and clarify whether it meant Doug, Malcolm, Ian and Baby Steve too.

That evening during the debrief I learnt that Romero had called in the CH53 chopper as an emergency extraction for him and Athansa only: he had lost communication with us and was convinced we'd been obliterated by the MOAB. It also transpired that he had not received my last signal calling for the MOAB to be dropped, and neither had he sent the command to drop it, so who had? It had been bloody good luck that it was dropped when we had wanted it.

When we sat down to dinner, I couldn't eat. My stomach was still in knots and I was nauseous. As I sat there staring at my plate, Tosh came in and said that the order applied to me only. The others would be stood down for seven days, awaiting new orders, then retasked for further operations. We all knew there was more to this order, sending me home alone, than met the eye but none of us had a clue what. After dinner we all sat round a big table and I raised a toast to our good health, then spat up more blood.

We threw a party of sorts. Malcolm and Baby Steve took on Pilot Steve's aircrew in a drinking match. Pilot Steve had seriously overextended his flight hours to return to our FOB that evening. Athansa drank and drank and drank, but it seemed to have no effect on him. Romero got totally hammered and made me promise that if anything happened to him I would get a message to his wife and daughter telling them how much he loved them. Guss drank Kero, a cereal drink – it turned out that he was a strict Mormon.

As I looked at the team, I knew that this was our very own club. We would be connected with each other for ever on a level that few in civilian life could ever understand. I would miss them all terribly and I felt as if I was deserting them in returning to the UK, but Doug said I was mad even to think it. After everyone had crashed out I packed my kit, giving Doug my sweets and razor blades. I felt angry that I alone was being recalled, but I had a lot of serious questions to ask and I wanted answers. I went to the signals tent and sent a message asking why I was returning to the UK and not the others. While I waited for a reply I heard a helicopter land and went to see who it was.

As I stood on the landing area watching a US Sea Hawk chopper put down, Doug came over to stand by my side. Dan Meany got out of it so I went back to the signals tent. He was the last person on earth I wanted to see. I knew my nerves were shot and that I might try to kill him if we ended up in the same room. But just after Doug and I had reached the tent I heard the door pulled across and Dan came in. As soon as he clapped eyes on me he knew I was less than happy to see him. 'You packed yet? I'm here to give you a lift to Konya,' he blurted out.

'Is that to ensure I leave?' I responded icily.

Dan hesitated. 'No. I thought you couldn't wait to get outta here, so as I was passing, dropping off some new blood, I thought I'd offer you a lift.'

'That's fucking bullshit if ever I heard it,' Doug said.

'Ah, fuck off, guys,' Dan snarled. 'Jeez, you got some cheek. By rights I could've had you hauled over the coals for your stunt telling the Peshmerga commanders we intended to slot them if they didn't play the game. You any fucking idea the shit that caused?'

'Don't try to turn this on me,' I retorted, anger rising. 'You were the arse so hell bent on having them slotted – and don't go giving me all that shit about the bigger picture again.'

'You are outta here, buddy,' Dan sneered. 'This is my ballpark, as I told ya from the start. You can't play by my rules, then you're no use to me and I want you gone, d'ya hear me?'

He dropped into a seat, stretched out his legs and put his hands behind his head. I told myself not to rise to his provocation, but I was boiling inside as I gazed at his smug face.

'Well, we're certainly good enough to be used as bait when you need some,' I said.

'Hey, you were an asset that could be used so I used you,' Dan replied. 'What can I say?'

'Really? And what about Wajy?' I countered. 'I still reckon you had something to do with his death, and if I ever find out you did, you'd better hope you got somewhere good to hide.'

Dan started to rock himself back and forth on his chair. 'Oh? And what will you do then, Mr Holier-than-thou? Shoot me? As I told you already, I had nothing to do with it. And even if I did, so what? You can't prove nothing. And, hey, it sure as hell made the other Pesh leaders think twice about staying in Kirkuk.'

Doug moved towards him but I raised my arm across his chest, stopping him. His were eyes blazing.

'I got you outta here,' Dan said. 'You done your job and I don't need you no more. That's why you're going home.'

'He leaves, I go too, you fuckwit,' Doug snarled.

'Oh, yeah, I forgot, you're his faithful poodle.'

'Don't give him the satisfaction,' I growled to Doug, as I held him back.

'You two still don't get it, do you?' Dan smirked. 'Niall, your job is done. Shit, this time you may even get medals for your endeavours. And, Doug, you go home now, what you gonna do, huh? Get pissed for a month? 'Cause if you leave now when we ain't telling you to, I can promise you won't ever work in this game again.'

'Tell me who authorised us to be sent into Tikrit as bait,' I countered, trying to ignore Dan's remarks about Doug. 'Someone, somewhere knew it was a trap, so who and why?'

'Like I said, you were an asset and used accordingly,' Dan replied. 'We knew the Republican Guards were somewhere around there, just couldn't tell where.'

'Just one more question, Dan.' I was trying to keep my temper in check. 'Why didn't your people come and give us some support when you were buzzing about in a chopper just minutes away?'

Dan paused. Then: 'Who said it was my people? Could've been any number of choppers. Anyways, someone had to be eyes in the sky to confirm troop numbers once the Iraqis came up outta their positions.'

'You bastard!' Doug exploded. 'You were there fucking sight-seeing and did nothing to help when we needed it.'

'You can cry about it all you like but your fucking boss there asked Quigly for this one – remember?' Dan retorted.

I knew that if I stood out of the way, Doug would quite probably kill Dan on the spot.

'Anyhow, who said we didn't help?' Dan added. 'Who was it told Romero and Athansa to bug out of there, and who'd you think ordered the MOAB to be released?'

What the hell was Dan on about, saying Romero had been ordered to bug out? Romero had never mentioned it to me or put it down in his debrief notes. I trusted Romero 100 per cent and now Dan was telling me something different. 'You're lying, Dan, so stop your fucking games,' I told him. 'All I want is the truth. Is that so fucking difficult?'

Dan started to laugh. 'Truth? Fuck, what is "the truth" any more? Was I there or was I not? Did Romero get told to bug out or not? Truth is, you were a disposable asset – as well as a fucking loose cannon. Always were and always will be.'

I knew he was deliberately winding me up now, and for what? He seemed to get real pleasure from messing with people's minds.

'I needed you for a purpose and you've now served it,' Dan continued. 'So, time to go home to your lady – Tosh has got her wrapped round his little finger, by the way.'

I glanced sharply at Tosh, who had just joined us in the radio tent, wondering what the hell Dan was on about. Doug was staring at him too. Tosh shrugged his shoulders and shook his head in bemusement – or that was how it looked.

'See? You just don't know what to think, do you?' Dan added

vindictively. 'Who to trust and what's the truth? Told you years ago, this game wasn't for you unless you could follow orders from those who know how to play. Maybe now you'll get the hint and leave this business to those who can. You're a fucking liability and you're outta here.'

I couldn't believe what I was hearing. Then Dan turned his back on me with a dismissive wave. That was it. I blew. Doug saw me lunge forward and tried to stop me. Dan spun round, saw me going for him and smiled, as if he was glad he'd finally got to me. As he went to block me, I kicked down hard on his right knee. His leg buckled away to the right – I'd connected with it at an angle, and he went down on his knees. I raised my right arm high and back, swiped my elbow as hard as I could across his face, knocking him sideways on to the floor. As he rolled on to his side I stood above him, ready to smash his face as hard as I could, but Doug pulled me back. As Dan looked up at me, blood dripping from his mouth, he laughed. 'See, bud? You ain't no different from us really,' he said. 'Maybe there is a place for you, after all.'

He stood up, wiping his face. If I'd had a gun in my hand I think I would have shot him.

'You think too much, bud, and you sure as hell care too much.' He rubbed his jaw where my elbow had struck. 'That's why I wanted you here. I knew you'd do exactly as you have done. We knew you'd win over those Pesh thugs. We knew you'd volunteer your sad arse to meet the Iraqis in person. Well, you've done that now so you ain't required no more. Simple as that, really.'

I walked up close to Dan and looked into his eyes. 'Listen,' I said. 'If I ever see you again, I swear I'll kill you.' With that I walked out of the tent.

'Not if I see the fucker first,' Doug said, and followed me.

A few hours after Dan had left I caught a chopper ride from Cizre to Konya – the first leg of my journey back to the UK. As the lads lined up to see me on to my transport, I felt as if I was running out on them. I'd been with them for what felt like years, not just four months. A large part of me wanted to stay to see the whole thing through to the end but, as Doug pointed out, the end of this war was a long time off in the future.

'If your chopper goes down, boss, we'll all know it was Dan's doing,' Doug told me, as we said goodbye. 'I'll hunt the fucker down. He can run but he'll just die tired.'

As I threw my kit aboard the Black Hawk, Romero grabbed me and gave me a bear-hug. 'You make a life for yourself with that lady of yours, you hear me?' he shouted.

As the chopper lifted off I gazed out of the doorway at Romero, Athansa, Baby Steve, Guss, Malcolm, the two Ians and Doug. They looked shattered – except Doug, who was standing ramrod straight. He raised his arm in farewell and I could feel my bottom lip quivering. I knew that if I opened my mouth to speak I would burst into tears. They shielded their eyes from the downdraught as we pulled away, then disappeared from view. I sat back in my seat. I still had a million questions to which I wanted answers, but I knew I'd probably never get them. That was the way things were in this game.

When we touched down at Konya, the snow had melted and it was warm. As I stepped off the Black Hawk I was amazed to find Quigly waiting for me. He'd heard about my showdown with Dan and had decided to meet me at Konya to put a few things straight. My flight to the UK wasn't due for several hours.

'Dan's a dinosaur, and it's him whose days are numbered in this game,' Quigly informed me over coffee.

He also explained that, in his eyes, I had done a great job, well beyond the call of duty. I had scared the crap out of everyone when I had told the Peshmerga commanders of our orders to slot them if they insisted on taking Kirkuk, but it was a gamble that had paid off. I asked Quigly how high up the chain of command that order had come from, and he told me it was better I didn't know.

He told me I should be proud of how we had rooted out the Iraqi Republican Guards unit on our last mission. As a result, many more Ahmeds would now return home to their families and, more importantly, many more US and British soldiers too. He sounded sincere as he said all of this, but I no longer knew what to think or whom to believe.

Later he asked if I would come and work full time with him, as he was earmarked for greater things back in the US. I told him I'd think about it. Finally I boarded a C17 transport aircraft for my flight home. I never normally slept while travelling, no matter how far I was going, but I did then – almost all of the way.

EPILOGUE

After my return from the Iraq war I have asked myself countless times what we were really fighting for. I have been asked a thousand times whether I believe that Saddam Hussein had WMD. All I can say is that intel showed he had had them in the past, and had used chemical weapons. He was certainly determined to acquire bigger and deadlier types of WMD. My gut instincts still tell me that perhaps WMD apparatus and equipment will be found, dumped in the depths of the great Buhayrat ath Thartha lake, west of Tikrit. It's just a feeling, and maybe I'm wrong.

Should Saddam have been removed? Definitely. And the bereaved families of those who lost their lives in the conflict should know that their men did not die in vain. If they still feel they did, please try to picture hundreds of women trying desperately to protect and reassure their children, babies held close, while they were herded into trenches and Saddam Hussein's men, under his orders, bulldozed tonnes of earth on to them, burying them alive. They were helpless, defenceless . . . and no one lifted a finger to stop it. That was what Saddam did to the Kurds and countless other of his enemies, and that was what decent service personnel and civilians gave their lives for in Iraq – to stop it happening again and again, as Saddam continued unopposed. Those who died did not do so in vain.

Two issues still anger me: the unnecessary wholesale bombing of Iraqi divisions who could have been spared, and, worse still, that the Iraqi armed forces and police were disbanded before the country had been stabilised. They should have remained in place to maintain law and order after the conflict. The consequences are now all too apparent.

Recently, Quigly sent me details of how the US forces had discovered Magdi's hideaway train carriage, which contained his few personal items along with a hand-drawn map showing the pumphouse where we were supposed to meet the general: it was on the north-western side of the Tigris river, north of Tikrit. Problem was, however, the general's informant, who passed on the map, appears to have not drawn in any bearings for north and south. He had put on GPS co-ordinates, which Guss had been given. Turn the map upside-down and you have a map showing the pumphouse on the south-east of the Tigris river, south of Tikrit. (See map.)

When we had approached the pumphouse, Guss had been checking his co-ordinates – and we took the piss out of him as it was clear the pumphouse was in front of us. Guss had not been satisfied that we were at the correct co-ordinates and had been embarrassed to tell us so in case it made him look to us like an inexperienced fool. Yet in retrospect he might have been right and ourselves the fools. It might have been the wrong pump-house. When I told Doug, he said, 'How fucking convenient.' I don't know how much to read into Quigly's intel. I probably never will.

According to Quigly's intel, Grey Fox members and one of their – Dan's – helicopters had, indeed, been in the immediate area of the pumphouse siege. They had assumed we were initially at the southern pumphouse until our frantic requests for CAS came through. By that time it was too late to cancel the MOAB attack. Once we had confirmed the exact location of the hidden Special Republican Guards, the decision was taken to deploy the MOAB. With major US forces advancing fast upon Tikrit, the prospect of a last-stand fight to the death by Special Republican Guards had to be avoided at all costs. The development of the MOAB certainly meant that the last stand never happened because so many Iraqi troops were put out of action.

After the war I was informed that it would be claimed officially that no MOABs had been deployed. We were warned that if we spoke of it or took matters further regarding the whole affair, our credibility would be seriously questioned. As MOABs leave no crater, there was little evidence that such a weapon had been used. Besides, the US Marine Corp of Engineers cleared away the debris and the dead rapidly. Unfortunately for the US military, they forgot to give the official line to the people in the US Department of Defense (DoD) who manage the website – that no MOABs were used. Consequently it appeared on the website and the DoD were forced to admit publicly that MOABs had indeed been used.

My colleagues and I were also made aware of the legal ramifications that would result if we published accounts of it or of our operations in Iraq. If we did we were warned that 'all' measures would be implemented to discredit our reputations, as well as to ruin our present and future careers. Where's democracy and freedom of speech? Hadn't the war aimed to defend those very principles against the people who wished to take them away?

Weeks after I'd returned to England, Doug managed to check on Ahmed who was still convalescing at the BMFH (British Military Field Hospital) in Basra, southern Iraq. War is war and amongst the Iraqi dead, many were just like Ahmed, but he was symbolic in a way in revealing that we were not just trained soldier spies without a heart or emotion or compassion for the enemy. Ahmed was almost a redeemer for our consciences. In my opinion he was certainly the only decent thing to come out of the Tikrit incident. Doug joked it would become known as the 'Tikrit Pump House action' as famous as the Iranian Embassy siege or the battle of Mirbat. I reminded him that officially we weren't there. As 'K' operators (code given to members on deniable operations), officially our little branch attachment doesn't exist. No glory, no recognition. 'Medals not conferred', as we were informed upon joining the team. Ahmed passed on a letter to Doug to give to me written in Arabic on a bluey (forces self seal blue letter envelope). When I finally received the letter and its English translation I was deeply moved. Ahmed was recovering well. He was being spoilt by his eight sisters, was getting married in the July and his family were going to read out a prayer of thanks to the anonymous Mr Big Boss at his wedding. That letter was all the recognition, glory or medal I would ever need.

Sadly, months after I'd returned from Iraq, I received terrible news of Romero. Having received the orders that sent him home, he hopped aboard a helicopter rather than waiting to go by road, which was considered dangerous. He made a split-second decision so that he could get home quicker to his wife and daughter. The helicopter next to his swerved to avoid an RPG round and the aircraft collided, killing all on board, including Romero. When I heard about it I was gutted, but I'll always remember his last words to me as I boarded the helicopter to leave Iraq. 'You make a life for yourself with that lady of yours, you hear me?' I certainly intend to.

Months after my return to the UK, Doug warned me about Tosh's intentions, with Victoria telling me of their developing relationship which had started while we were in theatre. He explained that on the occasion when Tosh rushed from his signals tent to tell me to talk to Quigly urgently, he had left his email open on screen. Doug had read it, including the other correspondence from Victoria, which had become very personal, and explained why Doug's attitude had turned positively hostile towards him. He had not told me at the time for fear it would cloud my operational judgement and ability to remain focused, but it had put him in an uncomfortable position. Victoria and I have since worked through it and got over it. Romero's last words to me helped weather the storm – even in death his wise counsel had again guided me. For that alone I am forever grateful to him.

As for Dan Meany, it turned out that he had never had the authority to give any orders that even hinted we should stop the Peshmerga taking Kirkuk. He had the authority to advise us that they shouldn't do so, but not to order us physically to stop them. Quigly had tried to cover up Dan's behaviour out of loyalty to him, but eventually Dan had abused that trust once too often. The question of whether he had any involvement with the blue-on-blue that killed Wajy still remains unanswered in my mind. A full military inquiry vindicated the pilot and the FAC operators on the ground. Dan was returned to the US just two days after I left Iraq, and strongly advised to take voluntary early retirement, which he did.

With Bush now waving a big stick at North Korea and Iran, Quigly offered me a job in the US as UK liaison officer to his department for global operations. I turned it down – despite a huge financial inducement.

After the war General Franks wrote a book on how he won it. He didn't pull any punches with his condemnation of some senior US administrators and planners, whose interference had proved a major hindrance during and after major ground engagements. Satellite imaging also confirmed that the majority of Iraqi divisions and Republican Guards Units in northern Iraq had stayed put, thanks to the April Fool operation he instigated. Franks also confirmed mass bombings of Republican Guards, claiming it was the most effective bombing campaign in the history of warfare. This had happened during a huge sandstorm when everyone, especially the armchair warriors and ex-generals, said the war was bogged down and stuck.

What of the Kurds? On 14 December 2003, I nearly died with laughter when I heard on the news that Kosrat Rassul and his Peshmerga, with an ordinary US infantry unit, had located and captured Saddam Hussein in Tikrit – just as Kosrat had vowed he would. What a player. Grey Fox and other covert US units played no part in it.

It is interesting to note that the Kurds now want English to be taught as their national second language, and that Massoud Barzani – the late Wajy's brother – became president of the entire Kurdish region of Iraq. On 6 April 2005, Jalal Talabani was elected president of all Iraq, and this was what he said of Tony Blair and Britain in Iraq: 'Britain's intervention in Iraq is one of the UK's "finest hours". History will judge Mr Blair as a champion against tyranny. Of course, the liberation of Iraq has been controversial. Iraqis sometimes wonder in amazement what the debate abroad is about. Why do people continue to ask why no WMD were found? The truth is that Saddam had, in the past, used chemical and biological weapons against his own people, and we believed he would again. Of course Saddam himself was, in the view of those who opposed him, Iraq's most dangerous WMD. Sadly, in this case war was not the best option. It was the only option.'

As for me, well, I'll continue with my medical endeavours, build a future with Victoria and my children, and kick up whatever fuss I can to make people aware of the very real and bigger threat of global warming that we *all* face, something I feel strongly about. Failing that, I'll enter politics as I once threatened some senior ministers I would!

In Memory

Captain Adrian Romero
Wajy Barzani, KDP Special Forces
Lieutenant Colonel Ian 'Tanky' Smith
Magdi
and to *all* those who died in Iraq and continue to do so. It is not in
vain.

GLOSSARY:

AWACS: Airborne Warning and Control Systems
AN/PVS 70: twin-eye night-vision goggles
AN/PVS 14: single-eye night-vision goggles
ASASR: Australian Special Air Service Regiment
Blue-on-blue: accidental attack on own forces
Brew: mug of tea
CAS: Close Air Support
Cam: camouflage
Casevac: casualty evacuation
Cent Com: Central Command
Comms: communications
Claymore: anti-personnel mine
Cops Vest: covert operations vest
CSAR: combat search and rescue
CT: counter-terrorism
CTR: close target reconnaissance
DEVGRU: Developments Group
Director: officer commanding Special Forces (brigadier)
DZ: drop zone
DS: directing staff
DOD: Department of Defense (US)
ERV: emergency rendezvous point

EMU: electronic module unit; encryption device
Ex-fill: Exfiltration
E4A: surveillance division of Special Branch
FMB: forward mounting base
FOB: forward operating base
FLIR: forward looking infrared
GPS: global positioning system (navigation aid)
GPMG: 7.62mm general purpose machine-gun
Gimpy: slang for GPMG
Green Army: regular forces
Head Shed: Special Forces (SAS) boss and staff/headquarters
Heads Up: informal meeting
ID: identification/identity
Incoming: incoming fire
Intel: intelligence information
K: operator on deniable operations
LAW 80: 94mm light anti-armour weapon
LMG: light machine-gun
LUP: lying-up point
LZ: landing zone
M60: 7.62mm US machine-gun
Magellan: name of GPS system
Maggot: green army sleeping-bag
MI5: Military Intelligence Five
MI6: Military Intelligence Six
MoD: Ministry of Defence
MSR: main supply route
NAVSPECWARCOM: Naval Special Warfare Command.
ND: negligent discharge
NVA: night-viewing aid
NVG: night-vision goggles
OC: officer commanding
OP: observation post
Opsec: operational security
PE: plastic explosives
PGMs: precision guided missions

PNGs: passive night-vision goggles
PUP: pick-up point
QRF: quick reaction force
REMF: rear-echelon motherfucker
RFA: Royal Fleet auxilliary
RTI: resistance to interrogation
RTU: return to unit
Rupert: officer
SAM: surface-to-air missile
SARBE: search and rescue/surface to air rescue beacon
SAS: Special Air Service
SAW: squad assault weapon 5.56mm M249
SEAL: Sea, Air and Land US Special Forces Unit (navy)
SF: Special Forces
SIS: Secret Intelligence Service
SS: Secret Service
Sitrep: situation report
SOP: standard operating procedures
SPIE: special procedures insertion extraction
Spook: Intelligence Corps analyst/spy
SSM: squadron sergeant major
Stag: sentry duty
STRABO: specialist tactical recovery airborn operations
Tab: forced march over long distance carrying heavy load
TACBE: tactical beacon/emergency radio
TCG: tasking and co-ordination group/tactical control group
TOG: time on ground
VHF: very high frequency radio (PRC 319)

Photographic Acknowledgements

Part 1: © Niall Arden. The author pictured with a fire retardant suit and 7.62mm M60E3. Part 2: © Anastasia Taylor-Lindt. A Kurdish Pershmerga soldier from the PUK (Patriotic Union of Kurdistan). Part 3: © Fabrique Nationale. The US M240 7.62mm General Purpose Machine Gun (GPMG, also affectionaly known as the Gimpy). Although heavy at 26lbs, its effectiveness and unrivalled stopping power saved our lifes. Below: © Niall Arden. Ahmed's letter of thanks, written on a standard-issue 'bluey'.

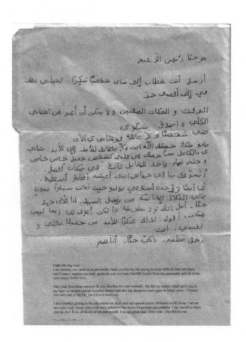

INDEX

347